MANCHESTER UNITED
THE MAKING OF A FOOTBALL DYNASTY
VOLUME ONE

1878-2021

by JOHN D T WHITE

EMPIRE
PUBLICATIONS

First published in 2021

EMPIRE PUBLICATIONS
1 Newton Street, Manchester M1 1HW
© John White 2021

ISBN: 978-1-909360-87-7

CONTENTS

ACKNOWLEDGMENTS

Thank you to Gerry and Geraldine McCollum and Eugene McCusker for proofreading my work.

DEDICATION

I am dedicating this book to two of the biggest Manchester United fans I know. My two sons, Marc and Paul. I love you both, Dad x

INTRODUCTION

The story of Manchester United is one long history book. It has twisted and turned through time since 1878. It's a book of moments; moments that make us leap out of our seats; moments that send shivers down our spine. Special Moments that make us cry with joy and no club has given their fans more.

It has been a roller-coaster ride of memories. In the history of Manchester United we have watched surprises unfold every season. There were disappointments we had to endure, but there were are also triumphs we celebrated and we had to rebuild after a tragedy but like the Phoenix, Manchester United Football Club rose from the ashes of the 1958 Munich Air Disaster.

There were moments that leapt off the page and became Legend but the greatest thing about this book is that there is no final chapter, no final page, no final word... the history of Manchester United continues.

Many managers tried to step out of the shadow of Sir Matt Busby, the Father of Manchester United, but only one man was able to follow in his footsteps and that man, Sir Alex Ferguson, wrote his own chapters in the club's history. And now Fergie's legacy seeks the man who will take United forward as he did.

Each season brings a new challenge to capture our imagination. With every new season we await in anticipation of witnessing greatness. Heroes of old are fondly remembered whilst new Legends are yet to be made and long to be woven into the very fabric of Manchester United history.

Every player dreams of standing on the top step with previous

United Greats, dreaming of becoming immortal in the minds of the fans. The Theatre of Dreams remains an open stage. Some Manchester United players were born with grace. One Legendary player fell from grace.

And so, this book remains open because we, the fans, are left wondering what is yet to unfold. What will be the next Chapter in the history of Manchester United?

As Manchester United fans we will continue to flock to Old Trafford hoping to be seduced with dreams in our heads, our hearts full of hope, of watching the next memorable game and the next player who will become a legend in the history of the club.

All Reds await the next entry of the club's story which will show the world why Manchester United is football history, why Manchester United is Legend.

John D T White

FOREWORD

I was delighted when my fellow Belfast man, John White, asked me to write the Foreword to this, his eighteenth book about the club we both love, Manchester United.

I first met John in 1997 when he invited me up to a function to raise monies for "Guide Dogs For The Blind" which he organised as the Branch Secretary of Carryduff Manchester United Supporters' Club, Northern Ireland's largest official branch. I was a Patron of the Charity at the time. Making a memorable moment for yourself is not such a big thing but when you are the key person in another person's most memorable moment in their life then that is an everlasting thing. I have lost count of the number of times a Manchester United fan, including John, has thanked me for giving them a special memorable moment by scoring the only goal of the game in the 1985 FA Cup final. That game will always be special to me and I will never tire of being thanked by the United fans for playing my part in our win over Everton at Wembley.

John's "The Making of a Football Dynasty: Manchester United 1878-2021" is one of those must-have books for all Manchester United fans. Some football matches are memorable because United recorded a big win, or enjoyed an important victory, or because it marked a player's debut, or it was the beginning of a manager's career at Old Trafford or because it was a game which produced a trophy for the club.

John sent me his draft manuscript and as I began to read about each game which helped form United's quite unique and unrivalled history, he drew me deeper and deeper into his work.

What I like most about John's book is his particular writing style. There is no doubt about it with 18 books to his name about Manchester United, John is one of the most knowledgeable writers and historians about the club. In essence John's compilation of 100 games is a history of Manchester United which has never before been written in this format. The games are not in chronological order or divided into competitions or categories because John will take you from a game played by Newton Heath in 1892, to the 1999 UEFA Champions League final, to the famous Busby Babes last game on English soil on 1 February 1958, to the 1909 FA Cup final, to a Division Two game in 1934 when United almost dropped into Division Three, to the club's first ever game in the European Cup in 1956 to the 1993-94 Double winning season, to the 1968 European Cup final and games played by United's famous Triumvirate of Denis Law, Bobby Charlton & George Best, to Sir Alex Ferguson's last season in charge of the club in 2012-13 when we won our 20th English League title, to the three great sides built by Sir Matt Busby in the 1940s, 1950s and 1960s or to Fergie's Fledglings who in season 1995-96 won the Double for the second time in United's history even though a famous ex-Liverpool defender and BBC Match of the Day pundit infamously said: "You can't win anything with kids."

At the end of every game, which John writes about with so much attention to detail, he gives us a little teaser in his "Did You Know That?" ending to the game. And, I must admit I did not know most of the 100 trivia comments which John has given us. Did you know that the football anthem "You'll Never Walk Alone" was first sung by United fans on the terraces of Old Trafford five years before the fans of Liverpool started to belt it out before home games at Anfield? I most certainly did not. But this is only one of those trivia entries that will leave you scratching your head in disbelief and thanks John for including the 1985 FA Cup final in your wonderful book, it was most definitely one of my most memorable games for Manchester United.

Norman Whiteside
Manchester United, 1982-89 – 274 Appearances, 67 goals

GAME NO. 1
GAINSBOROUGH TRINITY 0-1 UNITED
SECOND DIVISION
THE NORTHOLME, GAINSBOROUGH
6 SEPTEMBER 1902
ATTENDANCE- 4,000

A SHAGGY DOG STORY

On 6 September 1902, Manchester United travelled to Lincolnshire to play Gainsborough Trinity in the opening game of their 1902-03 Second Division season. The home side's ground, The Northolme, had opened in the 1850s and was originally a cricket ground. Gainsborough Trinity moved to The Northolme in 1884 and at the time the only spectator facility was a small covered stand in the south-west corner of the ground. Players used the nearby pub, The Sun Inn, for changing rooms, and the landlord built an extension to the building for use by the football club. A 200 seat grandstand was later added to The Northolme along the southern touchline and a covered terrace on the northern side of the pitch. Yet it was at this humble ground that Manchester United played their first ever competitive game, rising phoenix like from the ashes of Newton Heath FC.

Newton Heath had been on the verge of bankruptcy for some time and things were so bad that fans conducted whip-rounds to pay for the team's railway fares to play away fixtures during the previous season. The club had organised a Grand Bazaar at St James's Hall, Oxford Street, Manchester late in the season in an effort to boost finances and raise the £1,000 which was needed to prevent the club from becoming bankrupt. At the bazaar the club captain's St Bernard named Major walked around the stalls in the hall with a collection box fastened around his collar so children could drop some pennies in his box but his own, Harry Stafford, left the animal to his own devices one evening while he was at a local hostelry and when he returned it had disappeared. A panic-stricken Stafford placed an ad in the Lost and Found section of the *Manchester Evening News* and must have feared the worst until he was contacted by someone to tell him he had Major and would he like to come and see him. That 'someone' was local brewery owner and oil merchant John Henry Davies who was one of the richest men in Manchester.

When Stafford called to Davies's oppulent Cheshire home to collect Major, the John Henry made an offer – his daughter was already devoted to the animal and he asked Harry his price. Stafford told Davies that Major was not for sale but during their meeting Stafford told Davies about the reason for the hound going AWOL and a deal was quickly struck. Harry, perhaps sensing that Major could live the life of canine country squire and would be spoiled rotten, came to a deal with Mr Davies – he could have the animal if he helped Harry save Newton Heath FC!

In January 1902, the club's crippling debts amounted to £2,670 and a number of creditors, including several former directors, pressed for payment. The club simply did not have the money to discharge their liabilities and so Newton Heath Football Club was adjudged bankrupt. When the gates to their Bank Street ground were locked by their landlord, Stafford decided to call in Davies's promise to help. A meeting of the club's shareholders was held at Islington Town Hall, Ancoats on 18 March 1902. As the doom and gloom of the club's financial position was being relayed to downcast supporters, Harry saw his chance and took to the stage. Being something of a showman, Harry cleared his throat and dramatically announced that he "knew of four local businessmen who were each prepared to invest £500 to guarantee the existence of the club" in return they would take full control of the club. There was uproar and the meeting was adjourned while the offers were confirmed. Harry was the hero of the hour! After lengthy negotiations, the new board took control but the Football Association declared that the re-formed club would need to have a new name.

On 23 April 1902, Newton Heath beat Chesterfield 2–0 (scorers: Jimmy Coupar & Stephen Preston) at their Bank Street home and finished 15th in the table, it was their last league game under that name. Three days later, 26 April 1902, Harry Stafford captained Newton Heath in their last ever game, a 2-1 win in the Manchester Senior Cup final against Manchester City at their rival's Hyde Road ground. It proved to be his only winners' medal in his time at Bank Street.

"Each night, when I go to sleep, I die. And the next morning, when I wake up, I am reborn."

Mahatma Gandhi

Two days later a key meeting was arranged to form a new club. Present were directors, supporters and pressmen. The main order of business was to decide on a new name for the football club. Manchester Celtic and Manchester Central were both suggested, the former perhaps reflecting links with the Irish community in the city while the latter was rejected as there was already a train station named Manchester Central.

A few years earlier Harry Stafford had been given a testimonial and selected a team from both Manchester clubs (Newton Heath and Manchester City) entitled 'Manchester United'. It had a certain ring to it... Years later Louis Rocca*, who served the club as a tea boy in the 1890s and played for the Reserve Team a few times, claimed that he was the person who suggested the name. Through the mists of time it impossible to say who suggested it but the new named was carried unanimously as was the change of team colours to red jerseys with white shorts.

Harry Stafford and club secretary James West were placed in charge of all football related matters which effectively made Stafford club captain, joint manager and Director. However, now that he had a position on the Board, Stafford had to give up his professional status and revert to amateur status. Harry was the last ever captain of Newton Heath Football Club and the first ever captain of Manchester United and the only director/player in the club's history (perhaps in football history!).

The Manchester United side that took to the pitch to play Gainsborough Trinity wearing their brand new red shirts as follows: James Whitehouse, Harry Stafford (Capt), Thomas Read, William Morgan, William Griffiths, Walter Cartwright, Charles Richards, Ernest Pegg, Jack Peddie, Frederick Williams, Daniel Hurst

With the exception of Peddie, who was born in Hutchesontown, Glasgow, it was an all-English side. The game ended 1-0 with the visitors getting their season off to the perfect start thanks to a goal from Charles "Chas" Richards who holds the distinction of being the first player to score a goal for Manchester United. Richards was a one season wonder for United after joining from Leicester Fosse that August. He was something of a journeyman having had spells with Gresley Rovers, Newstead Byron, Notts County, Nottingham Forest and Grimsby Town. Richards left United for Doncaster Rovers in March 1903 having played 11 times and scoring two goals. He also scored in United's 7-0 victory over Accrington Stanley on 1

November 1902 in the Third Qualifying Round of the FA Cup.

Formed in 1873 as Trinity Recreationists, set up by the vicar of the Holy Trinity Church for young parishioners, Gainsborough Trinity became members of the Midland Counties League in 1889 losing their first match 2-1 to Lincoln City and going on to finish 7th out of eleven clubs. The club quickly became well known, and won their first Midland League championship in 1890-91 and after finishing runners-up the following season were elected to the Football League Second Division.

Ironically Gainsborough Trinity's first ever Football League match had been against Newton Heath. The Second Division game was played on 1 September 1896 at The Heathens' Bank Street ground with the home side running out 2-0. Trinity held on to their place in Division Two but based in an area with a small population it was always a struggle and the club returned to the Midland League in 1912. Here they were to settle and earn more success, winning the Midland Championship in 1927-28, 1948-49 and 1966-67, also finishing runners-up twice.

Did You Know That?

On 7 February 1903 Harry Stafford became the first Manchester United player to be sent off when he was given his marching orders in a First Round FA Cup tie against Liverpool at Bank Street which United won 2-1. Stafford took the decision to retire after United's 2-1 home defeat to Lincoln City on 7 March 1903 in Division Two. He played 200 games for Newton Heath and Manchester United, scored just 1 goal, in a 3-0 home win over Portsmouth on 5 January 1901 in the Intermediate Round of the FA Cup (William Griffiths and William Jackson also scored) but his contribution to Manchester United and the world of football was invaluable. Harry eventually settled in Canada where he died in 1944. For more information on his colourful life read *Harry Stafford – Manchester United's First Captain Marvel* by Ean Gardiner.

★ *Rocca is something of a Walter Mitty figure at the club cropping up at key moments in the club's history. He was a 'fixer' for the club through the early part of the 20th century before a financial crisis in 1931 led him to seek new investment which is how James W. Gibson came to be United's next owner. Rocca was then Assistant Manager to Walter Crickmer for two periods in the 1930s and became chief scout for the newly-formed MUJAC (Manchester*

4

United Junior Athletic Club) and is credited with discovering Johnny Carey,
Stan Pearson and several other key players in United's post-war renaissance.

After attempting but failing to sign Manchester City midfielder Matt
Busby in 1931, the pair stayed in touch and upon discovering that Liverpool
had offered Matt the manager's position, Rocca moved quickly to offer Busby
the United job. By the time Rocca died in June 1950 he had therefore seen
many of the players he had scouted and the manager he had recruited win
the FA Cup in 1948 and set United on a course to become the biggest club
in England. Something that would have been unimaginable at that historic
meeting back in 1902.

GAME NO. 2
UNITED 1-0 ASTON VILLA
FIRST DIVISION
BANK STREET, CLAYTON
1 JANUARY 1907
ATTENDANCE – 40,000

THE WELSH WIZARD

In October 1906, Manchester United manager Ernest Mangnall made one of the most important signings in the history of the club when he persuaded the Welsh international outside-right, William "*Billy*" Meredith, to join the club. Meredith was a household name in Manchester long before he arrived at United's Bank Street home having played for local rivals Manchester City since 1894. Born in Chirk, Wales on 30 July 1874, Meredith won Division Two winners' medals with City in 1899 and 1903 and an FA Cup winners' medal with them in 1904 when he captained the team. However "*Old Skinny*" as he was nicknamed due to his wiry frame, was involved in a bribery scandal in April 1905 when he was accused by the Aston Villa captain, Alec Leake, of offering him the sum of £10 to throw a match prior to kick-off. It was the final league game of the 1904–05 season and City needed to beat Aston Villa to stand a chance of winning the First Division title. Villa won the game 3-1 and finished fourth in the league, four points behind City who in turn finished a single point shy of runners–up Everton and two points adrift of champions Newcastle United.

Meredith always maintained that he was innocent of the charges but the FA threw the book at him by suspending him and fining him.

When Manchester City refused to pay his wages during the suspension Meredith retaliated and opted to tell the public exactly what was going on at Manchester City. In an interview with a sports journalist, Meredith said: *"What was the secret of the success of the Manchester City team? In my opinion, the fact that the club put aside the rule that no player should receive more than £4 a week. The team delivered the goods, the club paid for the goods delivered and both sides were satisfied."*

His statement caused shockwaves at the FA which had imposed a £4 per week maximum wage on all clubs in 1901. The FA acted immediately and carried out a thorough investigation at City and discovered that the club had made payments over and above the £4 ceiling to every player on their books. The club was fined £250, manager Tom Maley (elder brother of Glasgow Celtic manager Willie Maley) was handed a life suspension from the game (lifted by the FA in 1910) and 16 other players along with Meredith were fined and suspended until 31 December 1906. In order to pay the numerous fines imposed on the club by the FA, City were forced to sell their best players in an auction held at the Queen's Hotel, Manchester but canny Ernest Mangnall managed to snap up the star attraction before the auction even took place by secretly signing Meredith for £500 plus three of his City teammates Jimmy Bannister, Herbert Burgess and Alexander *"Sandy"* Turnbull. With these four players trading the blue of City for the red of United, the first golden era of Manchester City had come to an end and United's first golden era was just about to begin. Shortly after joining United, Chairman John H. Davies set Meredith up in business until he could resume his playing career and provided him with the funds to open a sports shop in St. Peter's Square, Manchester.

On New Year's Day 1907 a huge crowd of 40,000 fans poured into Bank Street to see the new quadruplet of players make their debuts for United in a First Division match against, of all clubs, Aston Villa. The new look United side lined-up as follows: Harry Moger, Robert Bonthron, Herbert Burgess, Dick Duckworth, Charlie Roberts (Capt), Alex Bell, Billy Meredith, James Bannister, Alexander Menzies, Sandy Turnbull, George Wall.

The vast majority had come to see Meredith and he did not disappoint them as he made his trademark winding runs down the wing, with a toothpick hanging from the corner of his mouth, followed by a perfect delivery into the opponent's box. Meredith claimed that the toothpick aided his concentration and that he preferred chewing tobacco but opted for the toothpick after the cleaning ladies refused to try and remove the stains from his jersey after games. Sandy Turnbull scored on his debut for the club to give the new recruits and United a 1-0 win after Meredith skipped past the Villa defence to deliver the killer pass. United's brand of stylish attacking football was the talk of the Division and they ended the campaign in a respectable 8th place.

After the match the *Manchester Guardian* reported the welcome Meredith received from suspension: *"It was a scene of wonderful enthusiasm, an amazing tumult of waving arms and handkerchiefs."*

City struggled during the 1906-07 season without their talented quartet of stars and finished 17th in the League, just two places above bottom side Derby County who were relegated. The following season, 1907-08, United were crowned Champions of England, First Division winners for the first time in the club's history, and repeated this title success in season 1910-11. In 1909 United won the FA Cup for the first time in the club's history with Sandy Turnbull scoring the only goal of the game in a 1-0 win over Bristol City at Crystal Palace. Mangnall left United in September 1912, after accepting an offer to manage City where he remained until the end of the 1923-24 season. His final game in charge of United was the Manchester Derby on 7 September 1912 when it was already known he would become the Blues' new manager. City won the First Division game 1–0 at Old Trafford and the media focused on Mangnall's delight.

After playing 335 games for United and scoring 36 goals, Meredith also returned to Manchester City in a free transfer that September aged 47 and played a further 34 games for the club. He was the oldest player ever to play for City, United and Wales.

Did You Know That?

Manchester United played their last game at Bank Street on 22 January 1910, beating Tottenham Hotspur 5–0 with Billy Meredith credited with scoring the last goal at the ground that had been the club's home for almost 18 years. Edward Connor and Arthur Hooper also scored with United captain Charlie Roberts scoring twice. Their next home game was played at their brand new purpose built home, Old Trafford, the beginning of a glorious new chapter in the history of the world's most famous football club.

GAME NO. 3
UNITED 2-1 GRIMSBY TOWN
FIRST DIVISION
MAINE ROAD, MANCHESTER
31 AUGUST 1946
ATTENDANCE – 41,025

MATT BUSBY APPOINTED MANAGER

When the 1946-47 season kicked off on 31 August 1946, Manchester United had a new manager in charge of the team, Matt Busby. It was the first competitive First Division season since the 1938-39 campaign when Walter Crickmer was the Secretary/Manager of United, Everton were crowned Champions of England (United finished 14th), Portsmouth beat Wolverhampton Wanderers 4-1 in the FA Cup final and the world was on the brink of war. When Great Britain declared war on Germany on 3 September 1939, the Football League introduced Wartime Leagues based on national regions, North and South. The atrocities officially came to an end on 2 September 1945 and the 1945-46 season was the last time the Wartime League was played. Sheffield United won the Football League North, Birmingham City were crowned Champions of the Football League South and Derby County won the 1946 FA Cup final after defeating Charlton Athletic 4-1 at Wembley.

On 15 February 1945, Matt Busby had been officially appointed as the new manager of Manchester United. In October 1930, with United in the middle of a record-breaking 12 successive defeats, manager Herbert Bamlett tried to sign Matt Busby from Manchester City. Bamlett asked his assistant, Louis Rocca, to contact City to see if they were willing to part with their Scottish right-half. Busby had become very good friends with Rocca as the pair were members of the Manchester Catholic Sportsman's Club. So Rocca telephoned Peter Hodge, the manager of City, and when he said he was interested in signing Busby Hodge said United could have him for £150. Rocca is believed to have replied: "*Peter, we haven't 150 cents, never mind £150,*" and so Busby remained at Maine Road. Rocca was no stranger to negotiating contracts. He was a shrewd businessman who owned an ice-cream manufacturing business in Manchester. At the end of the 1926-27 season, Rocca heard that Stockport County were hosting a bazaar to raise much needed monies for the club. United needed a half-back at the time and so Rocca offered three freezers of ice-cream to release Hugh McLenahan from his amateur contact. His offer was duly accepted and McLenahan was transferred to United.

Towards the end of the 1930s United were in desperate need of a manager to take over from Walter Crickmer (Club Secretary & Manager, 1937-45) who decided that he would relinquish his managerial responsibilities when the war eventually ended. A board meeting was called in December 1944 to look at candidates. Rocca reported that Liverpool had already offered Busby a job as right hand man to manager George Kay and it was he who convinced the United Board to leave it to him to approach his close friend Matt Busby. Rocca wrote a letter to Busby and addressed it to his army regiment. The letter was quite vague, referring only to a job offer just in case it fell into the wrong hands, namely the Board of Directors at Liverpool Football Club!

On 1 February 1945 Busby, still in his army fatigues, attended a meeting at Cornbrook Cold Storage, Trafford Park, a business unit owned by Manchester United Chairman James W. Gibson. United were still homeless, on the night of 11 March 1941 Old Trafford's Main Stand was completely destroyed by the Luftwaffe in a bombing raid on the nearby Trafford Park Industrial Estate. Much of the stadium's terracing was damaged as was the pitch. The damage meant that for the foreseeable future United would play their home games at Maine Road. Manchester City charged United £5,000 a year to use their facilities but they never allowed United use of the home team changing room when the teams met even when United were the home team!

On the face of it United were not an attractive prospect for a first time manager. They were practically penniless, had no home ground and their record between the wars had seen them yo-yo between the top two divisions. Nevertheless Busby was anxious to learn more about the job offer. As a player he had played for Manchester City (1928-36, FA Cup winner in 1934) and Liverpool (1936-41) and was capped once for Scotland in 1933 but he knew those days were over. He listened to what Gibson had to say and agreed to accept the job provided Gibson met his conditions. Busby made it clear from the outset that he, and only he, would be in charge of training, selecting the team and having the final decision in which players would be bought and sold and made it clear that he would accept no interference whatsoever from the club's directors, who, he believed, did not know the game as well as he did. At the time there wasn't a single club in England who offered their manager such a level of control over the team. It was totally unprecedented in the English game but Gibson was in no position to argue. Busby was originally offered a 3-year contract but the canny Scotsman managed to negotiate himself a 5-year deal after explaining to Gibson that it would take at least that long for his ideas to have a tangible effect.

Having agreed Gibson still needed the seal of approval of the Manchester United Board of Directors. On 15 February 1945 the Board of Directors met and unanimously agreed to offer Busby a 5-year contract to become manager following his demobilisation from the army. However, with the war in Europe still raging, it was not until 1 October 1945 that Busby officially took over the reins at the club. In the interim, Busby returned to the Army Physical Training Corps and in the spring of 1945, he took their football team to Bari, Italy. When he was there he took in a training session for a football team made up of non-commissioned officers which was led by Jimmy Murphy, a former pro who had played for West Bromwich Albion as a wing-half from 1928-39 and won 15 international caps for his native Wales (1933-38). Murphy was making a speech to a group of soldiers as Busby stood in the crowd and listened intently. Busby was so impressed with Murphy's speech that when it ended he walked over to him and introduced himself. The pair bonded immediately with the Scot persuading the Welshman to join him at Old Trafford when the fighting in Europe had ceased for good. Murphy accepted the offer and so after 7 years without a manager, no ground to play at and the club £15,000 in debt, Busby and Murphy set about turning Manchester United into the biggest club in England.

On his first day of training Matt Busby did something very few other football managers of the day did; he took to the training pitch wearing a tracksuit adopting a more hands on approach to management of his players. When asked about Busby's managerial style Johnny Carey, captain of Manchester United and the Republic of Ireland, said: "*When I joined United, Scott Duncan, with spats and a red rose in his buttonhole, typified a football manager. But here was the new boss playing with his team in training, showing what he wanted and how to do it. He was ahead of his time.*"

Busby was a football revolutionary and along with his right-hand man, Murphy, the former army buddies changed the course of English football. When Busby accepted Chairman James Gibson's offer to become the new Manchester United Manager, the club had not won a trophy in 34 years, the First Division Championship in season 1910-11, and were regarded as a yo-yo club; relegated to the Second Division at the end of the 1921-22 season they spent three seasons outside the top flight before finishing runners-up in the Second Division in season 1924-25 to win promotion. In season 1930-31, United finished bottom of the First Division having won only 7 of their 42 League games and conceded 115 goals. A sabbatical of five seasons followed in the Second Division and in season 1933-34, the unthinkable almost happened but relegation to the Third Division was averted on the last day of the season (United finished in 20th position). United returned to English football's top table in 1936-37 after clinching the Second Division Championship in 1935-36.

United opened the 1946-47 season on 31 August 1946 with a home game versus Grimsby Town at Maine Road. The Mariners were tough opponents at that time as iconic Liverpool manager Bill Shankly describes them in his autobiography, *"Pound for pound, and class for class, the best football team I have seen in England since the war. In the league they were in they played football nobody else could play. Everything was measured, planned and perfected and you could not wish to see more entertaining football."* High praise indeed from Shankly. Busby is quite justifiably regarded as the "Father of Manchester United" but Shankly could equally be described as a manager who may have been flawed, feared perhaps, but like Busby he was ultimately revered and did the same for Liverpool as Matt did for United.

The United side Busby selected was: Jack Crompton, Johnny Carey (Capt), Billy McGlen, Jack Warner, Allenby Chilton, Henry Cockburn, Jimmy Delaney, Stan Pearson, Jimmy Hanlon, Jack Rowley, Charlie Mitten

United beat Grimsby Town 2-1 with goals from Charlie Mitten and Jack Rowley. The man Liverpool wanted as George Kay's No.2 guided his Manchester United side to second place in the First Division in that first post-war season, a point behind Kay's Liverpool but in the long run Busby would transform the manager's role until it became central to every club in the world.

Did You Know That?

Matt Busby, Bill Shankly and the legendary Glasgow Celtic manager Jock Stein were all born with a 30-mile radius of each other in the central lowlands of Southern Scotland. Busby was born in Bellshill,

North Lanarkshire, Shankly in Glenbuck, East Ayrshire and Stein in Burnbank, South Lanarkshire. All three men were born into mining families. Their players would do anything for their manager such was the respect each one of the three commanded. They were the Three Kings of Scotland.

"No Scot ever made a bigger impact on a club than Bill Shankly. Others may claim an equal share of trophies and Matt Busby comes to mind with his wonderful record crowned by the European Cup, but not even Matt would claim the kinship with the fans that Bill enjoyed. He was what football was all about. I can't praise him higher than that." – Jock Stein

"Mr Williams (Chairman of Liverpool) said, 'How would you like to manage the best club in the country?' 'Why, is Matt Busby packing it up?' I asked." – Bill Shankly when he was offered the job of Liverpool manager

'John, you're immortal now' – Bill Shankly to Jock Stein after Glasgow Celtic won the European Cup in 1967

GAME NO. 4
WOLVERHAMPTON WANDERERS 0-1 UNITED
SECOND DIVISION
MOLINEUX
9 SEPTEMBER 1922
ATTENDANCE – 18,000

AS TOUGH AS SHEFFIELD STEEL

"When iron and carbon come together, there emerges steel! To be something stronger and better, you must mostly unite with something else and melt in something else!"

Mehmet Murat ildan

Frank Barson was the most controversial figure to play for Manchester United between the wars and arguably the toughest to pull on the famous red shirt. Forget your Keanes and Cantonas or even Captain Marvel himself, Barson was a bruiser in a class of his own and had the belligerence to go with it. Standing six feet one inch tall and weighing 12 stone 10, Barson was a fearsome ball of muscle unafraid of any opponent yet he played with enough class, style and brute force as a centre-half for Barnsley and Aston Villa to earn a call up for England. Off the pitch Frank was single-minded and freely mixed with some questionable characters not least Sheffield's notorious Fowler Brothers who were hanged for the murder of local boxer William Plommer in 1925.

He arrived as Manchester United embarked on a long downward spiral from which they wouldn't emerge until another world war had come and gone. By the summer of 1922 the club's glory era of a decade earlier had long since passed – United had finished bottom of the First Division the previous May and found themselves in the Second Division. They played in a palatial stadium capable of holding 70,000 but crowds rarely rose to half that. The recent world war had laid waste the cream of a whole generation and far from the Roaring Twenties experienced in the Home Counties, Manchester was struggling economically and thrills were few. Not only that but City were the bigger and better team.

Yet in signing Barson the club showed a rare glimpse of inter-war ambition to not only return to the First Division but compete with the powerhouses of the day. During the first war football had entrenched itself as the national sport – the story of German and British soldiers downing rifles to enjoy a mid-trench kick-about on Christmas Day struck a chord and the game quickly grew in popularity as attendances surged in the 1920s, everywhere that is except Old Trafford. While Evertonians were thrilling to the sight of goal machine Dixie Dean and Arsenal fans were going doe-eyed over dashing Ted Drake, United fans were limited to watching prolific striker Joe Spence and ten others either fighting relegation or trying to gain promotion on an annual basis. United's highest finish between the wars was ninth in 1925/26, the year they also reached the FA Cup semi-finals but were hammered 3-0 by City.

Born in Grimesthorpe, Sheffield, Frank had been an apprentice blacksmith and part-time footballer when he was recruited by Barnsley FC but before he could play for them he had to serve a two month ban following an ugly brawl against Birmingham City in a pre-season friendly. Later, having turned pro, he had to be smuggled out of Goodison Park when Everton fans wanted to confront him following several unsavoury incidents during a cup-tie. The smell of cordite was always at Frank's heels.

Having fallen out with the Barnsley board over his travelling expenses from Sheffield he joined Aston Villa in 1919 for £2,850 but Frank was never far from controversy and refused to move to

Birmingham despite the club's insistence that he should. He helped the Villains win the FA Cup in 1920, his only major medal, but before the match referee Jack Howcraft entered the Villa dressing-room and warned Barson that he would be sent off for any indiscretion. According to *The Essential Aston Villa*, "the normally unflappable Barson was taken aback and his performance was uncharacteristically cautious for much of the game." That summer Barson played his only game for England in a 2-1 defeat to Wales and was never selected again. He had the class alright but his hard-man reputation was impossible to shed.

Eventually his frequent clashes with the Villa board led him to hand in a transfer request and despite attention from much more attractive suitors Barson plumped for Second Division United whose owner John Henry Davies sweetened the £5,000 transfer deal by promising the new signing the landlordship of a pub should he secure the club promotion within the first three seasons.

United had started their Second Division campaign in fine fettle, winning 3 of their first 4 fixtures under manager John Chapman who had stepped into the job following the sudden death of fellow Scot Jack Robson the previous November and the signing of Barson had brought a bumper crowd of 30,000 to the opening game of the season, expectation for Frank's debut was huge. The Manchester United team that day read: John Mew; Charles Moore, John Silcock, Frank Barson (Capt); Clarence Hilditch, Neil McBain; Henry Thomas, John Wood, Joe Spence, Arthur Lochhead, Harry Williams.

Barson's reception was predictably mixed at Molineux, with Frank it came with the territory, and eye-witness reports suggest a degree of rustiness (he had not played for Villa for months because of the dispute with the board) but he had a hand in the late winner, cracking in a shot that was spilled and fell for Harry Williams who made no mistake.

Unfortunately it soon became apparent that Frank wouldn't be getting his pub that May as United endured a run of eight games without a win that autumn and never quite recovered, finishing fourth. Nor did he get it the following season when United hobbled in fourteenth but he finally got his hands on the keys to his pub in 1925 as United finished runners-up to Derby – they were back in the big time. That night the United fans flocked to Barson's pub in Ardwick Green to celebrate and according to Tony Matthews' account in *The Aston Villa Who's Who* "After 15 minutes behind the bar Barson, utterly fed up with the din, handed the keys over to the head waiter and walked out, never to return."

Although crowds were not Frank's thing, one-to-one contact certainly was and he received an eight week suspension in 1926 for punching Manchester City's Sam Cowan during an FA Cup semi-final which the Blues won 3-0. Barson eventually left United for Watford in May 1928 having made 152 appearances for United, scoring 4 goals. He was never sent off during his Old Trafford career which might say much for the relaxed nature of the officiating of the day rather than Frank's restraint on the pitch.

Did You Know?

Frank Barson only made 10 League appearances as captain of Watford, scoring once, because of his seven-month suspension he received in October 1928 for kicking an opposing forward and refusing to leave the pitch after the referee sent him off. On his return from suspension, he was placed on the transfer list on 19 April 1929. He then joined and became the captain at Hartlepool United FC on 17 May 1929 (9 League appearances, 2 goals), stepping up to player-coach before the season ended.

In April 1930, he was released and after an advertisement was placed in the *Athletic News* announcing his availability, Barson joined Wigan Borough FC as captain on 16 July 1930 and once again, a long suspension kept his League appearances down to only 19. He spent the 1931-32 season with Rhyl Athletic FC, appointed playermanager on 11 May 1932.

GAME NO. 5
UNITED 1-4 CARDIFF CITY
FIRST DIVISION
OLD TRAFFORD
4 APRIL 1953
ATTENDANCE- 37,163

THE BOY WONDER

After winning the First Division Championship in season 1951-52, Matt Busby's first as Manchester United manager, they inexplicably struggled to find the same form in season 1952-53. In their opening game of the 1952-53 campaign they beat Chelsea 2-0 at Old Trafford with goals from Johnny Berry and Johnny

Downie but they looked far from being champion material in their next four League games losing three and drawing one.

Busby did not seem to know his best team. He tinkered with his squad and over the course of the season he used no fewer than 30 different players in United's 42 First Division games including five different goalkeepers (Jack Crompton, Reg Allen, Les Olive, Ray Wood and Johnny Carey). Carey was a right back and captain of the team but with none of his goalkeepers fit at the time, Busby was forced to use his captain as a stop-gap goalkeeper. On 18 February 1953 Carey swapped his No.4 shirt for the green No.1 shirt and performed quite admirably in goal helping his team-mates draw 2-2 with Sunderland at Roker Park (scorers: Eddie Lewis aged 18, David Pegg aged 17).

The previous season he had only used called upon the services of a 24 man squad and pretty settled starting eleven but a year on and Busby realised that this was an ageing side and despite being loyal to the men who had served him so well over the previous five post-war seasons when they helped United to a fourth place League finish and four runners-up spots before finally landing the title in 1951-52, the time was right for youth to be given its chance.

Following a 2-0 defeat at home to Stoke City on 11 October 1952 United dropped to second bottom in the First Division table (Manchester City were rock bottom) and for the first time since he took charge of the club in 1945 the alarm bells were ringing at Old Trafford. Off the pitch Busby was receiving some heat from his Board of Directors who themselves were being pressed by the club's shareholders to turn things around and quickly but Busby wasn't a man who panicked under pressure and he knew something the club's shareholders didn't. Busby had an extra card up his sleeve which he was yet to play. In fact as time would tell he had more than the standard four Aces in his pack.

Over the summer of 1952 the forward thinking Busby, ably assisted by Jimmy Murphy, opened the doors of Old Trafford for a Summer School. These pupils were not taught their lessons in a classroom, they were taught on the training pitch. Manchester United became the first club to run a close season coaching course for promising schoolboys who dreamed of becoming a professional footballer. The boys were given their lessons by Murphy, Bert Whalley (coach), Joe Armstrong (scout) and Bill Inglis (trainer). Prior this Murphy and Whalley had travelled south on 31st May arriving at 23 Malvern Crescent, Holly Hall, Dudley at close to midnight - they were taking no chances. The home they were staking out belonged to the parents of Duncan Edwards whose prodigious talent had attracted interest from many clubs, including nearby Wolverhampton Wanderers, following a junior career that had seen him play regularly for Wolverhampton Street Secondary School, Dudley Schoolboys and Worcester County XI. Despite his accent and upbringing Duncan admitted that he had his heart set on playing for Manchester United and as the clock struck midnight the pair pounced. By the time the clock struck one they were on their way home with the hottest property in football – they had signed Duncan Edwards on amateur forms.

Amazingly it was Joe Mercer, a player with Arsenal at the time and the future manager of Manchester City, who had alerted Busby to the talent of Edwards telling his United counterpart that "'the boy would become a world beater." Duncan was one of the first to be enrolled for classes at the summer school and is famously pictured on his second day at the school, with Mrs Ann Davies, a club stewardess at Manchester United, pouring the shy, but immaculately attired Edwards a cup of tea. Innocent times they were.

During the 1952-53 season the Football Association introduced a new competition, the FA Youth Cup. Murphy signed the cream of the crop from the Summer School to United's youth set up to join other lads who had been spotted from around the British Isles. Murphy's mob strolled through that inaugural competition and reached the final. Ironically their opposition in the final was Wolves, still bitter about the loss of their local legend. To rub salt in the wound United beat them 7-1 at Old Trafford in the first leg on 4 May 1953 before a bumper crowd of 20,934 (scorers: Noel McFarlane 2, Lewis 2, Pegg, Albert Scanlon, Liam Whelan). The second leg was played at Molineux on 9 May 1953 before a crowd of 14,290. The kids from Manchester drew 2-2 (scorers: Lewis and Whelan) and won the trophy 9-3 on aggregate. The shiny new trophy was presented to the United captain, 16-year old Duncan Edwards, who won it again as captain with United in 1954 and 1955. Indeed, the United Youth Team in the late 1950s were untouchable winning the first five editions of the competition. The football lessons that were taught in the Summer School had most certainly paid off.

Yet raising this trophy above his head wasn't the highlight of Edwards season as on 4 April 1953 Busby gave the captain of his Youth Team his first team debut. Cardiff City were the visitors to Old Trafford for a First Division game and Edwards was handed the red No.6 shirt. The Manchester United team was: Jack Crompton, John Aston Jnr, Roger

Byrne (Capt), Allenby Chilton, Duncan Edwards, Thomas Gibson, Johnny Berry, Jack Rowley, Tommy Taylor, Stan Pearson, David Pegg.

The Welsh side won the game 4-1 with Roger Byrne scoring United's goal. Although the match proved to be the 16-year old's only senior game that season, Busby had seen enough. The United manager knew he had a star in the making and he wasn't going to rush his progress. Busby wasn't concerned about the value of the club's shares. His only concern was for his players. At the end of the season United finished in eighth place in a League won by Arsenal, their seventh title.

When United got off to a similarly dismal start in 1953-54 – winning 4, drawing 5 and losing 6 of their first 15 League matches, Busby turned to his youth set-up once again. On 28 October 1953, three days before United were due to play Huddersfield Town away in the League, Busby and Murphy had arranged a friendly match with Kilmarnock to celebrate the official switching on of the Scottish club's new floodlights at their Rugby Park home. Busby wanted to see just how good his young players were and how they performed against more experienced players. A few of the youth team players were selected to play; Eddie Colman (aged 16), Duncan Edwards (17), Wilf McGuinness (who had turned 16 three days before the game) and David Pegg (18). Jackie Blanchflower (20) and Jeff Whitefoot (19) also played although they had already made the step up into the first team. A youthful United team beat Kilmarnock 3-0 in front of 12,639 fans. It was the birth of the Busby Babes.

And when United travelled to Yorkshire on 31 October 1953, Busby made three changes to the team which had beaten Aston Villa 1-0 a week earlier at Old Trafford. Out went Henry Cockburn, Mark Pearson and Harry McShane and in came Dennis Viollet (aged 20) for his third start that season, Jackie Blanchflower and Edwards who had celebrated his 17th birthday four weeks earlier. Following the retirement of Johnny Carey at the end of the 1952-53 season, 24-year old Roger Byrne was made club captain. A 0-0 draw at Huddersfield's Leeds Road ground marked the start of the Busby Babes reign of English football in the remaining 26 League fixtures, Blanchflower (13 goals) and Viollet (11 goals) appeared in all 26. Duncan ran out a further 23 times in the League that season missing the 2-2 draw away to Aston Villa and the final two games, a 1-0 loss at Charlton Athletic and a 3-1 win against Sheffield United at Bramall Lane – United finished in fourth place in the First Division won by Wolverhampton Wanderers, the first of three titles they won in the 1950s.

Over the course of the following three seasons (1954-57) Duncan played 117 times for United in all competitions, scoring 15 goals, winning the First Division in seasons 1955-56 and 1956-57. He had also burst on to the international scene, winning his first senior England cap on 2 April 1955 aged 18 years and 183 days in a 7-2 rout of Scotland at Wembley Stadium in a British Home International Championship match.

During the 1956-57 season, several of Busby's young stars, notably Bobby Charlton and Duncan Edwards, were encouraged by their manager to follow in his footsteps and do their National Service. Charlton aged 19 and Edwards aged a year older like many professional footballers from the Midlands and north-west, were posted to Nesscliffe, Shropshire and played for the Nesscliffe Army Royal Army Ordnance Corps football team.

Duncan finished his National Service in 1957 and Bobby left Nesscliffe in 1958. Prior to the 60th anniversary of the Munich Air Disaster Derek Thorpe, who served with the Kings Shropshire Light Infantry at Copthorne Barracks, Shrewsbury was asked about his memories of the famous United pair when he played against them. "Because they were just up the road from us, we would play each other a lot. They were a cut above the rest. They had a lot of players from different clubs, there was a player from Everton, and another one from Blackpool," said Derek who himself was a nippy winger. Derek recalled one game in particular between the two army sides when his sergeant-major warned his team that the Nesscliffe lads had a few tasty players in their side. Not long into the game Derek was bearing down on goal when he was dispossessed by a strapping defender. Derek immediately set about paying his opponent back saying: "He tackled me early on, and I thought 'I'll have you next time'. I didn't half know about it, I landed about two yards further up the pitch than I did the first time." The player was none other than Edwards who was already a leading figure in the United side and had been capped by England three times. Derek said he was in total awe of the power, skill and speed of the Busby Babe. "Him and Bobby Charlton were both in the same team, and they really stood out. I thought Duncan Edwards was better than Bobby Charlton, and I later read that Bobby Charlton also thought he was. They were such great lads. Duncan was from Dudley, and I was from Dawley, so the lingo was pretty similar. After he had knocked me flying with his tackle, he came over to me, and said 'you all right, kid?'"

Brian Griffiths, who played at full back for Shrewsbury Town, also played for the Nesscliffe Army Royal Army Ordnance Corps football team. Charlton arrived at the Nesscliffe depot shortly after Brian and the pair were in the same platoon, 3 Platoon, and they shared the same billet. "Duncan was already there. He was a PTI, a physical training instructor. He was a corporal. We had a good old natter and he explained everything to us. I knew him as Dunc. He was a smashing lad. He was big, and so gentle, and yet when he said something, you automatically did it. He was not aggressive, and his football capabilities were just unbelievable," said Brian. The platoon trained at Shropshire Racecourse, Monkmoor Road, Shrewsbury. "We would do the normal training the soldiers did – marching, ammunition and so on – and then after that the footballers would do the football training. We were all mates and it was a good atmosphere," said Brian. Charlton played at inside-forward or centre-forward but Brian recalls that it took Edwards to get the best out of his United teammate. "Bobby does owe Dunc quite a lot. Over the time I knew him he improved to A1. He did not use his body like a defender does. He was always looking to try and pass people, even if they had the ball. He had no aggression – we used to say to him: 'Bloody get in!'" added Brian.

Derek was impressed with how the Busby Babes slotted in very easily to army life, and got on with all the other soldiers during their Shropshire army days. "They were great lads, they really were. You could talk to them easily, it was just normal army chat. At one point I was injured, and I finished up in the medical centre at Nesscliffe, and I remember Duncan and Bobby coming to visit me. They mucked in with everything and they never thought they were any higher than anybody else," added Derek.

Duncan Edwards was only 21 years old when he died and had the football world at his feet. In his short career he played 177 times for Manchester United and scored 21 goals. He also made 18 appearances for England, scoring 5 goals. There will never been another team like the Busby Babes or indeed, a player like Duncan Edwards.

Did You Know That?

When Duncan made his United debut he became the youngest player to play for the club in the Football League aged 16 years and 185 days. When Duncan played for United in the 1955 FA Youth Cup final he became the first international player to play in the final. He has two streets named in his honour, Duncan Edwards Close in Dudley and Duncan Edwards Court in the Newton Heath area of Manchester.

GAME NO. 6
WEST BROMWICH ALBION 1-4 UNITED
FIRST DIVISION
THE HAWTHORNS
18 JANUARY 1964
ATTENDANCE- 25,624

UNITED'S THREE MUSKETEERS

The French author Alexandre Dumas's historical adventure novel, "The Three Musketeers," written in 1844 can be classified in the swashbuckler genre. The story is about heroic, chivalrous swordsmen who fight for justice in France in the early 17th Century. Set between 1625 and 1628, the novel recounts the adventures of a young man named d'Artagnan after he leaves home to travel to Paris, hoping to join the Musketeers of the Guard. The Musketeers were a fighting company of the military branch of the Maison du Roi, the Royal Household of the French monarchy whose famous motto was "All for one and one for all!".

As United went into the 1963-64 season, hoping to build on their FA Cup final win over Leicester City the previous season, manager Matt Busby had a constant thought in his head. It occupied his thoughts prior to every game United after they opened their 1963-64 First Division season with a 3-3 draw against Sheffield Wednesday at Hillsborough on 24 August 1963. A week earlier Busby's FA Cup winners had been on the end of a 4-0 beating against champions Everton at Goodison Park in the FA Charity Shield and left Busby with a major dilemma – what do you do when you have players such as Bobby Charlton, Denis Law and a 17-year old wonder kid named George Best at your disposal? The answer is quite simple really. You play them all, although in George's case he might have to wait.

Bobby Charlton had been a member of the first team squad since making his debut on 6 October 1956 when he scored twice in a 4-2 win over Charlton. Denis Law was just starting his second season with United having cost a British record transfer fee of £115,000 when

United bought the Scottish international striker from the Italian side, AS Torino, on 12 July 1962. Law, who had played for Manchester City from 1960-61 scoring 21 times in 44 games, cost Busby £27,000 less than the £142,000 which Inter Milan shelled out to Barcelona to acquire the services of Luis Suarez in the summer of 1961. Suarez, a Spanish international, won the Ballon d'Or in 1960 ahead of Ferenc Puskás (Real Madrid) and Uwe Seeler (Hamburg). In his first season at Old Trafford Law scored 29 goals in 44 games for United. Law scored in United's 3-1 win over Leicester City in the 1963 FA Cup final, David Herd scored twice.

Matt Busby gave 17-year old George Best his debut on 14 September 1963 wearing the No.7 jersey in a 1-0 win over West Bromwich Albion at Old Trafford – Law missed the game but Charlton played in it. Best's second match came against Burnley on 28 December 1963 and The Belfast Boy tortured the opposition that day scoring his first professional goal and helping United to a comfortable 5-1 win but again Law did not play. Busby kept George in the team when United travelled to Southampton in defence of the FA Cup but once more Law was absent. On 4 January 1964, United defeated The Saints 3-2 at The Dell in the Third Round, George wore the No.11 jersey. A week after the FA Cup win, United lost 2-1 at home to Birmingham City in the League and this time it was Charlton who missed the game. George's room-mate David Sadler deputised for him and scored his fourth goal of the season with George retaining the No.11 jersey. So it wasn't until a fortnight later that Matt Busby was able to name Best, Law and Charlton in the same team.

Busby's team to face The Baggies at The Hawthorns was: David Gaskell, Tony Dunne, Noel Cantwell (Capt), Bill Foulkes, Maurice Setters, Pat Crerand, Graham Moore, Bobby Charlton, George Best, David Herd, Denis Law.

In the main Busby favoured a 4-2-4 formation, Law took a central role up front and Best was handed the wide right role (No.11). Charlton played as the more advanced of the middle two with Crerand sitting just behind Law with Herd and Sadler making up the front four. United were on a different planet that cold and windy afternoon in the West Midlands; Charlton was unflappable in the United midfield, a player who just oozed composure and confidence as he directed the play in front of him, Bobby glided across the pitch effortlessly with the same grace and composure displayed by Rudolph Nureyev on the stage. Law was Busby's menace up front, a striker who was fearless and always up for a scrap if defenders started using dirty tactics on him. Denis was as good in the air as he was on the deck possessing a deft touch to match the precision of his shooting and his pace and he scored goals, lots of goals. Defenders hated playing against him and it came as no surprise when along with his tag of "The King" United fans also nicknamed him "Denis the Menace" after the archetypal badly behaved schoolboy from the comic *The Beano*. Just as *The Beano*'s Dennis waged a constant campaign of terror against a gang of 'softies', Law terrorised defences in England and Europe.

In many ways Best was a hybrid of Charlton and Law possessing the grace and composure on the ball of Charlton and the athleticism and speed of Law. Despite his tender age, and his waif like look, the kid who grew up on the streets of east Belfast could handle himself. From an early age the young Best was used to playing against much bigger and stronger opponents but he always outwitted them. Throughout his playing career no player was kicked or singled out for special treatment by hardened defenders more than George Best. He was similar to Real Madrid's legendary outside-left, Francisco Gento (1953-71), who the *Morning News* newspaper in Houston, Texas once colourfully described thus: "The ball pants and twirls and laps at his feet as though it were a kitten trained in method acting." George possessed perfect balance, he was as tough as any player, he had an abundance of skill and he often made defenders look like they should contemplate pursuing a different career

The West Bromwich Albion players must have looked at the players in red standing beside them in the tunnel at The Hawthorns prior to kick-off and contemplated by how many goals they would lose the game. They will have remembered Best's debut for United against them four months earlier and this time they also had to face the threat of Law. Unlike United's narrow home win in September, this game was a stroll with United winning 4-1 and although all three of United's finally united stars scored it was Best who caught the eye and his goal after the interval capped a terrific display. With the game at 1-1, Charlton's opener being cancelled out by Terry Simpson just before the break, George latched on to a pass from Law and seemed heavily out-numbered but a drop of a shoulder and a burst of pace took him clear, although the angle was acute, geometry mattered little as Best slid the ball in with little difficulty. Law doubled United's lead minutes later and added a fourth in injury time, , his 19th league goal of the season, but this had been yet another star performance from the Belfast boy-wonder.

Yet it was a season of frustration for United as they ended 1963-64 potless, finishing runners-up to Liverpool in the league, beaten by West Ham on a quagmire at Hillsborough in the FA Cup semi-finals and were dumped out of the Cup Winners' Cup 5-0 by Sporting Lisbon. Nevertheless Law finished the season with an incredible 46 goals in all competitions in just 42 appearances, while Best scored 6 in 26 and Charlton 15 in an incredible 54. Law's exploits for United earned him the coveted Ballon d'Or award in 1964 winning 61 votes, in second place was Inter Milan's Luis Suarez with 43 while Real Madrid's Amancio was in third place with 38.

Following their 5-Star performance against West Bromwich Albion, United's Three Musketeers would be box office draws up and down the country and abroad for the next eight years as United teammates. Busby had the golden touch and his selection of Law, Best and Charlton signalled the beginning of the assembly of his third and final great United team and a new golden age for the club.

Did You Know That?

When Manchester United beat Sunderland 4-1 at Old Trafford on 18 January 1969, they had in their team a unique trio which no other football club in Europe could match. When the team took to the pitch they had three Ballon d'Or winners in their line-up: Denis Law (1964), Bobby Charlton (1966) and the Belfast Boy, George Best, who was named the best player in Europe with 61 votes at a ceremony in Paris, France on 28 December 1968. United's Northern Ireland international beat teammate Bobby Charlton, to the award by 8 votes. Red Star Belgrade's Dragan Dzajic was in third position with 46 votes. It was the first time three Ballon d'Or winners had played in the same team. It would be another 24 years before another club side could field three European Footballers of the Year when AC Milan had Ruud Gullit (winner in 1987), Marco van Basten (winner in 1988, 1989 & 1992) and Jean-Pierre Papin (winner in 1991) in their 1992-93 squad. Papin was at Olympique Marseilles when he won the award. Two other winners of the Ballon d'Or have played for United: Michael Owen, who was at Liverpool when he picked it up in 2001, and Cristiano Ronaldo who scooped it in 2008 after helping United to winning the Premier League and UEFA Champions League in season 2007-08.

GAME NO. 7
UNITED 5-1 SWANSEA TOWN
SECOND DIVISION
OLD TRAFFORD
4 DECEMBER 1937
ATTENDANCE- 17,782

TOP GUN

"The question isn't who is going to let me; it's who is going to stop me."

Ayn Rand

Wayne Rooney, Bobby Charlton, Denis Law, Dennis Viollet, George Best, Ryan Giggs, Mark Hughes and Paul Scholes are all Manchester United Legends. Their exploits for the club are legion, historic even. Eight of the greatest ever players to be honoured with wearing the world famous jersey of Manchester United Football Club. And they occupy 8 of the Top 10 places in the table of players who scored the most number of goals for United. Perhaps an unknown United Legend to a lot of United fans, Joe Spence, is No.7 in that elite list with 168 goals in 510 appearances after arriving at Old Trafford from Scotswood, now known as Newcastle Blue Star Football Club, in March 1919. Spence left United to join Bradford City in June 1933 but his successor as United's main goal-getter was the man who occupies the No.4 place - Jack "Gunner" Rowley.

Scott Duncan bought 17 year-old Jack Rowley from Bournemouth & Boscombe Athletic Football Club in October 1937 for a mere £3,000 and in his 18 years at United (1937-55), which was interrupted by World War II, Rowley was the club's undisputed goal king scoring 211 goals in 424 appearances. Rowley was a strong, compact striker who possessed a powerful and accurate shot and was decent in the air.

He had began his football career as a youth team player with Cradley Heath and aged 15 he was signed by his local club side, Wolverhampton Wanderers then managed by Major Frank Buckley, a former United player but before he kicked a ball for the West Midlands club he was on his way back to Cradley Heath who played in the Birmingham & District League. Playing for Cradley Heath the 17-year old began to draw the attention of several Football League clubs one of which was Third Division South side Bournemouth who signed him in February 1937. He scored 10 goals in his first 11 games for The Cherries and his total of 12 goals in 22 League appearances helped them to their highest ever finish of eighth. The same season United were relegated from the top flight having spent just one season back. United's problem seemed obvious, they were poor in attack and even worse in defence! The club had scored a meagre 55 goals in 42 League games while conceding 78. Scott Duncan knew he needed a new striker if United were to make an immediate return to the First Division, the club's top goal scorer in 1936–37 was Tommy Bamford with 15 in the League and 1 in the FA Cup. He was a decent striker scoring 11 times for United in 1934–35, 16 times in 1935–36 and 15 times the season they went down but Duncan wanted a prolific forward in the mould of such stars of the Thirties as Everton's Dixie Dean, Middlesbrough's George Camsell and Arsenal's Ted Drake, These players were the pin-up boys in an era when record breaking scoring feats seemed to be a weekly occurrence.

Duncan knew that United had some promising youth players coming through the ranks, not least 18 year-old Salford lad Stan Pearson who would make his debut later that season but United's hopes of making an instant leap back up into the First Division were looking slim after their opening 11 League games, they had won 4, drawn 2 and lost 5, scored 14 and conceded 11. Only four different players had found the net: Bamford 5, Thomas Manley 5, William Bryant 2 & Ronald Ferrier 2. Following United's 1–1 draw away to Blackburn Rovers on 16 November 1937, Duncan liked what he seen in Rowley and persuaded his Chairman to stump up the money to get him before another club nipped in and signed him. Duncan gave the teenager his Manchester United debut a few days later on 23 October 1937 a 1–0 (Ferrier) home win over Sheffield Wednesday. It was a huge decision for Duncan who dropped Tommy Manley after he had played in the previous 11 games. Rowley had no airs and graces about him and was an open and honest player but he knew his own mind. After making his debut he asked Duncan to put him back in the reserves as he felt he was not quite ready yet for playing in the second tier of the English League.

Duncan acceded to his young signing's request but by the time Rowley made his second appearance for the club his manager had resigned on 9 November 1937. The club's Secretary, Walter Crickmer, took charge of first team affairs in tandem with his role as Secretary of Manchester United. It was not the first time Crickmer had been asked to fulfill both roles at Old Trafford, following United's relegation to the Second Division at the end of the 1930-31 the directors opted not to renew the contract of manager Herbert Bamlett and Crickmer took charge, them to 12th place in the League. Duncan was appointed Manchester United manager on 13 July 1932, leaving Crickmer to return to his day job.

Amid the turmoil at the end of Duncan's reign, Rowley had missed five games, United winning 3, drawing 1 and losing 1 - they scored 13 times and conceded 5 with Bamford netting 5 times and Manley twice. One of the victories was a 7-1 destruction of Chesterfield at the Recreation Ground, Chesterfield on 13 November 1937. The game marked the debut of Stan Pearson. Pearson scored in his next two League games and on 4 December 1937, Crickmer unleashed Pearson and Rowley on the Second Division. Swansea Town were the visitors to Old Trafford. Crickmer selected his team: Jack Breedon, Herbert Redwood, William Roughton, George Vose, William McKay, Bert Whalley, William Bryant, Harry Baird, Jack Rowley, Thomas Bamford, Stan Pearson.

Swansea Town was founded in 1912 and joined the Football League in 1921. In 1969 the club changed their name when they adopted the name Swansea City to reflect Swansea's new status. Yet that afternoon the Swans were run ragged as the youthful duo of inside-forward Pearson and centre-forward Rowley ran the Swansea players into the ground on the back of a 5-1 hiding. "Gunner" Rowley bagged four and Bryant scored the other goal. Crickmer's belief that the pair of young strikers would work well together reaped immediate dividends.

Rowley now knew he had what it took to make it in the professional game. All of his dreams were about to come true in the famous red jersey of Manchester United and alongside Stan Pearson the pair would terrorise defences either side of the looming World War. Rowley only missed one of United's remaining 24 League games of the season, a 1-0 loss at home to Tottenham Hotspur on 19 February 1938. In his 25 League outings he scored 9 goals but failed to find the net in the four FA Cup games he played in for United. Pearson scored twice in 11 League games and once in his only FA Cup appearance of the season. The pair helped United to second place in the table, four points behind Champions Aston Villa, and promotion back to the First Division.

Another player Duncan signed that season was Johnny Carey

who would go on to captain Manchester United in the post-war era while the following season Crickmer acquired Allenby Chilton from Liverpool, both, along with Rowley and Pearson, would form the nucleus of United's post-war team after Matt Busby accepted in 1945.

By the time Rowley left Old Trafford in February 1955 he had played 424 games for Manchester United scoring 211 times, a ratio of a goal every two games. He won the FA Cup with United in 1948, scoring twice in the 4-2 win over Blackpool in the final, and a First Division Championship winners' medal in season 1951-52 when he scored 30 times in his 40 League outings making him United's top goal scorer in a season for the fifth and last time of his Old Trafford career (Pearson scored 18 goals in 1952-53, Tommy Taylor netted 23 times in 1953-54 and Dennis Viollet was top marksman in 1954-55 with 21 strikes). He also won the FA Charity Shield in 1952. Yet the most remarkable aspect of Rowley's story is that he wasn't even the most prolific striker in his family, his younger brother George scored 434 goals in 619 league games for West Bromwich Albion, Fulham, Leicester City and Shrewsbury Town, which is still a record for the most number of goals scored in the history of English League football,.

Jack moved on to become player/manager at Plymouth Argyle for three seasons, scoring 15 times in 58 games, before concentrating solely on managing the club. Despite relegation from the Second Division in 1955-56, the Pilgrims bounced back up in 1958-59 but within 10 months of guiding the Pilgrims to the title he was sacked in March 1960 with Argyle teetering in the relegation zone at the bottom of the table. Rowley then moved on to Oldham Athletic and steered the Lancashire club to promotion to the Third Division after finishing runners-up to Brentford in the Fourth Division in 1962-63. When he was invited to become manager of Ajax Amsterdam for the 1963-64 season he jumped at the chance. When he arrived at Ajax he soon discovered the talents of a 16 year-old named Johann Cruyff but by the time he made his debut, 15 November 1964, Rowley was already back in England after only managing to guide the Dutch club to fifth place in the 1963-64 Eredivisie. More managerial roles followed at Wrexham 1966-67, Bradford Park Avenue 1967-68 and a return to Oldham Athletic 1968-69 before he quit football in December 1969 to manage a sub Post Office in Oldham.

Rowley was capped six times by England making his debut versus Switzerland at Wembley in an international friendly match on 2 December 1948. Rowley scored in the game, a 30 yard left foot shot in the 55th minute to put England 4-0 up in a game that ended 6-0. His United teammates also played in the game, John Aston Snr making his third appearance and Henry Cockburn winning his 8th cap. Rowley's rocket of a shot was hailed as a masterpiece by the English press. He scored four against Ireland in a 9-2 mauling of the Irish at Maine Road on 16 November 1949 with Pearson scoring twice. Rowley was only selected for the game due to an injury suffered by Newcastle United's lethal centre-forward, Jackie Milburn. Ireland's goalkeeper, Hugh Kelly of Fulham had to pick the ball out of the back of his net 28 times in his last five internationals for his country. In May 1949, he played in a 'B' international for England and bagged a hat-trick in a 4-0 win versus the Netherlands 'A' team at Amsterdam's Olympic Stadium.

Rowley's sixth and last goal for his country was against Italy at White Hart Lane on 30 November 1949, a game England won 2-0, Rowley's scorcher of a goal was set-up by Pearson Although he was also selected to play for the Football League select side in representative matches against Northern Ireland, Republic of Ireland and Scotland, his ability to regularly find the back of the net deserved more international recognition. He was not selected for England's 1950 World Cup squad which ultimately cost England as they only scored two goals in their three Group 2 games and were on the first plane home from Brazil.

The Manchester United Legend and club's fourth all-time leading goal scorer sadly passed away on 28 June 1998.

United's all-time Top 10 goal scorers are: 1. Wayne Rooney 253; 2. Bobby Charlton 249; 3. Denis Law 237; 4. Jack Rowley 211; 5. Dennis Viollet 179; 6. George Best 179; 7. Joe Spence 168; 8. Ryan Giggs 168; 9. Mark Hughes 163; 10. Paul Scholes 155

Did You Know That?

During World War II, Jack Rowley served in the South Staffordshire regiment and participated in the D-Day landings. During the war he appeared as a guest player for Tottenham Hotspur, Wolverhampton Wanderers, Aldershot, Shrewsbury Town and Belfast Distillery in Northern Ireland. In 1942 he helped Wolves win the Football League War Cup scoring twice in their 4-1 win over Sunderland at Molineux in the second leg of the final after drawing the first leg 2-2 at Roker Park. The Wolves manager was Major Frank Buckley. His goal scoring exploits during the war, 8 in one game for Wolves, and 7 in a game for

Spurs, earned him a wartime cap for England versus Wales on 6 May 1944. England won the game 2-0 at Ninian Park.

GAME NO. 8
UNITED 3-1 LIVERPOOL
FIRST DIVISION
OLD TRAFFORD
1 JANUARY 1989
ATTENDANCE – 44,745

NEW YEARS HONOURS

By New Years Day 1989 Alex Ferguson was over two years into his Old Trafford reign and fans were struggling to see any progress - the old guard who had been mainstays under Ron Atkinson were still first team regulars with the likes of Norman Whiteside, Paul McGrath and Gordon Strachan still at the club but the team didn't play the kind of expansive football they had grown accustomed to under the previous manager. United seemed to have an identity crisis, they were duller to watch than under Big Ron and didn't even have the results to show for it.

Early performances under Fergie had been all about aggression, a highlight being a 2-0 victory over Arsenal in January 1987 where the team appeared to have been sent out to kick The Gunners out of their stride. It worked as Norman Whiteside, oozing aggressive intent from the kick-off, wound the Arsenal players up so much that they lost control and David Rocastle was sent off. Otherwise performances had been underwhelming.

Fergie's first significant signings had been Viv Anderson who arrived from Arsenal for £250,000 and Brian McClair from Celtic for £850,000 in the summer of 1987 with centre-half Steve Bruce following in December from Norwich for £825,000. McClair had settled in well registering 31 goals during the 1987-88 season as United finished a distant second to an all-conquering Liverpool team that most pundits rated as one of the greatest of all time.

Ahead of the 1988-89 season Fergie spent £450,000 on goalkeeper Jim Leighton and £1.8m on bringing back crowd favourite Mark Hughes from Barcelona and hopes were high that the club could go one better but, having got off to a reasonable start, United endured an horrific autumn registering just one league win in twelve games. By then Luton defender Mal Donaghy and winger Ralph Milne had been signed and neither looked likely to turn the club into title challengers.

Milne turned into a sort of terrace anti-hero. He had been a devastating winger for Dundee United but, playing before a United Road crowd who had grown up watching the likes of Best, Morgan, Coppell and Hill, the criticism and catcalls seemed to get to him. However a goal against Charlton Athletic in United's only win for three months, brought astonishment then acclamation. There wasn't much else to shout about. The attendance that day was a mere 31,173. Under Ron Atkinson there would have been another 10,000 there at least. Admittedly Margaret Thatcher's newly introduced ID scheme didn't help with a membership card required to enter certain sections of the ground but the dwindling attendances chimed with the growing sense of ennui surrounding the club. Following a 2-0 win over Nottingham Forest on Boxing Day before a bumper crowd of 39,582, all eyes were on the New Years Day game against champions Liverpool.

At least under Big Ron United fans could always rely on the team turning up against the scousers. Under Atkinson United only lost 3 times against the best team in the country in 15 games. Fergie had won his first two games against Liverpool as United boss but after a couple of draws the previous season, including a famous comeback from 3-1 down at Anfield in April, United had lost the game at Anfield earlier in the season to a Jan Molby penalty. Alex knew he'd have to get the better of Dalglish's Liverpool to stay in the job.

United were not at full strength - 17 year-old Lee Sharpe, a £185,000 signing from Torquay United, deputising for Colin Gibson at left-back while 19 year-old Lee Martin was quickly establishing himself at right-back and 20 year-old Russell Beardsmore filled in for Paul McGrath, still recovering from a long-term knee injury, who only made the bench alongside prolific youth team striker Mark Robins.

Manchester United: Jim Leighton, Lee Martin, Lee Sharpe, Steve Bruce, Russell Beardsmore, Mal Donaghy, Bryan Robson, Gordon Strachan, Brian McClair, Mark Hughes, Ralph Milne. Subs: Mark Robins (for Strachan 33 mins), Paul McGrath (for Martin 66 mins).

The New Year brought new hope for United fans and what better tonic could there be to ring in 1989 than a victory over Messrs Dalglish, Aldridge, Barnes and Beardsley. Despite their poor recent form, United had only lost one home game all season, a 2-1 defeat to Norwich back in October, while Liverpool were on a run of nine unbeaten games but began the game in an accustomed fifth place 9 points behind leaders Arsenal. United were three points and six places behind the visitors.

The first half saw plenty of ambition from United with Liverpool stand-in goalkeeper Mike Hooper forced into a sharp save from McClair early on but injury concerns mounted as Gordon Strachan was forced off after 33 minutes with a knee injury and replaced by Mark Robins as an auxiliary attacker with McClair dropping into midfield. Liverpool's front three of Barnes, Beardsley and Aldridge were a growing threat as the first half progressed and McClair was forced to clear from his own six-yard area as Beardsley threatened to find a way through just before the break.

A re-jig in the second half saw Beardsmore move on to the right wing and McClair return to his accustomed centre-forward role and the switch nearly paid immediate dividends as the diminutive Beardsmore jinked past his full-back and McClair's volley was beaten away by Hooper. Then United broke forward following a Liverpool corner and Hughes shot narrowly wide. Liverpool turned up the pressure with Beardsley getting the better of Steve Bruce once again and Donaghy clearing the ball off the toes of Aldridge. Then a hopeful ball into the box saw Hughes latch on to a loose ball and hit a post and, following in, Robins forced Hooper into a fine save.

Then, just minutes after his introduction in place of Lee Martin, Paul McGrath gave the ball away and Beardsley played in Barnes who turned back onto his right foot and chipped the ball over Leighton. It was a goal very much against the run of play but typical of Liverpool at the time and the home crowd feared the worst. The visitor's lead didn't last long though - straight from the kick-off Beardsmore jinked past Gary Ablett once again, cut the ball back and McClair scored with a spectacular scissor kick past Hooper. Just minutes later Beardsmore was at it again, latching on to a long ball that ran towards Steve Nicol but the Liverpool defender panicked and slipped and Mark Hughes seized on the loose ball and fired it under Hooper. Then, just two minutes later, Robson and Milne worked it down the left and played in the willing Sharpe whose cross eluded Hughes and Robins but fell for Beardsmore just 6 yards out and his cool finish made it three. The old ground hadn't seen excitement like this in years! The 44,745 in the stadium had just witnessed United score three goals in seven minutes against a team rated one of the greatest of all time. The rest of the game was played out to a soundtrack of cheers and disbelief.

For Alex Ferguson this was a priceless victory against a club that he knew would have to get the better of if he was to succeed as United boss. Typically, United played Middlesbrough the following day at Ayresome Park and it was a case of after the Lord Mayor's show as they succumbed to a tame 1-0 defeat but Ferguson's team selection that day saw appearances for more academy players as United's injury crisis deepened – midfielder Tony Gill replacing Lee Martin at right-back and David Wilson coming on as a sub for Gill in the 79th minute.

Gill and Wilson both appeared in the goalless home FA Cup tie against QPR and Gill and striker Deniol Graham both scored in the replay at Loftus Road the following Wednesday in a 2-2 draw. Gill scored again in the league game against Millwall on the following Saturday in a 3-0 win with Wilson and winger Jules Maiorana both coming off the bench to play a part. The press quickly dubbed the young players 'Fergie's Fledglings' and the tag stuck. Yet by the time United played West Ham in the next league game the first team players had returned to full fitness and the juniors had returned to A team and reserve team duties but they had helped the club through a tough period. United now won 6 matches in a row including a 4-0 win over Oxford in Round 4 of the cup before 47,774 supporters and a 1-0 win in a Fifth Round replay against Bournemouth that attracted 52,422 with thousands locked out. All of a sudden the gloom had lifted even if defeat in the next round to Nottingham Forest (attendance: 55,052) brought an abrupt end to the jollity.

A year later, when the knives were out for Fergie and the press were predicting his sack if they lost to Nottingham Forest in the FA Cup, United chairman Martin Edwards would recall this brief period when the Scot placed his trust in youth and Fergie's Fledglings responded with terrific performances that changed the atmosphere around the club and paved the way for a stirring cup run.

Did You Know

None of Fergie's original Fledglings had long, illustrious careers at Old Trafford with injury forcing Tony Gill into premature retirement, David Wilson moving on to Bristol Rovers and Deniol Graham moving on to Barnsley. Russell Beardsmore had the most impact, making 73 appearances during 4 seasons at the club scoring 4 goals. He will always be fondly remembered for New Years Day 1989 when he tore Liverpool apart and, given that the Anfield club lost the title by a solitary goal that season, ultimately cost them the league.

GAME NO. 9
BLACKPOOL 2-4 UNITED
1948 FA CUP FINAL
WEMBLEY STADIUM
24 APRIL 1948
ATTENDANCE- 99,000

BUSBY'S FIRST TROPHY

During his 25 year reign as United manager Matt Busby built three great teams. Most supporters know about The Busby Babes of the 50s and the United Trinity of the 60s but the team that immediately proceeded the end of the Second World War was arguably the most important as it set the blueprint for United's style of play and gained the club a nationwide following.

Imagine there was no professional football for six years! Well this was the situation after all league games were suspended after just three games of the 1939-40 season when Nazi Germany invaded Poland and Prime Minister Neville Chamberlain gravely announced that the country was at war. It wasn't until 7 May 1945, a few days after VE day, that it was announced that the FA Cup would resume and the 22 clubs which had played in the First Division and Second Division in season 1938-39 would be divided into two leagues, the Football League North and the Football League South for 1945-46. United finished that season fourth in Football League North which was won by Sheffield United while Birmingham City won the Football League South. It has to be remembered that a lot of players were being demobbed so squads were initially filled with the fit and willing, not necessarily the brightest and best.

United played all their 'home' games at Maine Road until 1949 as Old Trafford had been bombed out in the blitz and that season's FA Cup games were played over two legs. United drew 2-2 away at Accrington Stanley in their Round 3, 1st leg tie at Peel Park on 5 January 1946. The game marked the competitive United debut of goalkeeper Jack Crompton who had signed for the club as a trainee in June 1944 and as a professional in the week before the game. The Football League North was not considered to be a fully accredited official competition as it was a combination of teams who had played in the First and Second Division Championships when a full season was last completed, 1938-39. Crompton actually played his first game for United on 16 September 1944 and conceded four goals. United drew 4-4 with Stockport County at Edgeley Park in a Football League North game, however appearances in the Football League North do not count in players' official records. The second leg of the cup tie was played four days later at Maine Road and United won 5-1. On 22 January 1946, United beat Preston North End 1-0 at Maine Road in a first leg, Fourth Round encounter with a goal from James Hanlon. The second leg was played at Deepdale four days later with United losing 3-1 after extra-time to exit the competition with a 3-2 aggregate defeat. United played Blackburn Rovers, Burnley, Bury, Chesterfield, Manchester City, Newcastle United, Sheffield United and Sheffield Wednesday in the League in 1945-46, all of whom had been playing in the Second Division before the war. Blackburn Rovers had won Division Two in 1938-39 with Sheffield United finishing runners-up (Manchester City were fifth). Birmingham City and Leicester City finished in the two relegation places in the First Division in 1938-39 which was won by Everton.

In season 1946-47 the First and Second Division Championships were reinstated and United finished runners-up to Liverpool by a point and for the second season in a row United were knocked out of the FA cup in Round 4, this time losing 2-0 at Maine Road to Nottingham Forest. Before the season Busby bought his first player as manager of United when he paid Glasgow Celtic £4,000 for his fellow Scot Jimmy Delaney.

Going into the 1947-48 season Busby was in buoyant mood with how well his team had performed in the League during the previous campaign and was hopeful that United could go one better this time and bring the First Division Championship back to Old Trafford for the first time since 1910-11. Or in United's case the trophy would be displayed before fans at Maine Road, their temporary home. Busby's squad included John Anderson (Aged 25), John Aston Snr (25), Ronnie Burke (26), Allenby Chilton (26), Henry Cockburn (25), Jimmy Hanlon (29), Samuel Lynn (26), William McGlen (25), Charlie Mitten (26), Johnny Morris (23),, Stan Pearson (28), Jack Rowley (27), John "Jack" Warner (35) and Harry Worrall (29).

Back then club allegiances were not what they are today, supporters would often watch other local teams if their club was playing away from home and support was not quite as entrenched. A glance at United's attendances at Maine Road suggest that the Manchester public were switching over from blue to red in huge numbers. City had been comfortably the better supported team before hostilities but the long break and the misery of war had left supporters yearning for pure entertainment and Matt's side delivered during this period playing a fast attacking style with wingers Delaney and Mitten feeding inside-forwards Pearson and Morris and prolific striker Jack 'Gunner' Rowley.

United got off to a decent start in the League in 1947–48 winning twice and drawing once in their first four fixtures, 2–2 draw at Middlesbrough, a 2–0 home win over champions Liverpool, a 6–2 battering of Charlton Athletic at Maine Road, with all three of Busby's forwards scoring, and a 2–2 draw with Liverpool in the return at Anfield. Then, quite inexplicably, United endured a winless run of 8 games which saw them lose 5 and draw 3. Twelve goals in the first four games were followed by only six in the next 8. The first loss came against Arsenal at Highbury (2–1) on 6 September 1947. It was The Gunners' fifth consecutive League win of the campaign with 17 goals for and only 5 conceded. The London club were in devastating form and were unbeaten in their first 17 games which produced 12 wins and 5 draws. The Gunners were back to the form that had seen them dominate the 1930s when they were crowned champions five times and were FA Cup winners in 1936.

Reigning champions Liverpool won 5, drew 5 and lost 7 of their opening 17 games whereas United won only 4 times, drew 8 and lost 5 which was not title winning form for either club. The reigning champions were already 14 points behind The Gunners whilst United were 13 points behind. In the end The Gunners romped to the title by 7 points over United while Liverpool ended the 1947–48 season in a lowly 11th place.

Yet in the FA Cup United flourished. The draw for the Third Round was not kind when they were handed an away trip to Aston Villa on 10 January 1948. Busby's forwards had recently returned to goal scoring form with Rowley scoring a hat-trick and Mitten scoring twice in a 5–0 thumping of Burnley at Maine Road on New Year's Day 1948 and two days later Morris and Pearson scored in a 2–1 win against Charlton Athletic at The Valley. The cup game proved to be a tonic for Midlands football fanatics as Villa and United served up a goal feast before 58,683 bewildered Brummies. Within 13 seconds of the start United found themselves a goal down when George Edwards scored for the home side. Conceding so early sparked the visitors into life and by the time the referee blew his whistle for half-time the home team could not wait to get back to their dressing room; United led 5-1 with goals from Rowley (8 mins), Morris (17 & 31 mins), Pearson (29 mins) and Delaney (43 mins). The Villa players didn't know what hit them and many Villa fans may have been thinking about leaving early. Typically United were caught napping once more in the opening minute of the second half when Edwards scored again and when Leslie Smith scored in the 70th minute and Richard Dorsett converted a penalty for the hosts in the 81st minute it seemed that all was not lost for Villa. Cheered on by their fans they attacked United in search of an equaliser and perhaps even a winner. Villa's constant bombardment of United finally produced the game's tenth goal but it was United who scored it as Villa had left themselves too exposed at the back as Stan Pearson netted his second of the game. United were in the hat for the Fourth Round draw although Villa had restored some pride at least with a valiant second half display. Yet the incredible events at Villa Park were overshadowed by Second Division Bradford Park Avenue producing one of the biggest shocks in FA Cup history when they beat Arsenal 1-0 at Highbury.

United drew Liverpool at home next round. With their chances of retaining their First Division title a pipe dream given Arsenal's rampant League form, Liverpool were hoping for a good run in the cup, a competition they had yet to win. In the Third Round they had beaten Nottingham Forest 4-1 at Anfield. Two of Liverpool's goals were scored by Albert Stubbins who was famously depicted on the front cover of The Beatles' seminal album "Sgt. Pepper's Lonely Hearts Club Band," the only footballer to appear on the sleeve. However, as Manchester City had also been given a home draw in Round 4 it meant United could not use Maine Road to host Liverpool and agreed to switch the tie to Goodison Park as Everton were drawn at Wolverhampton Wanderers in Round 4. 74,000 fans piled into the ground to watch the Lancashire rivals do battle and United cruised into the Fifth Round draw on the back of a 3-0 victory with goals from Mitten, Morris and Rowley. It was Rowley's 20th goal of the season. Elsewhere Manchester City beat Chelsea 2-0 and Everton beat Wolves 3-2 after a replay.

United were given another home draw for the Fifth Round against FA Cup holders Charlton Athletic but with City also drawn at home United would have to play elsewhere, this time the setting was Leeds Road, home of Huddersfield Town. Charlton had disposed of Newcastle United 2-1 at The Valley in the Third Round and Stockport

County 3-0 in another home game in the Fourth Round but their defence of the cup ended in West Yorkshire as goals from Warner and Mitten gave United a 2-0 win. City lost 1-0 to Preston North End on the same day while Everton went out of the competition after losing 1-0 to Fulham at Goodison Park in a replay.

United were awarded their third consecutive home draw in the Sixth Round and, as with their previous three games in the competition, the opposition were a fellow First Division side, Preston North End but with City no longer in the FA Cup it meant United could play the match in Manchester, and United beat their Lancashire rivals 4-1 at Maine Road before 74,213 supporters.

Before the semi-final draw took place United knew two things: they would be playing an FA Cup tie at a fifth different venue that season as the semi-finals were staged at a neutral venue and once more they would be facing a top flight side as the other three sides still left in the competition were Blackpool, Derby County and Tottenham Hotspur. United avoided Lancashire neighbours Blackpool and faced Derby at Hillsborough and United proved just too strong for their opponents who could not control Mitten's mazy runs on the right wing while in Stan Pearson United had a forward at the top of his game who on his day could run defences ragged with his class and power as he scored a hat-trick in United's 3-1 triumph. The other semi-final at Villa Park produced the same score line after extra-time, and once again a hat-trick was scored, this time by Blackpool's prolific centre-forward Stan Mortensen.

And so on 24 April 1948 an army of Lancastrians invaded London to see the 1948 FA Cup final contested by Blackpool and Manchester United. Blackpool had finished ninth in the league and for the fourth year in a row Stan Mortensen was their top goal scorer with 21 in the League and 9 in the FA Cup. Before seeing off Spurs in the semi-finals, The Seasiders beat Leeds United 4-0 at home in the Third Round, Chester were beaten by the same score at Bloomfield Road in the Fourth, then Colchester United were dispatched 5-0 and in the quarter-finals they defeated Fulham 2-0 at Craven Cottage. Mortensen had scored in every round but all eyes were on Stanley Matthews, then regarded as the greatest player in the world. Matthews had joined Blackpool on 10 May 1947 in a £11,500 transfer from his hometown club Stoke City where he had made his debut as a 17-year old on 19 March 1932, a 1-0 win over Bury at Gigg Lane. He had made 379 League appearances for Stoke City and from his outside right he had scored 17 times. On the night before the final, 23 April 1948, Matthews, whose nicknames included "The Wizard of the Dribble" and "The Magician", was named the inaugural Football Writers' Association Footballer of the Year but aside from a Second Division Championship winners' medal with Stoke in 1932-33 his unquestionable talent. Matthews was 33 and many thought this represented his last chance at a major medal★.

Goals seemed assured as both finalists had scored 18 times on their way to the final but whereas United's defence had been breached 7 times, Blackpool's defence had proved impregnable. When the teams emerged with Busby leading out United and Smith leading out Blackpool, the fans saw their players in a change strip. United's red shirt was deemed too similar to Blackpool's tangerine so United wore blue shirts, white shorts and blue socks and their opponents opted for white shirts, black shorts and their traditional tangerine socks.

Manchester United's 1948 FA Cup final team was: Jack Crompton, Johnny Carey (Capt), John Anderson, Allenby Chilton, Henry Cockburn, John Aston Snr, Jimmy Delaney, Johnny Morris, Charlie Mitten, Jack Rowley, Stan Pearson.

It was the North's big day out as both sides were introduced to King George VI before kick-off. It was a beautiful sunny day in the capital. United kicked off and the 99,000 fans in attendance did not have long to wait for the first goal to be scored and with United on top early on, it looked like the side in blue would score first but in the 15th minute Mortensen, who was always a threat in the area, was chopped down from behind by Chilton. The referee, C. J. Barrick of Northamptonshire, pointed to the spot and Blackpool's right-back Ernie Shimwell scored the resulting penalty kick making him the first full-back to score a goal in the show-piece final. Fifteen minutes later United were on level terms; Delaney passed the ball to Rowley who looped it over the head of the advancing Joe Robinson in the Blackpool goal and then quite coolly side-footed it into the net. United's equaliser spurred The Seasiders into action and in the 35th minute they were back in the lead. A free kick outside United's box saw the ball arrive at the feet of Mortensen but he was so far wide of the right hand post it looked an impossible angle to score from but somehow his cross evaded Crompton and found the left hand corner of the United net. Busby had his work cut out at half time and Blackpool almost went 3-1 ahead not long into the second half when their captain, Harry Johnston, tried a speculative long range shot which Compton pushed over his head only to turn and watch the ball roll out for a corner.

Matt Busby's half-time message was simple: he told his players to relax as he sensed that the big occasion had got to a few of them. When United resumed they were much freer and slowly took control of the game. Blackpool were defending well until the 70th minute when Morris took a quick free-kick out on the left and Rowley darted in between two static defenders to score with a powerful header. It was no more than United deserved. Both teams were starting to suffer from the heat and the Wembley turf began to sap their energy but ten minute later the game produced a major turning point when Crompton saved a shot from Mortensen and within seconds the ball was in the Blackpool half of the pitch. Mitten started the move on the left wing and passed infield to Rowley who squared the ball to Stan Pearson. Pearson's shot from 20 yards out flew into the net off the inside of the left hand post and wide of a diving Robinson. The United players suddenly looked to be full of energy and two minutes after going ahead Anderson made it 4-2 and United had won the cup!

United were well worth their victory, their defence had snubbed out any threat from Matthews and they won 12 corner kicks to Blackpool's four. Blackpool boss Joe Smith was criticised for leaving striker Jimmy McIntosh out of his team despite the fact that he had scored five times in the five ties which took Blackpool to the final. Four days after the final the teams met again in a re-arranged First Division game at Bloomfield Road which the home side won 1-0, McIntosh the scorer. United's season came to an end on 1 May 1948 with a 4-1 win over Blackburn Rovers at Maine Road. United had scored 103 goals in the season, 81 of them coming in the League which was also the same number of League goals scored by champions Arsenal. Rowley was United's top scorer on 28, Pearson 26 and Mitten 21.

Many FA Cup finals do not live up to expectation or match the hype surrounding them. Some call it "Wembley Nerves," the importance of the occasion just too much for some players. There were no nerves on show in the all-Lancashire FA Cup final of 1948 which is considered by football connoisseurs to be one of the best exhibitions of football ever seen at Wembley.

Did You Know That?

Six months after the 1948 FA Cup final, 9 October 1948, Mortensen and Pearson would be teammates. The pair played in England's 6-2 demolition of Ireland at Windsor Park, Belfast in the British Home International Championships. Ireland (as opposed to Northern Ireland or the Republic of Ireland) were captained by United captain Johnny Carey, whilst Billy Wright was captaining his country for the first time. Wright went on to captain England a record 90 times in his 105 games for his country. Mortensen scored a hat-trick against the Irish, his teammate Matthews also scored as did Newcastle United's Jackie Milburn and Stan Pearson also found the back of the net for England. United's Henry Cockburn also played in the game.

★ Remarkably on 18 December 1956 Matthews was named the winner of the inaugural Ballon d'Or beating Real Madrid's legendary striker Alfredo Di Stefano, who in season 1955-56 had helped the Spanish giants win the inaugural European Cup while Stade de Reims and France striker Just Fontaine was third in the voting. Matthews played his last First Division game aged 50 years and 5 days and remains the oldest player ever to play in the top flight of English football and he is the oldest player ever to represent England at international level aged 42 years and 104 days.

GAME NO. 10
SL BENFICA 1-5 UNITED
EUROPEAN CUP, QUARTER-FINALS, SECOND LEG
ESTADIO DA LUZ, LISBON, PORTUGAL
9 MARCH 1966
ATTENDANCE – 75,000

THE NIGHT GEORGE BEST LIT UP THE STADIUM OF LIGHT

On 9 March 1966, United visited Lisbon, Portugal to play Benfica in the quarter-finals of the European Cup. During the 1965-66 season a few niggling injuries meant George Best missed 11 League games but he still managed to find the net 9 times in the other 31 and laid on many of the 45 goals scored by Bobby Charlton, David Herd and Denis Law. George also missed the 1-0 FA Cup semi-final defeat to Everton at Burnden Park, Bolton but one game he made sure he did not miss regardless of what his body was telling him was United's two tussles versus Benfica in the quarter-finals of the 1965-66 European Cup. The Portuguese Champions,

European Cup runners-up to Inter Milan in 1964-65, and Champions of Europe in 1960-61 and 1961-62, arrived in Manchester on 2 February 1966 for the first leg in confident mood. Benfica had beaten Barcelona 3-2 in the 1961 European Cup final to prevent a Spanish club from lifting the first six editions of this relatively new trophy. The all conquering Real Madrid won the inaugural European Cup final in 1956 and then successful defended it four times in a row. In season 1960-61, the five times winners surprisingly exited the competition in the First Round going down 4-3 to their Spanish contemporaries after drawing 2-2 at their Estadio Santiago Bernabéu home in the first leg and losing 2-1 at Camp Nou in the away leg. At the time only the winners of their domestic League Championship gained entry to the following season's European Cup but the tournament's organisers permitted the winners to defend their crown regardless of where they finished in their League campaign. Los Blancos, Real Madrid's nickname, took full advantage of this European "Get Out of Jail Free" card in season 1959-60 when they defeated Eintracht Frankfurt 7-3 at Hampden Park, Glasgow, Scotland in the 1960 final. Incidentally, it was the first time a German Club, East or West, had reached the final. The aristocrats of Spanish football finished second in the Spanish League in season 1958-59, La Liga, to Barcelona. The 1960 European Cup final is generally accepted by football connoisseurs to be the greatest ever European Cup final. Mind you, many Manchester United fans would direct that particular barometer to the 1999 final, not for the goals scored, but for the Hollywood movie finale to the game.

But for the European Cup script writers, a new chapter in this 11-year football odyssey of Europe's premier competition was about to be written in a game which would rival the exploits of Real Madrid's demolition of Eintracht Frankfurt. In the previous two rounds of the 1964-65 competition Benfica won three of their ties and drew the other scoring 23 goals in the process (Stade Dudelange 18-0 & Levski Sofia 5-4). United's path to the Last 8 saw them defeat Finland's HJK Helsinki 9-2 over two legs and a trip behind the Iron Curtain to East Berlin where they beat Vorwarts Berlin 2-0 followed by a 3-1 win in the return leg at Old Trafford in Round 2.

United drew first blood against Benfica winning the first leg 3-2 in front of a packed audience of 64,035 at Old Trafford on 2 February 1966 with goals from David Herd, Denis Law and an unlikely goal scorer, centre-half Bill Foulkes. It was a slender lead to take to the capital city of Portugal on 9 March 1966 with the Portuguese giants just needing to win 1-0 at their famous Estadio Da Luz (Stadium of Light) home to progress to the semi-finals. When United arrived in Lisbon for the game very few sports commentators gave them a chance of making it through to the semi-finals whilst the Portuguese press gleefully reminded United of the last time they had visited the city and went home with their tails between their legs on the end of a 5-0 hammering at the feet of Sporting Lisbon in the quarter-finals of the 1963-64 European Cup Winners'

To make the task for United all the more difficult Benfica, like United, had never lost a European Cup tie at home but this was a different United team than had been trounced by Sporting. Not only were Manchester United now the reigning English League Champions, but in George Best they possessed a player who could win a game on his own if he was in the mood. The Belfast Boy had more moves than a Chess Grandmaster. Prior to kick-off the stadium announcer whipped the home crowd up into frenzy and the sound was deafening when their star player, Eusébio da Silva Ferreira, was invited out on to the pitch to be presented with the 1965 European Footballer of the Year Award (Ballon d'Or). Standing watching Eusébio was Denis Law who had won the coveted award the previous season and Bobby Charlton who would succeed Eusébio as Europe's No.1 player when he won the award for season 1965-66. As for Best, he was itching for the game to get underway and his coronation as Europe's best player was still two years in the making.

Eusébio was a prolific striker, one of the most feared front men in European football, a player who had finished top scorer in the Portuguese League in the previous two seasons. United knew only too well that if they were to hold out for the 0-0 result which would see them reach the semi-finals of Europe's top club football competition for the third consecutive time from the three times they participated in it, then Eusébio had to have a stinker on the night or be kept quiet by the United back-line. How could United handle the unenviable task of stopping the newly crowned King of European football from adding to his tally of seven goals which he bagged in the first two rounds?

The United team was: Harry Gregg, Shay Brennan, Tony Dunne, Bill Foulkes, Paddy Crerand, Nobby Stiles, Bobby Charlton (Capt), John Connelly, George Best, David Herd, Denis Law

Busby sent his team out and gave them strict orders to be cautious and hold the home side for as long as they could in the hope that United could wear them down and either grab a vital away goal or hang in there for a scoreless draw. Best must have been in the toilet at the time or else he was tuned into a different frequency to that of his manager because he clearly either did not hear what his manager had to say or else he just decided to ignore it. For George, this was moment that the Lisbon public saw the real Manchester United and the real George Best. The young Irishman swooped all over the defence of the *Águias* and within 13 minutes United were in the driving seat in the tie having scored two magnificent goals. In the 6th minute George soared high into the air above the Benfica defence to head a free-kick past Costa Pereira in the Portuguese goal. Less than seven minutes later he collected a flick on from Herd just inside the Benfica half, the teenage Irishman looked up and surveyed the path ahead to goal with six white shirts in front of him blocking his way. George could have laid the pass off to a team-mate and found space higher up the pitch for a return pass closer to the opposition's net, he sometimes did, but not on this occasion. This night was his chance of payback, an opportunity to announce himself on the European stage. For some people their future is defined by a certain moment in time, their chance to show what they can do, and this was most definitely George's moment. With the ball at his feet he took off and headed straight for the goal. For those watching inside the Stadium of Light or on TV at home, it must have looked like time stood still for everyone on the pitch except George. It was if George was in a Ferrari and the Benfica players were trying to catch him in a tank as he raced through the Portuguese defence to fire into the net and put United 2-0 up on the night and 5-2 ahead on aggregate. Best cut through their rearguard like a hot knife cutting through butter. \

The home side now needed four goals to win the tie on aggregate and the heads of the Benfica players slumped into their chests. The crowd quickly realised the enormity of the task before their team and their nervousness seemed to spill down from the huge stands on to the pitch. Within minutes United were 3-0 up when Connelly hammered a pass from Best beyond a well beaten Pereira. Suddenly the game resembled a match being played behind closed doors as 75,000 voices fell silent, dumbstruck by what was unfolding on the pitch before their very eyes as Best toyed with the Benfica players like a matador teasing a bull before he moved in for the kill. Best possessed the ability to make the ordinary look extraordinary.

Half-time could not have come too soon for the home side who left the field to a chorus of incessant boos. However, for the small pocket of United fans so stuck high up in the corner of one of the huge stands, things could not have been better as United were on the verge of the European Cup semi-finals yet again. When a Manchester United player scored the fourth goal of this pulsating tie no more than a feint whimper could be heard from the home fans as Brennan had put through his own goal, scoring against George's Northern Ireland international teammate, Gregg but Best and United had not finished with their hosts yet and added two more goals in the 78th minute (Crerand) and 89th minute (Charlton) to clip the wings of the famous Eagles of Lisbon with an 8–3 aggregate victory. When the final whistle sounded the home fans who had bothered to stay and watch their team humiliated for the full 90 minutes, hurled cushions down on their crestfallen players as they trudged off the pitch totally demoralised. However, there was no doubting the fact that Manchester United's demolition of the Portuguese Champions is one of the greatest ever attacking displays by a team away from home in European competition and it was the dazzling skills of the Belfast Boy, and not Eusébio, who looked the best player in Europe on the night. And for George and his United teammates the agony and despair experienced by them in the Portuguese capital two years earlier had well and truly been exorcised.

After the game a fan ran on to the pitch with a knife and made his way towards George. Thankfully, he was brought to the ground before he could get anywhere near United's two goal hero and afterwards it was discovered that he had intended to claim a lock of George's hair. When Matt Busby was interviewed after his side's 5-1 win he was asked what his plans had been going into the game trying to protect their slender one goal advantage and said: "*Our plan was to be cautious, but thankfully somebody must have stuffed cotton wool in George's ears.*"

Eusébio had scored 48 goals in the previous season including 9 in 9 European Cup games, and this was supposed to be his big night but he was too well marshalled by the United back four, his performance a mere flicker compared to George who illuminated the Stadium of Light in flashing streaks of red lightning. This was Best's night, 90 minutes of rampage during which he taught the Benfica players a "lição," the Portuguese word for lesson.

The ghosts of two years before for United in Lisbon had well and truly been eradicated on what proved to be a Night of Horrors for the home side. Nobody saw this result coming including the Portuguese press. It caused shock-waves throughout the country which was only mirrored by Portugal's quarter-final game against North Korea in the 1966 World Cup finals hosted by England. Having won Group 3 at a canter, hardly breaking sweat after defeating Hungary 3-1 at Old Trafford, Bulgaria 3-0 at the same venue and rounding off their Group games with a 3-1 victory over reigning World Cup winners from the previous two editions of this global tournament, Brazil. Eusébio scored twice against the South American champions and in the quarter-finals Portugal were drawn against the surprise outfit of the competition, North Korea, who had finished runners-up in Group 4 to the Soviet Union who won all three of their matches. North Korea's 1-0 win over Italy, two times Jules Rimet winners (1934, 1938), at Ayresome Park, Middlesbrough sent a shock-wave to the other nations competing as if a tsunami had just arrived on English shores but no one gave them a prayer against Eusébio and Portugal.

On 23 July 1966, Portugal met North Korea at Goodison Park. The outcome seemed a mere formality, an annihilation of their Asian opposition by a European powerhouse, or maybe not. North Korea were World Cup final stages virgins and no other team from Asia had ever progressed beyond the Group Stages in the competition since the inaugural World Cup held in Uruguay in 1930. But after twenty-five minutes of the game the Koreans had raced into a 3-0 lead. It was at this point that the "Black Panther" revealed his claws and scored four goals (including two penalties) in his side's 5-3 victory. But their hopes of being crowned World Champions were ended by England and one man in particular, Bobby Charlton who scored both goals in a 2-1 semi-final win at Wembley Stadium. Portugal beat the Soviet Union 2-1 in the Third-Place play-off at Wembley Stadium, Eusébio scored yet another penalty, his third in the tournament, whilst England defeated West Germany 4-2 after extra time at the same venue, the otherwise known as Empire Stadium. With 9 goals, Eusébio won the Golden Boot as the top goal scorer.

As the Manchester United team home touched down in Manchester Airport the next day, the sea of press waiting for them were only interested in speaking to and photographing one player – George Best. The 19-year old who was born in east Belfast stepped off the plane and looked like a movie star. He was wearing a black leather jacket, dark sunglasses and a souvenir sombrero covered his long black hair. The Portuguese media quickly dubbed him "El Beatle" a monicker which the English press instantly adopted naming George as the "Fifth Beatle" – the world was now literally at his feet.

There is absolutely no doubt that George Best was football's first superstar. Diego Maradona named Best as his all-time favourite player and the legendary Brazilian striker, Pelé said that George Best was the best player in the world. Who would dispute Pelé's endorsement of George? After all he won the World Cup three times with Brazil (1958, 1962, 1970) and scored a staggering 1,281 goals in 1,363 games during his glittering career including 77 for Brazil in 92 international appearances.

Many years later, when George looked back on the game, he realised that it was perhaps the watershed moment of his career which would shape the rest of his life on and off the pitch. "On nights like that, good players become great players and great players become gods. It was surreal stuff," said George.

Little did George know it but whilst he may have been halfway to heaven, he was just a half mile from hell.

Did You Know That?

When George Best was dazzling the Portuguese public in their own backyard, back home in the UK Nancy Sinatra was No.1 in the UK Singles Chart with the song *These Boots Are Made For Walking*. Nancy was the eldest daughter of the legendary crooner Frank Sinatra and she spent four weeks at the top of the charts (17 February 1966 to 17 March 1966). Her boots may well have been made for walking but George's boots were most definitely made for scoring goals. Coincidentally, when United beat Benfica 3-2 in the first leg, the UK No.1 single was *Michelle* sung by the Overlanders, a song taken from The Beatles' album *Rubber Soul*.

GAME NO. 11
LEEDS UNITED 1–0 UNITED
FA CUP SEMI-FINAL, SECOND REPLAY
BURNDEN PARK, BOLTON
26 MARCH 1970
ATTENDANCE– 56,000

THE WARS OF THE ROSES

The Wars of the Roses (1455–85) were a series of Civil Wars for control of the throne of England and were fought between the houses of Lancaster and York. The wars were named after the crests worn by the contending parties, the red rose of Lancaster and the white rose of York. In the 1909 FA Cup final Manchester United wore a red rose badge on their white shirts when they beat Bristol City 1–0 at Crystal Palace. Leeds United crests since 1984 have incorporated a white rose.

In season 1969–70 Manchester United had five wars with Leeds United and the word 'war' is used advisedly. Leeds were renowned as a tough-tackling team and by this stage United had their own share of players who were prepared to leave their foot in. The cross Pennine rivals met twice in the First Division a 2–2 draw on 6 September 1969 at Elland Road with George Best scoring twice and another 2–2 draw in the return at Old Trafford on 26 January 1970. Both games were seen as a litmus test for United's new manager Wilf McGuinness who had taken up the Old Trafford hot-seat following the retirement of Sir Matt Busby.

Born in Collyhurst, Manchester, Wilf had signed for United as a trainee in January 1953 after leaving school aged 15. He made his debut for United at Old Trafford on 8 October 1955 in a 3–2 victory over Wolverhampton Wanderers just 17 days shy of his 18th birthday. He was yet another product that seamlessly made their progression from the junior side to the senior side. Fortunately he missed United's ill-fated trip to play Red Star Belgrade through injury but a serious leg fracture forced him to retire because of injury in 1961. Wilf moved into coaching and assisted Jimmy Murphy with the youth team and was selected by Alf Ramsey to be one of his assistants during the 1966 World Cup Finals. Wilf was no mug as a coach as his work with the national team proved but taking on the biggest job in English football in succession to the man who invented modern football management was always going to prove an almost impossible task.

By 1970 Leeds manager Don Revie had turned the Yorkshire team into the major force in the land. Champions in 1968-69 they were never out of contention until Revie left for the England job in 1974. When Busby announced his retirement in January 1969 there were rumours that Revie was being lined up to succeed him but the Leeds boss flatly refused the advances of United chairman Louis Edwards and dedicated his time to making Leeds United the greatest club side of all time. History will show that Revie never quite fulfilled that dream but during his reign he steered Leeds to the Second Division Championship in 1963-64, League Cup in 1967-68, Inter-Cities Fairs Cup in 1967-68 & 1970-71, First Division Championship in 1968-69 & 1973-74, the Charity Shield in 1969 and FA Cup in 1971-72.

In McGuinness's first season United finished a disappointing eighth in the league but in the domestic cup competitions they enjoyed good runs. They reached the semi-finals of both cups, losing to Manchester City in the League Cup, losing over two legs, and battled their way past Ipswich, Manchester City, Northampton Town and Middlesbrough, after a replay, and were drawn to face Leeds at Hillsborough in the semis of the FA Cup. Leeds were a side packed with an abundance of talent with players such as Paul Reaney, Norman Hunter, Mike O'Grady, David Harvey, Gary Sprake, Paul Madeley, Eddie Gray, Rod Belfitt, Jack Charlton, Mick Jones, Terry Cooper, Terry Hibbitt, Billy Bremner, Johnny Giles, Mick Bates, Peter Lorimer and a player who won the FA Cup with United in 1963, Johnny Giles. After winning the First Division title in 1968-69, manager Don Revie had splashed out a British record transfer fee of £165,000 to sign striker Allan Clarke from Leicester City and now set his sights on winning all four competitions the club were involved in: League, League Cup, FA Cup and the European Cup. During the season they broke the First Division record for games unbeaten thereby bettering the Football League record of 31 set by Liverpool in the Second Division in 1894.

On 14 March 1970, the third War of the Roses of the season resulted in a 0-0 draw in the FA Cup semi-final. Nine days later the teams met again, this time at Villa Park, and it was goalless again and so, in the words of William in *Henry V* (Act 3, Scene 1): "Once more unto the breach, dear friends, once more" on 26 March 1970 United and Leeds went into battle for a fifth time that season with the semi-final second replay taking place at the home ground of Bolton Wanderers, Burnden Park.

The United team lined–up as follows: Alex Stepney, Paul Edwards, Tony Dunne, David Sadler, Nobby Stiles, Paddy Crerand, Willie Morgan, Carlo Sartori, Bobby Charlton (Capt), Brian Kidd, George Best. Substitute: Denis Law for Sartori

Over the three games it took 217 minutes for the deadlock to be broken and it was the Leeds United captain, Billy Bremner, who scored in the 7th minute of the second replay, turning in a spectacular shot from the edge of the box past Stepney in what proved to the only goal of the tie to send Leeds into the final against Chelsea who beat Watford 5-1 at the first time of asking.

However the most infamous incident surrounding this game didn't happen on the pitch but emerged in the tabloids over the next few days when stories appeared claiming that George Best had picked up a woman at the bar of the team hotel on the afternoon of the game and taken her back to his room. United manager Wilf McGuinness found out about it just as the deed was being done and stormed to George's room to find the door locked and the curtains closed. He immediately shouted through the door to tell Best he would not be playing that night, however as soon as Matt Busby found out about it Best was reinstated, completely undermining the manager. Things got even worse for George on the pitch as the Leeds players had found out about it and were soon taking every opportunity to mention it. Late in the game with United a goal down Best was put clean through on Leeds' goal but fluffed his chance. Whether the events of that afternoon affected him or not is anyone's guess but George would never appear in an FA Cup final and this was as close as he ever got.

Don Revie failed in his bid to land all four trophies: Leeds lost 3-1 to Glasgow Celtic over two legs in the semi-finals of the European Cup, finished runners-up to Everton in the First Division and then lost 2-1 to Chelsea in the FA Cup final replay which was played at Old Trafford after their first encounter ended 2-2 at Wembley. They had been beaten in the Third Round of the League Cup early in the season.

As for poor old Wilf… McGuinness's reign never recovered from the interference of his predecessor. After being denied transfer targets in the summer of 1969 Busby continued to veto some of Wilf's team selections and the Best incident before this game was the beginning of the end for the likeable Mancunian. Having been appointed as 'Head Coach' he was given the title 'Manager' the following season but was sacked at Christmas 1970 with United languishing near the bottom of the table. Sir Matt came out of retirement to steady the ship and steer United to mid-table safety but in truth he had never relinquished control.

Did You Know That?

The 1969-70 FA Cup was the first time a Third Place Play-Off game was introduced for the competition for the two losing semi-finalists. On 10 April 1970, the day before the 1970 FA Cup final, United beat Watford 2-0 at Highbury thanks to two Brian Kidd goals. The extra game was discontinued in 1974.

GAME NO. 12
UNITED 3-0 FC BARCELONA
EUROPEAN CUP WINNERS' CUP,
QUARTER-FINAL, SECOND LEG
OLD TRAFFORD
21 MARCH 1984
ATTENDANCE- 58,547

A NIGHT TO REMEMBER

Sometimes in life obstacles are placed in our way to test us, to see if what we want is really worth fighting for. In the 2nd leg of their 1983-84 quarter-finals European Cup Winners' Cup tie versus Barcelona, Manchester United went into the game knowing they had to win by three clear goals after losing the 1st leg 2-0 in Camp Nou a fortnight earlier. In Spain Graeme Hogg, making his European debut, had a nightmare scoring an own goal in the 37th minute to send the partisan 94,000 crowd into a frenzy while Bryan Robson, Frank Stapleton and Ray Wilkins all missed chances to draw United level. Then the killer blow when Barcelona sealed victory with a goal in the 89th minute from Juan Rojo. Gary Bailey in the United goal had no chance of stopping a thunderbolt from the Spanish striker and United's dreams of reaching the semi-finals looked more than remote. One of the headlines in the British press the following day read: "HOGG's HORROR: Boob adds to United agony" but other papers sounded a more upbeat note with one headline reading "Down But Not Out". United needed a comeback to rival Muhammad Ali's in the Rumble in the Jungle against George Foreman in 1974. Foreman was the reigning World Champion, Ali the challenger, and the punters' money was on Big George to retain his title, after all he was unbeaten and Ali was rated a 4-1 outsider yet Ali won the contest in the 8th Round after adopting his famous "Rope-A-Dope" tactics and United would have to fly into the Catalans at Old Trafford from the first whistle.

What made things more difficult was that United needed to score at least three goals and prevent the visitors from scoring. Barcelona had not lost by a three goal deficit in any of their previous games during the season. Nobody gave them a chance of overturning Barcelona's advantage, it was just too big of a obstacle to overcome and the Catalans had never squandered a two goal advantage in Europe before.

Barcelona qualified for the 1983-84 European Cup Winners' Cup after beating Real Madrid 2-1 in the final of the Copa del Rey the previous season. They also won the Spanish Super Cup after beating La Liga Champions Athletic Bilbao. United qualified by beating Brighton and Hove Albion 4-0 in the 1983 FA Cup final replay after the first game ended 2-2. Prior to facing United in the last 8 of the competition, the Spanish side beat 1. FC Magdeburg 5-1 away and 2-0 at home for a 7-1 aggregate victory. In season 1982-83, the Royal Spanish Football Federation only permitted La Liga clubs to have three foreign born players in their squad so as to encourage member clubs to nurture young home grown players. Barcelona's three foreign stars were the 19-year old striker Jorge Luis Gabrich from Argentina. Gabrich helped Argentina to second place in the 1983 FIFA World Youth Championship in Mexico winning the Bronze Boot as the tournament's third highest goal scorer with 4 goals. He joined Barcelona from Newell's Old Boys (Argentina) in June after the 1983 FIFA World Youth Championships. The second foreigner was West Germany's Berndt Schuster nicknamed "der Blonde Engel" (the Blond Angel) who joined Barcelona from 1. FC Koln in 1980, the same year he finished runner-up to his fellow countryman, Karl-Heinz Rummenigge (FC Bayern Munich), for the Ballon d'Or. Schuster bossed the Spanish side's midfield and helped them beat Standard Liege (Belgium) 2-1 in the final of the 1981-82 European Cup Winners' Cup. The third foreigner in their ranks was the world's most expensive player, 22-year old Diego Armando Maradona, who cost £5 million when he was signed from Boca Juniors after he played for Argentina at the 1982 FIFA World Cup finals in Spain. Maradona scored a hat-trick in the 5-1 win over 1. FC Magdeburg with Schuster also finding the net in the game. In Round 2, Barcelona beat NEC

Nijmegen (Netherlands) 5-2 over the two legs.

Manchester United had met Dukla Prague in Round 1 with the first leg played at Old Trafford. United found their Eastern Bloc opponents a difficult proposition and in the 60th minute of the game the Czech outfit took the lead with a goal from Tomas Kriz. Ray Wilkins spared United's blushes on the night scoring a penalty in the 89th minute to salvage a 1-1 draw. It was a close call for United who had never lost a European game at home since they first entered European competition in season 1956-57. With an away goal in the bag, Dukla Prague were favourites to progress to Round 2. On 27 September 1983, United faced a stern test in the Czech capital and they got off to the worst possible start conceding a goal by Frantisek Stambachr after only 11 minutes. Captain Marvel Bryan Robson made it 1-1 in the 33rd minute so it was game on once again for both sides with the aggregate score 2-2 and no side holding an away goal advantage. When Frank Stapleton found the back of the net in the 79th minute the up to then noisy home crowd fell silent, the tables had turned and it was now United who held the crucial away goal advantage but more importantly their opponents had to score twice in the remaining 11 minutes to win the tie. The home side threw everything at the United defence of Mike Duxbury, Arthur Albiston, Kevin Moran and Gordon McQueen. And when Vaclav Danek drew his team level with 7 minutes to go the 25,000 fans inside Stadion Juliska woke up and found their voices once again but United held on to progress into Round 2 with a 5-4 aggregate victory.

The United fans' opinion was divided as to who they would like to see next at Old Trafford. Some of the teams they could be drawn to play were Aberdeen (Scotland), Alex Ferguson's defending Champions of the European Cup Winners' Cup after defeating Real Madrid 2-1 after extra-time in the previous season's final, Barcelona (Spain), Porto (Portugal), Glasgow Rangers (Scotland), Juventus (Italy) and Paris Saint-Germain (France). When the draw was made United were handed another trip behind the Iron Curtain, this time to Bulgaria. On 19 October 1983, United beat Spartak Varna 2-1 at the Yuri Gargarin Stadium in Varna with goals from Robson and Arthur Graham and in the return leg two Stapleton goals gave United an easy passage into the last 8 having won the tie 4-1 on aggregate.

The Manchester United team given the task of overhauling the visitors' advantage by Big Ron was: Gary Bailey, Mike Duxbury, Arthur Albiston, Graeme Hogg, Kevin Moran, Ray Wilkins, Bryan

Robson (Capt), Remi Moses, Arnold Mühren, Norman Whiteside, Frank Stapleton. Substitute: Mark Hughes for Whiteside, 70 mins

"Destiny is not a matter of chance, it is a matter of choice; it is not a thing to be waited for, it is a thing to be achieved."

William Jennings Bryan

United's destiny in the competition would be revealed in 90 minutes of football. Norman Whiteside had recovered from injury to replace Mark Hughes, who played in the 1st leg, in attack and United entered the game on the crest of a wave as they had just hammered Arsenal 4-0 at Old Trafford to go top of the league. They were now unbeaten in 16 games and led Liverpool by a point.

Atkinson sent United out to attack from the start and they dominated the opening 20 minutes but Atkinson knew his team could not afford to risk too much early in the match for the fear of being caught on the counter attack. Their opponents were happy to sit back and let United dictate the pace of the game, safe in the knowledge that if they conceded a goal or less, their place in the semi-finals was assured. They also knew that a United goal would whip the already raucous and expectant crowd of 58,547 into a frenzy. With no away fans Old Trafford was a cauldron of noise as every touch of the ball by a red shirt was cheered and every touch by a Barcelona player jeered. The visitors looked visibly nervous of the hostile reception and after a cagey start the ground exploded – Graeme Hogg, making amends following his disastrous debut in Barcelona, flicked a corner on at the near post and Bryan Robson stooped to head home.

It was clear that the atmosphere seemed to be getting to the visitors, Diego Maradona was a shadow of himself while Schuster found a match in Moses who never left his side for the full 90 minutes. Nevertheless United went in at the interval a goal up and knew they had unsettled their Spanish visitors who looked rather shaky in defence, particularly their goalkeeper Javier Urruti.

Sure enough five minutes into the second half it was a mistake by Urruti which led to United's equaliser in the tie. Barcelona tried to play their way out of trouble only to lose possession and a shot from Wilkins rebounded off the hapless keeper and Robson penalised him for his error. Now the noise inside the stadium almost lifted the roofs of all four stands – United had lift off! The Spaniards were rattled as an English Armada attacked them mercilessly having smelt their fear. United were in search of blood and went straight for the jugular. When Stapleton scored a third United goal a minute later after Whiteside headed a pass from Albiston across the front of the goal for the Republic of Ireland international to toe poke into the net from one yard out. A sea of faces in the Stretford End seemed to suck the ball into the net. The goal produced a wave of emotion that flowed from stand to stand inside Old Trafford. A tidal wave of passion from the United fans overwhelmed the Barcelona players who were now in unchartered waters. The tie was turned on its head just two minutes later, Robson found full-back Arthur Albiston in acres of space on the left, his first time cross was headed back across goal by Norman Whiteside and Frank Stapleton pounced from 2 yards out to put United ahead on aggregate for the first time.

Barcelona now pushed for the away goal that might turn the tie their way but the closest they came was a Schuster curler that went just wide of Gary Bailey's left hand post. At the final whistle United's joyous fans invaded the pitch to mark a special performance from their team and a night that has gone down in club folklore as two-goal Captain Marvel was carried off the pitch shoulder high by his adoring fans

The semi-final draw matched United with Juventus. The Italian outfit were formidable opponents and had a team crammed full of skill and talent with players including Zbigniew Boniek (Poland), Antonio Cabrini (Italy), Claudio Gentile (Italy), Paolo Rossi (Italy) who was the top goal scorer in the 1982 World Cup finals, their captain Gaetano Scirea (Italy), Marco Tardelli (Italy, scored in the 1982 World Cup final) and a Football Master, France's Michel Platini. Platini had joined Juventus from Saint-Etienne in 1982 and went on to win the coveted Ballon d'Or in three consecutive years with "The Old Lady" in 1983, 1984 and 1985.

Yet by the time United faced the Italians they would be without their talisman, Bryan Robson. The first leg of the semi-final ended 1-1; Paulo Rossi opened the scoring for the visitors in the 14th minute with a deflection off the luckless Graeme Hogg that left Gary Bailey stranded but 24 minutes later United equalised when a high ball into the Italian's box fell for Alan Davies who tapped into an empty net. Davies had come on as a substitute for John Gidman who received an injury after only 10 minutes. It was only Davies seventh appearance for United and his first game since he played in the 1983 FA Cup final and replay against Brighton and Hove Albion. The visitors never really tested United after conceding and were happy to adopt the Italian style of defending, "Catenaccio," (often referred to as the door-bolt) confident that they could see off United at Stadio Communale a fortnight later.

All looked lost for United in the second leg when a long ball from Platini sent Boniek through on Gary Bailey in the 13th minute and the Pole converted to send the 64,655 crowd into scenes of celebration. In the 63rd minute Atkinson replaced Frank Stapleton Norman Whiteside in his place. The Italian defenders were cast from iron but Big Norman, like so many of the famous ocean liners that were built in the Harland and Wolff Shipyard in the city of his birth, was made from steel. Then United were back in the tie, Arthur Graham crossed the ball towards the penalty area and Paul McGrath, deputising for Robson in the number 7 shirt, shot toward goal but the deflected and fell of Big Norm who hammered home from close range. Suddenly the once jubilant home fans were now reconsidering their travel plans. Hughes came close with a header before Gary Bailey made an incredible clearance to deny Rossi. Then, just as as the game looked like it would go into extra-time, a Scirea shot from the edge of the box took a deflection and fell for Paolo Rossi who made no mistake from 6 yards. The United players were devastated, they had been within touching distance of the final only to have it snatched from their grasp by The Old Lady.

Yet United fans could look back on an incredible cup run and that night when they overturned a two goal deficit against the most experienced team in European football amid an atmosphere that would never be forgotten

Did You Know That?

Arnold Mühren was 31-years old when he signed for United in August 1982 from Ipswich Town but Ron Atkinson knew the Dutch midfielder had a few more seasons left in the tank. After Ipswich Town beat Arsenal 1-0 in the 1978 FA Cup final, their manager, Bobby Robson, swooped to sign Mühren from the Dutch side FC Twente and paid the paltry sum of £150,000 for his signature. It proved to be an inspired signing by Robson who added Mühren's fellow Dutch international and FC Twente teammate, Frans Thjissen, the following season. The Dutch combination helped Ipswich Town win the UEFA Cup in season 1980-81 when they defeated AZ '67 (Netherlands) by a score line of 5-4 over a two legged final. A future United player,

Alan Brazil, also starred in the final for "The Tractor Boys". But this was not the Dutch midfielder's first winners' medal. He played for Ajax Amsterdam from 1971-74 and with them he won the Eredivisie (Dutch First Division) in 1971-72 & 1972-73, the KNVB Cup in 1972, the Intercontinental Cup in 1972, the European Cup in 1973 and the UEFA Super Cup in 1973. He also won the KNVB Cup with FC Twente in season 1976-77. When Mühren played in United's 1983 FA Cup final draw versus Brighton and Hove Albion he became the first Dutch player to play in a FA Cup final and when he scored a penalty in United's 4-0 win over Brighton and Hove Albion in the reply, he became the first foreign born player to score in the FA Cup final. He left Old Trafford after the 1985 FA Cup final, in which he did not play, having lost his place in the team to Danish international Jesper Olsen, and returned to Ajax Amsterdam aged 34. Mühren played four more seasons for Ajax helping them win the European Cup Winners' Cup and Ajax reached the final again the following season but this time they were beaten 1-0 by Mechelen. Having won practically everything at club level, Mühren was, at 37-years old, a key figure in the Netherlands' team which won the 1988 European Championships.

GAME NO. 13
LIVERPOOL 2-0 UNITED
FIRST DIVISION
ANFIELD, LIVERPOOL
26 APRIL 1992
ATTENDANCE – 38,669

SO NEAR, YET SO FAR

"The ultimate measure of a man is not where he stands in moments of comfort and convenience, but where he stands at times of challenge and controversy."

Dr Martin Luther King

By the end of the 1991-92 season every Manchester United player and supporter came to know the true meaning of this quote. This gut-wrenching defeat at Anfield was arguably the nadir of Sir Alex Ferguson's reign because the club looked near-certainties to win the league for most of the season before a disastrous run-in saw them fade and allow rivals Leeds to pip them to the prize.

There were two games of the season left to play and United were sitting second in the table, a single point behind leaders Leeds United, 76 points to 75. In their penultimate game United played Liverpool with Leeds also facing a trip to Yorkshire neighbours Sheffield United. Both games looked tricky and the destination of the title, the last ever First Division Championship, hung in the balance.

United had not won the title since the halcyon days of Law, Best and Charlton a quarter of a century earlier while Leeds had not be crowned Champions of England since 1973-74, the season United were relegated to the Second Division. That season saw the end of Leeds United's dominance of English football under manager Don Revie who left the club to replace Sir Alf Ramsey as manager of England at the end of the season.

While United bounced straight back by winning the Second Division Championship in 1974-75 and have remained there ever since, Leeds went into decline following Brian Clough's infamous 44 day reign as manager. They reached the European Cup final the same year under Jimmy Armfield (losing to 2-0 to Bayern Munich) but were never a force in English football again and were relegated at the end of the 1981-82 season after 18 consecutive years in the top flight. It took Leeds eight years to get back among the big boys when they won the Second Division title in 1989-90.

In season 1990-91 Leeds had finished fourth in the First Division, United ended up in sixth place but won the European Cup Winners' Cup and all was looking well for the Old Trafford club going into season 1991-92 as the title seemed to be the next logical step for Ferguson's squad but Leeds were an improving side managed by Howard Wilkinson and going into their game at Bramall Lane they had lost just four league games to United's five. In their ranks Leeds had ex-United player Gordon Strachan who was playing arguably the best football of his career, the previous season he won the Football Writers' Association Player of the Year award.

When the two Uniteds met in the League during the season both games ended 1-1 and on 8 January 1992, United beat Leeds 3-1 at Elland Road in the quarter-finals of the League Cup with goals from Clayton Blackmore, Andrei Kanchelskis and Ryan Giggs. A week later the sides met again at Elland Road, this time in the Third Round of the FA Cup, United beat Leeds 1-0 with a goal by Mark Hughes, to knock them out of both domestic cup competitions. Those victories would prove to be a mixed blessing...

United eventually lost 4-2 on penalties to Southampton at Old Trafford in an FA Cup Fourth Round replay but beat Nottingham Forest 1-0 in the League Cup final on 12 April 1992 two weeks before they faced Liverpool at Anfield in the League.

United were top of the League table on 18 April 1992 with 75 points after drawing 1-1 with Luton Town at Kenilworth Road. That same day Leeds drew 0-0 away to Liverpool and were second in the table on 73 points, United also had a game in hand over their title challengers and hadn't lost since going down 1-0 at Nottingham Forest on 18 March 1992 but before their trip to Luton their form was a cause for concern as they had drawn three games in a row including a 1-1 draw in the Manchester derby at Old Trafford where City equalised late on via a Keith Curle penalty.

By now United were suffering for their cup exploits, they would play 7 games in April (including the League Cup Final) and were fading fast. A 1-0 home win against Southampton the Thursday after the final brought respite but it was followed by that draw at Luton before a disastrous defeat to Nottingham Forest on Easter Monday which left them a point behind Leeds, albeit with a game in hand. Two days later United travelled to Upton Park to face bottom of the table West Ham. A victory looked assured but the Hammers produced a performance described by a frustrated Alex Ferguson as 'obscene' as a fortunate Kenny Brown goal and an inspired defensive performance gave the hosts a 1-0 win.

Like an exhausted boxer United no longer packed a punch, meanwhile Leeds seemed to be inspired and had won two, drawn two and lost one of their previous five matches. The reason for the contrast in form was Leeds signing of Eric Cantona from Nîmes. The Frenchman had made his debut on loan on 8 February in a 2-0 loss to Oldham Athletic but when he scored his third goal for Leeds in a 3-0 home win over Chelsea on 11 April 1992, Wilkinson signed the Frenchman permanently. Wilkinson liked the partnership his new French international striker had established with striker Lee Chapman who had scored six goals playing alongside him since his arrival including one in the victory against Chelsea. While United were losing to Forest, Leeds beat Coventry City 2-0 at Elland Road and following United's defeat at West Ham there were two games left to play and Leeds led by a single point and were 4 goals better off in terms of goal difference.

The games at Anfield and Bramall Lane were both played on

Sunday and both televised live by ITV. Leeds would kick-off at Midday meaning that a win would give them a huge psychological advantage. The Yorkshire derby was helter-skelter: Alan Cork gave the Blades the lead before a deflection off Rod Wallace brought Leeds level. In the second half Gary McAllister's free-kick was headed home by Jon Newsome but the hosts equalised minutes later with Lee Chapman putting through his own goal. A draw would have meant the league going to the final game of the season but with 13 minutes to go Blades defender Brian Gayle misjudged a cross in the blustery conditions and headed over his own keeper. Leeds held on meaning that United had to get something at Anfield to keep their faint hopes alive.

Manchester United: Peter Schmeichel, Mal Donaghy, Denis Irwin, Steve Bruce, Gary Pallister, Bryan Robson (Capt), Andrei Kanchelskis, Paul Ince, Ryan Giggs, Mark Hughes, Brian McClair. Substitute: Mike Phelan (for Pallister 31 mins).

Mal Donaghy was not fully fit but Alex Ferguson had to take a chance with him as his first choice at right-back, Paul Parker, was injured and Bryan Robson was making a comeback after missing six games through injury. Paul Ince replaced Mike Phelan in the side who, like Donaghy, was not fully fit.

After 12 minutes the portents were not looking good. Prolific Liverpool goal-scorer Ian Rush had never scored against United before in his previous 24 games but now he put the hosts ahead with a typically calm finish. The Liverpool supporters reacted as if they'd won the league themselves as United continued to try and find an equaliser. Paul Ince hit a post with a blistering drive and both McClair and Kanchelskis struck the crossbar with a header and a volley respectively while Peter Schmeichel made some tremendous saves. To add insult to injury Michael Thomas added a late goal for Liverpool and it was as if all the scouser's Christmases had come at once! At the final whistle Ferguson took to the pitch, applauded the United fans and told his players to go and salute their supporters while the home fans taunted their rivals with shouts of "You lost the title on Merseyside".

It was a bitter pill for the United fans inside the ground to swallow, not only losing against your bitter rivals but losing the title at their ground. Liverpool had been Champions for the 18th time in 1989-90 but slumped to sixth in season 1991-92, their first finish outside the Top 2 since 1980-81. United left Anfield as runners-up as Leeds were four points clear with a game to play. Leeds won their final game of the season, a 1-0 home win over Norwich City, and United defeated

Tottenham Hotspur 3-1 at Old Trafford. West Ham United finished the season bottom of the First Division and went down with Notts County and Luton Town.

That Pyrrhic win over Spurs was the last ever competitive game at Old Trafford in front of the terraced Stretford End. Work commenced on it a few days later to make it an all-seater stand. The game also marked the end of the Manchester United career of Belfast-born Norman Whiteside. Ironically, the last ever game at Old Trafford before the Stretford End was demolished was United versus Everton the day after the Spurs game for Stormin' Norman's Testimonial, the team he had just signed for.

And so the hopes and dreams of Manchester United once again being crowned Champions of England would have to go on for one more season. Alex Ferguson had to take a deep breath, pick up his players, dust them off, and start all over again in the first ever Premier League season in 1992-93.

> *"Winners are not afraid of losing. But losers are.*
> *Failure is part of the process of success.*
> *People who avoid failure also avoid success"*
>
> Robert T. Kiyosaki.

In season 1992 the team that lost at Anfield and failed to land the First Division title learned a valuable lesson and within a year they made Manchester United Champions once again.

Did You Know That?

Howard Wilkinson was the last English manager to win the Premier League/First Division Championship. The following season the Yorkshire outfit won just 12 of their 42 league games (they failed to win a single away game), had a goal difference of –5 and finished 17th in the inaugural Premier League season (51 points), two points above the relegation zone.

GAME NO. 14
UNITED 6-1 ARSENAL
FIRST DIVISION
OLD TRAFFORD
26 APRIL 1952
ATTENDANCE- 53,651

IF AT FIRST YOU DON'T SUCCEED...

After accepting an offer to become the manager of Manchester United in February 1945, Matt Busby guided United to runners-up place behind Liverpool in the First Division in his first full season in charge, 1946-47 and over the next four seasons Busby assembled the first of three great United teams with United finishing runners-up on another three occasions and for Busby's high standards, a lowly fourth place finish in season 1949-50. During these five seasons after the war he also won the club's first trophy in 37 years when they lifted the FA Cup in 1948.

Having finished runners-up again in 1950-51 (this time by 4 points to Spurs) few fancied United to finally go one better in 1951-52. By now the illustrious '48 team were regarded as well past their sell-by date: goalkeeper Jack Crompton was 30, club captain Johnny Carey was 32, centre-half Allenby Chilton would be celebrating his 33rd birthday on 16 September 1951, left-half Henry Cockburn would turn 30 just two days before Chilton's birthday, wing-half Billy McGlen was 30, John Aston Snr would be 30 on 3 September 1951 and winger Harry McShane was 31. His two main strikers were both aged 32, Stan Pearson and Jack Rowley. Whilst these players were all seasoned professionals, Busby knew that if his team were to be crowned Champions of England, a fresh injection of youth was needed to compliment the experience his older players possessed.

Before the season got underway Busby brought in winger Johnny Berry, aged 25, from Birmingham City for a club record £25,000, Busby's most expensive signing to date breaking the record held by John Downie who Busby had spent £18,000 on from Bradford Park Avenue in March 1949. Downie was still at United in season 1951-52, playing 32 times and scoring 11 goals. When it came to spending the club's money Busby was quite frugal, doing so only when he felt it was absolutely necessary, preferring instead to develop players from his Youth Team and during this campaign he would look to the junior ranks in order finally bring United their third league title.

Partly through desire but mostly through necessity, Busby tried to do what few other managers had tried before him; blend the experience of the older players with the youth players already at the club. It was on the pitch at United's Cliff Training Ground in Salford where Matt and his assistant Jimmy Murphy would assess which players were capable of graduating to the first team and this marriage of experienced players with those of youthful exuberance would prove to be the key to United's success.

United's 1951-52 season began with a trip away to West Bromwich Albion on 17 August 1951, a game United drew 3-3 with Jack Rowley scoring a hat-trick. Rowley was out to show that he still had what it took to be a top notch striker in the top flight and he sent a clear message to his fellow strikers at United. Four days later Middlesbrough visited Old Trafford and Rowley was a man on fire scoring another hat-trick with his fellow "old boy," Pearson, also scoring in an emphatic 4-1 victory. The Gunner collected another match ball following a 4-0 win against Stoke at Old Trafford leaving United third in the table but level on points with leaders Portsmouth and second placed Bolton. Rowley had scored 14 goals in 7 games!

Form was mixed over the next few months as United lost 5 of their next 11 games, so for the next game on 24 November 1951, Busby gave two of his younger players, Roger Byrne (aged 22) and Belfast-born Jackie Blanchflower (aged 18) their United debuts in a 0-0 draw away to Liverpool. Byrne had joined United as a trainee in August 1949 while the young Irish player, who was adept at half-back as he was at inside-forward, signed for United as a trainee in May 1949 aged 16. Following a 3-1 home win over Blackpool the following week, United travelled to London to play Arsenal, their 21st game of 42 League games which marked the half-way point of the campaign. Portsmouth, Champions in 1948-49 & 1949-50, were top of the table on 3o points with Arsenal second on 26 points, one place above Bolton Wanderers who had the same number of points but an inferior goal difference to The Gunners. Preston North End, United and Tottenham Hotspur, the reigning Champions, sat in fourth, fifth and sixth places respectively on 24 points. United's encounter at Arsenal Stadium was a four-pointer game at a crucial stage of the season – defeat would almost certainly spell curtains for any title challenge but Busby's mix of youth and experience saw United triumph 3-1 at Highbury. The result proved to be a turning point as Busby's men and boys embarked on a 14 match unbeaten run that took them two points clear of The Gunners at the top of the table.

When United beat Chelsea 3-1 (scorers: Carey, Pearson, own goal) at Old Trafford in their second last League game of the season on 21 April 1952, the title was practically secured. After 41 games United topped the Division on 55 points, two ahead of their nearest challengers, Arsenal, who were sitting second with 53 points. United's final League game of the season, their expected Coronation as First Division Champions, produced a finale which caught the attention of the British sporting public. Before Busby's first great side could finally discard the bridesmaid's dress they had worn for six long years they had to see off Arsenal at Old Trafford on 26 April 1952. Regardless of the outcome of the game the title was surely United's, their first since two World Wars had come and gone, season 1910-11. Or was it a formality? In addition to their two points advantage, United also carried a huge advantage on goal average – 1.745 to Arsenal's 1.436. The visitors needed to win 7-0 to steal the title from United's grasp which seemed highly unlikely but The Gunners had just thumped West Bromwich Albion 6-3 at Highbury. Arsenal also had one eye on the FA Cup final which they would contest a week later against Newcastle United.

Jack Rowley was United's top goal scorer of the season having scored 27 League goals but Arsenal also had a striker who could score at will - Doug Lishman had netted 23 league goals as well as 6 in Arsenal's cup run to Wembley.

Busby sent out his team to win the League: Reg Allen, Thomas McNulty, John Aston Snr, Johnny Carey (Capt), Allenby Chilton, Henry Cockburn, Johnny Berry, John Downie, Roger Byrne (No.11, in an unaccustomed role on the wing for his 25th game of the season). Jack Rowley, Stan Pearson

The gates were locked an hour before kick-off as United supporters squeezed into every available space within Old Trafford. They had come to acclaim the first United champions for 40 years since the days of Billy Meredith and Charlie Roberts. From the off the home side were all over the visitors and George Swindin in the Arsenal goal was forced into action early and often. Jack Rowley got the ball rolling in the 8th minute on his way to his fourth hat-trick of the season while partner-in-goals Stan Pearson bagged a brace and Roger Byrne, now firmly in ownership of the number 11 shirt, made it a round half dozen. Freddie Cox scored for the visitors late on but there's no doubt that United were worthy champions. They ended the campaign with 23 wins, 11 draws, 8 defeats, scored 95 and conceded 52 to finish on 57 points, four points clear of runners-up Tottenham Hotspur who had the same number of points as Arsenal, 53, but enjoyed a better goal average – Arsenal's 6-1 loss on the final day not only cost them the title, it also cost them runners-up spot. The Gunners ended the season without a trophy when Newcastle United defeated them 1-0 in the 1952 FA Cup final at Wembley.

By winning the 1951-52 First Division Championship title, Busby had finally scaled the summit of English football but it was the promotion of youth players that would point the direction for the rest of the 1950s.

Did You Know That?

During the 1951-52 season Busby played five teenagers in his first team: Brian Birch (19), Jackie Blanchflower (18), Laurie Cassidy (18), Mark Jones (18) and Jeff Whitefoot (18). Busby's decision to blood his younger players with his older players had paid off and was the start of his continued investment in youth with the likes of Geoff Bent, Eddie Colman, Ronald Cope, Duncan Edwards, Edward Lewis, David Pegg, Albert Scanlon and Dennis Viollet, being promoted from the junior ranks over the next few seasons. Colman, Cope, Edwards (Capt), Lewis, Pegg and Scanlon were members of the Manchester United Youth Team which won the inaugural FA Youth Cup final in season 1952-53.

GAME NO. 15
UNITED 2-1 MANCHESTER CITY
PREMIER LEAGUE
OLD TRAFFORD
6 DECEMBER 1992
ATTENDANCE – 35,408

I AM NOT A MAN, I AM CANTONA!

Eric Cantona had been through so many changes in his life before joining Manchester United. He had reached some incredible highs and then again he had suffered more than a few lows in a career that had promised more than it had delivered.

Eric was a member of the France Under-21 side which won the Under-21 European Championships in 1988, scoring a hat-trick their quarter-final win against England but there were already warning signs that he was a law unto himself when he was fined by his club, Auxerre, for punching his teammate, Bruno Martini in the face in 1987. Eric felt unloved in his native country. He was a man who placed less value on lucrative contracts, despite the fact that he joined Marseille in 1988 for a record transfer fee of 22 million Francs. Eric was a loner and his career seemed to lack direction and purpose, with no team to love and no fans to love him. Behind him he left a trail of destruction as loan moves to Bordeaux and Montpellier and a transfer to Nîmes all ended in tears as Eric pressed the self-destruct button time and again.

Eric's last chance seemed to be a move away from France where he was vilified and after interest from Sheffield Wednesday he eventually wound up at Leeds United. He played a key role in helping the Elland Road club win the league in 1991-92 but when manager Howard Wilkinson dropped him for a game against Arsenal, a furious Cantona refused to train and faxed a transfer request to the club on 24 November 1992 requesting a move. Cantona stated he was willing to join Arsenal, Liverpool or Manchester United but his bad boy image was enough to put most clubs off buying a player who possessed such a volatile temper.

And that was when Manchester United came into his life. On 24 November 1992, Bill Fotherby, the Chairman of Leeds United, was asked by Wilkinson to telephone his opposite number at Manchester United, Martin Edwards, to inquire about the possibility of signing their Republic of Ireland international left back Denis Irwin. Irwin had begun his professional career with the Yorkshire club in 1983 leaving them in 1986 to join Oldham Athletic before arriving at Old Trafford at the end of the 1989-90 season. Alex Ferguson was in Edwards' office when Fotherby made the call and told his Chairman that Irwin was part of his future plans and that he wanted to keep him. Ferguson then prompted Edwards to ask Fotherby if Leeds were willing to sell Cantona as United would be without their new £1 million striker Dion Dublin who had signed for United from Cambridge United on 7 August 1992 but then broken his leg on 2 September 1992. Fotherby said he would speak to Wilkinson and return shortly with his manager's answer. Messrs Ferguson and Edwards were stunned that the move was not immediately ruled out. A few minutes later Wilkinson said he was prepared to let his French striker leave and so on 26 November 1992 Eric Cantona signed for Manchester United in a £1.2 million transfer.

When Cantona left Leeds United for Manchester United he was considered toxic, pundits all over the country claimed that Fergie had lost the plot big time and more than one of them predicted that the Frenchman would be the Scotsman's final gamble in the Old Trafford hot seat. Yet in Alex Ferguson Eric Cantona found the greatest man-manager in the history of the game. Alex knew how to handle his new signing and the Frenchman quickly recognised that Manchester United were not just another club. It was a marriage made in heaven – Eric was exactly what the club needed and the club was exactly what Eric needed.

On 6 December 1992, Eric Cantona made his debut for Manchester United as a substitute in the Manchester derby Old Trafford. Manchester United: Peter Schmeichel, Paul Parker, Denis Irwin, Steve Bruce, Gary Pallister, Lee Sharpe, Paul Ince, Bryan Robson (Capt), Brian McClair, Mark Hughes, Ryan Giggs. Substitute: Eric Cantona (for Giggs, 46 minutes).

After an even opening quarter United took the lead – Robson playing a free kick towards Hughes who found Steve Bruce. The big centre-half laid the ball back for Paul Ince on the edge of the box who beat Tony Coton at his near post. Sky TV cameras focused in on Cantona warming up in the tunnel at half time as the level of expectation rose and the Frenchman duly came on for Ryan Giggs. Mark Hughes made it 2-0 to United in the 74th minute with a spectacular volley – his initial header towards Cantona was only half clear and fell for him, the Welshman advanced and smashed the ball past Coton from the edge of the box. Just two minutes later City were back in at as Niall Quinn capitalised on indecision in the United back line to poke past Schmeichel. City piled on the pressure in the closing stages and the Great Dane was forced into a terrific point-blank save from David White in the dying moments.

In truth Cantona's 45 minutes were relatively uneventful and many United fans may have wondered what all the fuss was about. After all he was known to be a player who could cause disharmony in the dressing room and who was as turbulent as they come. The United fans did not have very long to wait to get the answer they were seeking. Cantona's debut may have been uninspiring but it didn't take him long to allay any fears supporters' may have had. Eric was handed the number 7 shirt for the hard-fought 1-0 win over Norwich the following weekend but then United faced a tough away trip to Chelsea. When they fell behind following a long-distance 68th minute free-kick from David Lee United supporters feared the worst but minutes later they got their first glimpse of Cantona magic. Sharpe's long cross was nodded back across the box to Eric and he swivelled and hit his shot clean as a whistle past Kevin Hitchcock in the Chelsea goal. It was the first of many decisive goals.

Prior to Cantona's arrival at Old Trafford United were in 5th place in the Premier League table having played 17 games, winning 7, drawing 6 and losing 4. Mind you, after the opening two games of the season they had been rooted to the bottom of the Premier League with no points, 1 goal for and 5 against after losing the season opener 2-1 away to Sheffield United and a 3-0 home loss to Everton. The club's dreams of winning a first League Championship since the heyday of Law, Best and Charlton looked to be over before the season had even properly started.

Now Cantona had an immediate effect. Starting with the derby United won 6 of their next 8 league after his arrival and romped to the title by 10 points from Aston Villa. The 25 year wait was finally over and never again would a newspaper question Alex Ferguson's hold on the United hot-seat.

Yet it was Eric's work away from the spotlight that had as much effect. He re-energised the club and gave a sense of purpose to United's youth team players, such as David Beckham, Nicky Butt, Gary and Phil Neville, Paul Scholes and many more who were all striving to get into the United first team. Cantona was without question the final piece in Alex Ferguson's jigsaw, an artist on the pitch who could picture a goal in his head many moves before it actually unfolded and the catalyst for United's domination of English football during the 1990s. Ferguson had pulled off a master stroke in persuading him to join United, a player who galvanised the team from his first day of practice with his new team-mates at the Cliff Training Ground.

In season 1993-94, Eric's first full season at Old Trafford, he produced some superb individual performances. He was articulate, eloquent, enigmatic, expressive, inspirational, magnificent, majestic, mesmeric, poetic and talismanic. He could also be moody, ill-tempered and on occasion violent to defenders who overstepped the mark. He was dismissed three times in 1993-94, receiving two red cards in four days in March which put the brakes on United's quest for the domestic treble and of course his temper would cost him and United much more the following season.

Nevertheless there's little doubt the Frenchman was Ferguson's greatest signing. Sir Alex Ferguson once said of Eric: "He was born to play for United. Some players with respected and established reputations are cowed and broken by the size and expectations. Not Eric. He swaggered in, stuck his chest out, raised his head and surveyed everything as if to ask: 'I'm Cantona, how big are you? Are you big enough for me?'"

At his peak, Eric was a charismatic footballer of fantastic skill, tremendous strength and superb vision. In 1994, Ryan Giggs released his autobiography in which he spoke about Eric's influence on United's 1993-94 Double winning side. Giggs was convinced that Cantona knew just how fast he, Andrei Kanchelskis and Lee Sharpe could run as he floated balls out to the wings so effortlessly and so perfectly it meant the gifted trio of United wingers did not even have to break stride to collect it. "I think he knows how fast the full back can run too and often when Eric gets the ball you can't conceive that a pass is on, but you have to make the run and get ahead of the defender because, just as it looks as if he's lost it, he'll pop it through his marker's legs and out to you," said Giggs.

Eric was the conductor whilst Giggs, Kanchelskis, Sharpe, Mark Hughes and Brian McClair were his orchestra. In the five years the United faithful had the pleasure of watching Cantona strut around the Old Trafford pitch, the collar of his No.7 shirt turned up, chest stuck out, his imperious look, theatrical swagger and consummate poise, the club won 4 Premier League titles, 2 FA Cups and 3 Community

Shields.

The only season the team did not win anything was 1994–95 when they finished runners-up to Blackburn Rovers in the Premiership and were beaten 1-0 by Everton in the FA Cup Final but then again United did not have Eric for the last four months of the season which effectively prevented the club from winning consecutive Doubles.

In an interview with *FourFourTwo* magazine Cantona was asked about his "Kung-Fu" attack after being sent off in an away game versus Crystal Palace on 25 January 1995, and said with regret: "I did not punch him strong enough. I should have punched him harder. I didn't watch it after on television. Because I knew. All I had was journalists around my house. That's all I could see. My house was small. They blocked the light." In the months that followed it took all of Alex Ferguson's powers of persuasion to stop Eric from moving to Inter Milan and the Scot was rewarded the following season with a different, calmer, more authoritative Eric as he led United's youngsters to the league and cup double. After Selhurst Park Cantona was never shown a red card again and he won the FWA Player of the Year in 1995–96.

Cantona was the catalyst that helped Manchester United to eclipse past glories. And Ferguson was 100% right, Eric Cantona was born to play for Manchester United, the United fans adored him and still do to this day. His passion for Manchester United was unconditional. Cantona wanted to please the fans and they loved him for it. Nowhere in the world will you find football fans more passionate than those of Manchester United and nowhere in the world will you find 75,000 fans singing the name of a former player at nearly every home game almost 20 years after he played his last game.

"You must be shapeless, formless, like water. When you pour water in a cup, it becomes the cup. When you pour water in a bottle, it becomes the bottle. When you pour water in a teapot, it becomes the teapot. Water can drip and it can crash. Become like water my friend."

BRUCE LEE

Bruce Lee was an inspiration for Eric and Cantona became United's water. He made the team flow freely. He gave life to Fergie's Fledglings. He quenched United's thirst for a first Championship in 26 years. He influenced the team's style of play as the current do in a river. He was a resource to his team-mates. He was sometimes uncontrollable. He could rage. He could flow gently. He could flow smoothly. He could flow effortlessly. He could flow with force. In a few games Eric was a Babbling Brook, in most he was Niagara Falls, occasionally he was a tidal wave that broke everything in his path.

He was not a man. He was Cantona. Il était magnifique.

Did You Know That?

Eric Cantona could have become a Liverpool player. On 6 November 1991 a spooky and unlucky 13 months to the very day before Eric Cantona pulled on the famous red shirt of Manchester United for the first time, Liverpool played Auxerre from France in a UEFA Cup, Round 2, second leg tie at Anfield. Liverpool were playing their first season of European football since the fateful Heysel Disaster at the 1985 European Cup final. Two weeks before the French outfit flew into Liverpool they won the first leg 2-0 at their Stade de l'Abbe-Deschamps home. After Liverpool beat their French opposition 3-0, Liverpool manager Graeme Souness received a visit in his office from the manager of the French national side at the time, Michel Platini and, in a strange twist of fate, it was Platini who scored the only goal of the game for Juventus when they beat Liverpool 1-0 in the 1985 European Cup final at Heysel.

In Souness's own words: "We had played Auxerre at home (in November 1991) and Michel Platini came to see me. He said he had a player - a problem boy but a proper player. Cantona. I said the last thing I needed was another problem player. I had 30-pluses that I was trying to get out so I didn't need more hassle. I said I was looking for something else. I said no thanks."

Thankfully, Alex Ferguson said "Oui," when Leeds United decided to offload their "Problem Boy." Merci Beaucoup Monsieur Souness.

GAME NO. 16
ASTON VILLA 3-1 UNITED
PREMIER LEAGUE
VILLA PARK
19 AUGUST 1995
ATTENDANCE - 34,655

YOU CAN'T WIN ANYTHING WITH KIDS

If there was ever a moment for Alex Ferguson to read poetry to his players before a game, then surely that moment must have taken place in the away dressing room at Villa Park on Saturday 19 August 1995. After losing the league and FA Cup final following in the wake of Eric Cantona's kung-fu kick, the Scot had just sold three key players before the 1995-96 season kicked off. United fans were staggered at the sale of Mark Hughes to Chelsea, Andrei Kanchelskis to Everton and Paul Ince to Internazionale of Milan and the only summer signings were 3 back-up goalkeepers. As if to emphasise the unease among fans, a poll in the *Manchester Evening News* suggested a majority of United supporters wanted the man who led them out of the 26-year title wilderness to be sacked! So when that first game of the season rolled around Fergie could have been forgiven for recalling the opening lines of famous poem 'If' by Rudyard Kipling.

If you can keep your head when all about you are losing theirs and
blaming it on you;
If you can trust yourself when all men doubt you, But make
allowance for their doubting too:
If you can wait and not be tired by waiting,
Or, being lied about, don't deal in lies,
Or being hated don't give way to hating,
And yet don't look too good, nor talk too wise.

Pundits seemed to have decided that United's summer business, or lack of it, marked the end of them as a title-winning threat, this was the first time since the inaugural Premier League season that bookmakers did not have United installed as favourites to win the League. The loss of Eric Cantona, the loss of the league to Blackburn Rovers on the last day of the season, the defeat to Everton in the FA Cup Final a week later, the loss of Kanchelskis, Hughes and Ince... The experts looked at United's squad and couldn't see how the promoted youth players could challenge the likes of champions Blackburn, a resurgent Liverpool and Kevin Keegan's Newcastle United for the league title.

Yet the same pundits were only dimly aware of events behind the scenes at the club. When he was manager of Aberdeen (1978-86) he entered his Youth Team in the first edition of the Scottish Youth Cup in season 1983-84 and his young charges went on to lift the cup in 1985 and 1986, the year Ferguson left Pittodrie for Old Trafford. Ferguson, along with ex-United player Brian McClair and Youth Team coach Eric Harrison, knew they had a group of very talented young players at their disposal. They won the 1992 FA Youth Cup final and by the summer of 1995 most of them had been blooded in the first team. However playing in the odd League Cup game against lower division teams was a world away from the slog of winning a Premier League packed with stars from across the globe. It was Ferguson's judgement that his lads were ready and the world would get their answer at Villa Park on the first day of the season.

The line-up included four members of the side which had lifted the FA Youth Cup four years earlier: David Beckham, Nicky Butt, Gary Neville and John O'Kane. Phil Neville, aged 18, and 20-year old Paul Scholes were also named in the squad along with seven established players: Peter Schmeichel, Paul Parker, Denis Irwin, Gary Pallister, Roy Keane, Brian McClair and 24-year old Lee Sharpe.

The Manchester United side Ferguson selected that day was: Peter Schmeichel, Paul Parker, Denis Irwin, Gary Neville, Gary Pallister, Phil Neville, Roy Keane, Nicky Butt, Lee Sharpe, Paul Scholes, Brian McClair. Substitutes: David Beckham for Phil Neville 46 mins, John O'Kane for Pallister 59 mins

The Aston Villa team, unlike United's, comprised players who had already established themselves as Premier League stars including future United goalkeeper Mark Bosnich, Gary Charles, Steve Staunton, Gareth Southgate, Ugo Ehiogu, Andy Townsend, future United striker Dwight Yorke and Manchester United Legend Paul McGrath. The United fans applauded their side on to the pitch and gave McGrath the welcome he always received from them a chorus of "Ooh, Aah, Paul McGra! I Say Ooh Aah Paul McGra!".

Villa had struggled in the two seasons since they finished 10 points behind United in that inaugural title race, finishing 10th in 1993-94 and 18th in 1994-95 and 'Big' Ron Atkinson had departed to be replaced by Brian Little in 1994. Even so, Villa would be confident going into this game as they could think back to their 3-1 1994 League Cup

Final victory over United just 18 months earlier.

With Giggs, Cole and Cantona all absent, Ferguson adopted a 3-5-2 set-up. The home side had their record £3.5 million signing in their side, Serbian striker Savo Milošević and the home side were off to flyer - after 14 minutes Dwight Yorke's cross flew across the box and when Gary Charles fired it back in Ian Taylor stooped to knock it past Schmeichel. On 27 minutes Dwight Yorke broke forward again finding Milosevic who in turn played in Draper, the striker beating the Great Dane at his near post. Just 10 minutes later Schmeichel brought down Milosevic and Dwight Yorke made no mistake from the spot. The young recruits looked like lambs to the slaughter and the team's embarrassing first half display was as grey as their new kit.

At half-time Ferguson sent on David Beckham for Phil Neville and on the hour mark John O'Kane replaced Pallister. The changes started to pay dividends as United looked transformed after the break, Bosnich saving a header from Keane and a chip from McClair before denying Keane again following a superb Beckham cross. Then, with just 6 minutes remaining, David Beckham took dead aim from 30 yards and swerved a superb shot past Bosnich who could only watch it sail past him. "Villa Park hummed with satisfaction," wrote the *Birmingham Mail*'s sportswriter Leon Hickman and most of the rest of the country seemed satisfied that United would not challenge for major honours in 1995-96.

These sentiments were most famously echoed on *Match of the Day* that evening as former Liverpool captain Alan Hansen was asked to comment on United's display, "I think they've got problems. I wouldn't say they've got major problems. Obviously, three players have departed, the trick is always buy when you're strong, so he needs to buy players. You can't win anything with kids." The "he" Hansen was referring to was Alex Ferguson. The former Liverpool man's personal criticism of Ferguson may have stemmed from Hansen's omission from Scotland's 1986 World Cup squad. Hansen had just won the double with Liverpool and was widely regarded as one of the best centre-halfs in Europe but he was overlooked. Yet Hansen wasn't alone in his criticism, he was just unfortunate in finding a memorable phrase that summarised pundit opinion of United's chances.

What happened after that fateful day at Villa Park is well documented. Eric Cantona returned from his suspension and played the finest football of his career, Peter Schmeichel became almost unbeatable in goal and the kids, chivvied by a dominant Roy Keane, edged out Newcastle United for the league title by four points after a legendary title race. Then they completed the double a week later by beating arch rivals Liverpool 1-0 in the FA Cup final.

As the final whistle sounded at Wembley, Alex Ferguson had been vindicated. Moreover, by selling three of his key men from the previous double winning team and replacing them with graduates of the youth system the club had been propelled into a new era true to the spirit of MUJAC and the Busby Babes – Manchester United were young, gifted and back!

Did You Know That?

Paul McGrath won the prestigious Professional Footballers Association Player of the Year Award in season 1992-93, the same season his previous club, Manchester United, won the inaugural Premier League title by 10 points over McGrath's new club, Aston Villa.

GAME NO. 17
UNITED 3-2 JUVENTUS
UEFA CHAMPIONS LEAGUE, GROUP B
OLD TRAFFORD
22 OCTOBER 1997
ATTENDANCE- 53,428

ROCAMBOLESCO UNITED

After winning the Premier League in 1996-97 for the fourth time in six seasons, Alex Ferguson knew that his legacy and that of his players could only be cemented in the history books by winning club football's biggest prize, the UEFA Champions League. United had not been crowned Champions of Europe in 30 years going back to the swinging sixties when the third great United side which Matt Busby built beat Benfica 4-1 after extra-time at Wembley in the 1968 European Cup final and Fergie's early campaigns in the tournament had been disastrous.

In 1993-94 they didn't even make the group stage. Having disposed of Hungarian champions Honved 5-3 on aggregate in the first round they drew Turkish champions Galatasaray and things seemed to be going to plan as United surged into a 2-0 lead at Old Trafford with less than a quarter of an hour gone but then it all started to go pear-shaped. The Turks pulled a goal back almost immediately,

Erdem looping a long-range shot over Schmeichel and were level by half-time following a disastrous mix up in the United defence. By now the Turkish champions were dominant and took the lead on the hour, Turkyilmaz turning in a close range rebound. Several impromptu pitch invasions added to the atmosphere of chaos and United were fortunate that they emerged with a 3-3 draw, Eric Cantona converting an 81st minute Roy Keane cross to preserve the club's long unbeaten home record in European competition that stretched back to 1956. The away leg has gone down in infamy as Galatasaray supporters greeted the United team at the airport bearing 'Welcome to Hell' banners and, after the visitors had failed to break Turkish resistance and as the home fans celebrated wildly, Cantona was sent off after the final whistle.

The following season wasn't much better. This time the format had changed slightly and United were selected in a tough group alongside Gothenburg, Barcelona and Galatasaray. After a 4-2 win over the Swedes and draws in Istanbul and at home to Barcelona, they crumbled in the return at the Camp Nou with Romario and Hristo Stoichkov running riot against a makeshift United defence limited by UEFA's 'three foreigner rule' that meant that United were forced to select one of Cantona, Keane, Schmeichel, Irwin and Kanchelskis and select only two of the 'assimilated players' in this case Mark Hughes and Ryan Giggs. So Gary Walsh was in goal and Nicky Butt played in place of Cantona. A 1-3 defeat in Gothenburg sealed United's fate and despite a satisfying 4-0 win over Galatasaray United were out before the tournament reached the sharp end again.

The Bosman ruling in 1995 put an end to the foreigner rule and United fared much better in their next Champions League campaign in 1996-97. United were drawn to play in Group C along with Turkish Champions Fenerbahçe, Rapid Wien the Austrian Champions and reigning European champions Juventus who had claimed their second European Cup after defeating Ajax 4-2 on penalties in the 1996 final. The opening Group match-ups meant a visit to Turin for United on 11 September 1996 to play Juventus at their famous Stadio delle Alpi home ground. The home side included: Antonio Conte, Croatian Alen Boksic, French international Didier Deschamps, Christian Vieri, playmaker Alessandro Del Piero and Zinedine Zidane, it was almost like facing a world eleven but then buying the best players in the world was never an issue for Juventus who were bankrolled by the Agnelli family who owned FIAT and on the night Juventus hit all of the right gears against United and won 1-0 with a goal by Boksic.

Following a 2-0 home win over Rapid Wien in their second group game, United were off to Istanbul again, this time to play Galatasaray's fierce rivals Fenerbahçe. The Turkish side, nicknamed "The Yellow Canaries" did not have much to sing about losing the game 2-0 but on 30 October 1996, 40 years and 34 days since first playing a competitive home European fixture, United's proud unbeaten home record fell when the Turks beat them 1-0. It was a sad occasion for the vast majority of the 53,297 who attended the game. Worse was to follow as Juventus beat United 1-0 at Old Trafford, a penalty scored by Del Piero and Fenerbahçe moved above them in the table after winning 1-0 at home against the Austrian Champions. United went into their final group game against Rapid Wien needing to win in Vienna and hope that Juventus, who were already through, could beat the Turkish champions in Turin. A point would be good enough to see United progress into the Knockout Phase on goal difference provided Fenerbahçe lost as United had the better goal difference. On a famous night in the Ernst-Happel-Stadion, United finally qualified although they were indebted to a wonderful save from Peter Schmeichel when the game was still goalless but a superb goal from Giggs on 24 minutes settled the nerves and when Eric Cantona scored midway through the second half United were there.

In the quarter-finals United drew FC Porto and dispatched the Portuguese champions 4-0 at Old Trafford in the club's most convincing European display since the 1960s. Following a goalless draw in Portugal they drew Borussia Dortmund in the semi-finals and were expected to progress but 1-0 defeats in both legs saw United crash out and by the end of the season Eric Cantona had retired.

In 1997-98 United were drawn with Feyenoord who were runners-up to PSV Eindhoven in the Eredivisie, Kosice who won the Slovak Superliga title in 1996-97 and who had come through two Qualifying Rounds already and Juventus again who, despite losing the previous year's European Cup Final 3-1 to Dortmund had won the Serie A title by two points from Parma. Could United, without talisman Cantona, finally reach the summit of European football?

United started well with a comfortable 3-0 win in Slovakia before the visit of the team most pundits rated the best in Europe to Old Trafford. Manchester United: Peter Schmeichel (Capt), Gary Neville, Denis Irwin, Ronny Johnsen, Gary Pallister, Henning Berg, Nicky Butt, David Beckham, Ryan Giggs, Ole Gunnar Solskjaer, Teddy

Sheringham. Substitutes: Paul Scholes for Butt 39 mins, Phil Neville for Solskjaer 48 mins

United captain Roy Keane was missing for United and so Ronnie Johnsen was handed the unenviable task of trying to shackle Zidane and when Del Piero scored after just 24 seconds, spinning around Berg to slide the ball wide of Schmeichel, United's task seemed impossible. Marcello Lippi's team were notoriously difficult to break down and had only conceded a single goal in their four Serie A games before the visit to Old Trafford but United fought their way back into the game and Sheringham put them level in the 38th minute rising high to sending a downward header from Giggs cross past Angelo Peruzzi in the Juventus net and two defenders on the goal line. The teams went in at the interval level and for the first fifteen minutes of the second half the away side looked content with their night's work but six minutes later their game plan went out the window when Didier Deschamps was shown a second yellow card for pulling Johnsen's shirt. Three minutes later Scholes put United in the lead when he rounded Peruzzi to score as the Italians protested for offside in vain. Scholes' goal unsettled the normally unflappable Italian back four and Giggs bedazzled them with his slalom like runs and with time running out Giggs sealed a famous victory for United when another of his twisting runs took him into the box where he fired a shot high up into the net at the near post. Zidane scored a consolation goal for the visitors in the 90th minute with a trademark free-kick from outside the box but this had been a huge victory for United as they had gone toe-to-toe with the best team on the continent and emerged victorious without Cantona. Fergie's young team, containing a nucleus of players brought through the junior ranks, had finally made their mark in Europe.

Unfortunately United went no further in the tournament, going out on away goals to AS Monaco in the quarter-finals and although Juventus reached their third consecutive final they were beaten 1-0 by Real Madrid in the Amsterdam Arena. Nevertheless they had well and truly learned from their two defeats against Juventus the previous season and their win on 1 October 1997 laid the foundations for the following season's exploits when they would eventually reach the summit of European football. United's performance against Juventus was *rocambolesco*, incredible.

Did You Know That?

The Ernst-Happel-Stadion was named in honour of Austrian footballer and legendary manager Ernst Happel, after he passed away on 14 November 1992. As a player, he won the Austrian Football Bundesliga six times, the Austrian Cup and the Zentropa Cup during his 15 years as a Rapid Wien player. He was also a member of the Austrian squad which finished third at the 1954 World Cup finals in Sweden, losing 6-1 to the eventual winners, West Germany in the semi-finals before beating Uruguay 3-1 in the Third Place Play-Off match. As a coach/manager he is considered one of the greatest of all-time winning the Dutch Cup with ADO Den Haag; the Eredivisie, the 1970 European Cup and 1970 Intercontinental Cup with Feyenoord; 4 Belgian Championships and the Belgian Cup with Club Brugge; the Belgian Cup and Belgian Supercup with Standard Liege; 2 Bundesliga Championships, the German Cup and the 1983 European Cup with Hamburger SV and 2 Austrian Championships and the Austrian Cup with Swarovski Tirol. He also guided the Netherlands to runners-up place in the 1978 World Cup finals where they lost 3-1 after extra-time to hosts Argentina.

Happel was the first of five managers to guide two different clubs to European Cup glory (Carlo Ancelotti – AC Milan & Real Madrid, Ottmar Hitzfeld – Borussia Dortmund & FC Bayern Munich, Jose Mourinho FC Porto & Inter Milan and Jupp Heynckes – Real Madrid & FC Bayern Munich). He is also one of six different managers to win a domestic League Championship in a least four different countries along with Ancelotti, Eric Gerets, Tomislav Ivic, Mourinho and Giovanni Trapattoni.

GAME NO. 18
UNITED 4-0 LEICESTER CITY
FIRST DIVISION
OLD TRAFFORD
21 DECEMBER 1957
ATTENDANCE – 41,631

THE HERO OF MUNICH

Manchester United, First Division Champions in 1956-57, got their defence of the title off to an excellent start in season 1957-58, winning five of their opening six games, scoring at will (22 goals) and conceding only 5 goals, three of which came in a 3-3 draw with Everton at Goodison Park in front of an astonishing crowd of 71,868. Liam Whelan and Dennis Viollet had scored six goals each with Tommy Taylor banging in four. Ray Wood was Matt Busby's first choice goalkeeper and had been since season 1954-55. Wood, aged 26, played in United's first 18 League games in 1957-58 but the team had started to leak goals, conceding 25 times since winning five of the opening six games. By the time United played Tottenham Hotspur at Old Trafford on 30 November 1957 Busby had decided to give 17-year old David Gaskell his second start in the No.1 jersey. United lost the game 4-3 and Busby then reinstated Wood for United's next game, a trip behind the Iron Curtain to Prague.

United had beaten Dukla Prague 3-0 at Old Trafford in the European Cup, First Round, first leg a fortnight earlier with Pegg, Taylor and Colin Webster all scoring and despite losing 1-0 in the Czech capital on 4 December 1957, United progressed to Round 2 with a 3-1 aggregate victory but United had fallen away in the League and had to close the gap between them and the two teams who were vying for United's crown, West Bromwich Albion and Wolverhampton Wanderers. Wood played in Prague and was in goal for United's next two League games, a 3-3 home draw with Birmingham City on 7 December 1957 and a 1-0 loss at Old Trafford a week later to Chelsea. United had fallen 10 points behind leaders Wolves and Busby, who had not bought a player in five years, knew he needed a new goalkeeper to maintain United's hopes of retaining their Championship title, win the FA Cup and challenge in Europe.

Busby's scouts were tasked with finding the club a new custodian, a player who would command his box, not be shy in barking orders at his defenders and be brave when confronting opposing forwards. It was a tall task indeed but within a week United had their man and he didn't come cheap. Manchester United's offer of £22,000 to Doncaster Rovers for their 25-year old goalkeeper Harry Gregg was instantly dismissed by Rovers manager Peter Doherty, so Matt Busby and his right hand man Jimmy Murphy drove to Yorkshire to ask Gregg in person to join United. At the time Harry was Northern Ireland's No.1 and had already been capped 9 times for his country. On the evening United lost 1-0 in Prague, Harry had played for Northern Ireland in a friendly against Italy. The game was actually supposed to have been a qualifying game for the 1958 World Cup finals in Sweden with the Italians only needing a draw to qualify whilst a win for the Irish would see them reach the finals. However on the eve of the match a drama unfolded when Hungarian referee, Istvan Zoltz, and his linesmen were unable to fly to Belfast due to heavy fog which had smothered Heathrow Airport near London. Billy Drennan, the General Secretary of the Irish Football Association, acted swiftly and arranged for highly respected English referee Arthur Ellis to sail from Stranraer to Larne as a standby. Thousands of tickets had already been sold for what was at the time the biggest game in Northern Ireland's history as they had never reached a World Cup finals tournament before. However the President of the Italian Football Federation, Dr Ottorino Barassi, refused to agree to let Ellis referee the game in the event that the Hungarian officials could not make it and was content to wait until the next morning to reassess the situation.

On the morning of the game the fog in London had not lifted sufficiently to permit flights to take off and early in the afternoon it appeared that the match would have to be abandoned as Barassi was adamant that under FIFA Rules all World Cup games had to be officiated by a neutral referee. Even had he agreed to Ellis ,it was too late for the English referee to make it to Belfast in time. However the abandonment of the game was not practical either as thousands of tickets had already been sold in advance as it was an afternoon kick-off at 2.15pm on a Wednesday, tens of thousands of workers at the world famous Harland & Wolff Shipyard had already planned to down tools and cheer their country on. Added to this the turnstiles at Windsor Park, Belfast had been opened early and a few thousand of the expected 50,000 fans had already taken up their places inside the ground. A compromise had to be reached or the organisers faced a riot from a disgruntled crowd, many of whom had taken the afternoon off work unpaid to see the game.

Zoltz was the manager of the Budapest Opera House and the drama surrounding the game rivalled an opera which premiered just 6 months before the game, "The Visitors." The Visitors is an opera in three acts which reflect and intensify the relationships between the protagonists. In this case the three acts, Zoltz and his two linesmen, did not play whilst the visitors, Italy, refused to play ball. At 2.00pm an announcement was made over the tannoy system: "The Hungarian referee has not arrived. A further announcement will be made later." The crowd began to boo and jeer. Five minutes before the scheduled kick-off time the two football Presidents, Barassi and Joseph McBride, signed an agreement to play the game using a local referee but downgrade it to an international friendly with the World Cup qualifier to be played at a later date. The tannoy system was switched on again and Billy Drennan, the General Secretary of the Irish Football Association, once again addressed the crowd saying: *"Due to the unfortunate circumstances of the non-arrival of the referee and linesmen an agreement has been reached whereby this match will be considered as an friendly international. The cup match will be played here on a date to be arranged. This is all that can be done in the circumstances to maintain friendly relations between the Associations."*

The crowd were far from happy and incessantly booed the Italian national anthem. The game ended 2-2 but it became known as "The Battle of Belfast," as a result of what happened during and after the game. The game was more of a mixed martial arts contest than a football match and there was certainly no *entente cordiale* on display. The Italians started the mayhem when their right-half, Giuseppe Chiapella, punched Irish captain Danny Blanchflower, who did not react. Blanchflower was a cultured player and was also the captain of Tottenham Hotspur. The crowd were incensed and baying for the blood of the Italians which also had Argentinian and Uruguayan players in their side who qualified to play for Italy after playing club football in the country for a number of years. Then Juan Schiaffino, who won a World Cup winners medal with Uruguay in 1950, hit Wilbur Cush. Blanchflower told Cush to forget about what had just happened and get on with the game but the "Little Iron Man from Lurgan" wasn't letting Schiaffino off with playing dirty and a few minutes later he tackled the Uruguayan with such ferocity the *Belfast Telegraph* later said "it even made hardened shipyard workers wince!" Windsor Park looked more like the iconic boxing amphitheater

Madison Square Garden than a football stadium as opponents squared up to one another.

Invigorated by his clash with Schiaffino, Cush scored both of the home side's goals and when the final whistle was blown by referee Tom Mitchell from Lurgan, several thousand enraged Irish fans invaded the pitch as the Italian players gathered in the centre circle to do their usual salute to the crowd, and attacked the visitors. Rino Ferrario, the villain of the peace in the Italian midfield, had to be carried off the pitch unconscious on a stretcher by two police officers. The police baton charged the fans in an attempt to restore some form of order whilst the Northern Ireland players had to escort their opponents to the safety of the tunnel. Gregg had to shield one of the Italian defenders who had been wrestled to the ground from receiving a beating while Manchester United's Jackie Blanchflower, Danny's younger brother, tried in vain to placate the Irish fans and the police had to place guards outside the Italian dressing room to prevent fans from battering the door down. Revenge would come swiftly for the Irishmen as just six weeks later on 15 January 1958 the Italians returned to Windsor Park and the Irish triumphed 2-1 meaning they had qualified for the 1958 World Cup as group winners and eliminated Italy in the process.

United knew that in Gregg they had a goalkeeper who could handle himself in the heat of battle. Harry was changing the way goalkeepers operated, as he was one of the first to venture out of his box to shout encouragement to his team-mates in front of him. At the time, most goalkeepers rarely left the goal line, but the innovative Gregg liked to bark orders to his defenders if he saw one or two of them out of position.

Busby and Murphy duly arrived up at Doherty's home just six days before Christmas to meet Gregg and discuss the terms of the transfer, Gregg liked what he heard and without a moment's hesitation the big Irishman agreed to move to United. A fee of £23,500 was agreed, the second time the club had broken the world record fee for a goalkeeper. Gregg received a paltry £30 from the transfer fee, but as he said himself he would have gone to United for nothing. However, Busby had the utmost faith that the young Irish international goalkeeper would be worth every penny, and Gregg did not let him down.

Henry "Harry" Gregg was born on 25 October 1932 in Magherafelt, County Londonderry, Northern Ireland. He played for Linfield Rangers, Linfield Swifts (also known as Windsor Park Swifts) and Irish League side Coleraine before he accepted an offer to sign for

Second Division Doncaster Rovers just before his 20th birthday. He was delighted to sign for a club whose player-manager was a Northern Ireland legend, Peter Doherty. Coleraine received £2,000 for releasing him. Gregg had played a total of 92 Division Two games for Rovers before Manchester United approached his club to sign him up. While he was at Doncaster Doherty was also in charge of Northern Ireland and awarded Gregg his first international cap in a 2-1 away win over Wales in Wrexham on 21 March 1954 in a World Cup qualifying game.

Two days after signing, Busby gave him his debut and he put in a commanding, almost flawless, performance as United ran out 4-0 winners over Leicester City at Old Trafford in Division One on 21 December 1957 (scorers: Viollet 2, Bobby Charlton, Albert Scanlon).

Manchester United: Harry Gregg, Bill Foulkes, Roger Byrne (Capt), Eddie Colman, Mark Jones, Duncan Edwards, Kenny Morgans, Bobby Charlton, Tommy Taylor, Dennis Viollet, Albert Scanlon. Kenny Morgans made his debut for United in the game.

Gregg's attitude to training and dedication to the task in hand were exactly what Busby was looking for and he retained his place in the team, playing in 18 of United's remaining 20 league games that season, which saw them finish ninth in the table.

By the time of the fateful Munich Air Disaster on 6 February 1958, United had not lost one of the ten games since Gregg's arrival, and everyone was in buoyant mood having qualified for the semi-finals of the European Cup the previous evening. Gregg, who had been reading The Whip by Roger MacDonald, put the book down and gazed out the window as the plane made a third attempt to take off got underway. The plane couldn't get off the runway and crashed into a building and burst into flames. Amid the wreckage and pandemonium, Harry clambered out of a hole in the fuselage to save himself then returned to the burning aircraft to rescue the survivors, despite the danger that the plane might explode at any stage.

In an interview with *The Times* sometime after the disaster Gregg said he could still remember how dark and silent it was after the plane crashed: 'I thought I was dead until I felt the blood running down my face. I didn't want to feel my head because I thought the top had been taken off like a hard-boiled egg. I was so confused. It was total darkness yet it was only three in the afternoon – it was hard to reconcile. The first dead person I saw did not have a mark on him.

It was Bert Whalley, the chief coach, who'd been taken with us as a bonus for developing all those great young players. At first I thought I was the only one left alive. In the distance I noticed five people running away, they shouted at me to run. At that moment, the aircraft captain came around from what had been the nose of the aircraft carrying a little fire extinguisher. When he saw me he shouted in his best English accent: "Run, you stupid bastard, it's going to explode."'

Then Gregg heard a baby crying: 'The crying seemed to bring me back to reality and I shouted at the people running away to come back. But they were still shouting at me to run. I could hear the child crying and felt angry they were running away, so I shouted again, "Come back, you bastards, there's people alive in here." For me to shout that was difficult because, at that time, I was a God-fearing man and wouldn't normally have cursed. But the people just kept running away.'

So he climbed back into the burning aircraft and found the baby: 'She was beneath a pile of debris and, remarkably, she only had a cut over her eye. I scrabbled back to the hole with her and got her out.'

After Gregg handed the baby to someone close by, he returned to the smouldering wreck and pulled the baby's mother, Vera Lukić, out of a hole in the fuselage. He then made a third trip back to the plane, ignoring cries for him not to given the likelihood that a further explosion could occur at any time. 'I began to search for Jackie Blanchflower and I shouted out his name. Blanchy and I had been friends since we played together for Ireland Schoolboys as fourteen-year-olds and I was desperate to find him.'

But in his frantic search for Blanchflower, he soon came across Bobby Charlton and Dennis Viollet, both of whom were unconscious. Gregg dragged his two team-mates out of the plane and laid them on the snow a short distance from the plane before resuming his search for Blanchflower and, much to his utter relief and joy, he finally found him. 'When I found Blanchy, the lower part of his right arm had been almost completely severed. It was horrendous, a scene of utter devastation.'

Quite amazingly, Gregg overcame the shock and horror of what he had seen and played in United's next match, on 19 February, a fifth-round FA Cup tie against Sheffield Wednesday at Old Trafford. Famously, the section in the match programme where you would normally see the United team was left completely blank, while Jimmy Murphy had the task of trying to find 11 players to wear the famous red shirt of United. He had missed the trip to Belgrade as he was in Cardiff at the time, coaching the Welsh national team for an important 1958 World Cup play-off game against Israel.

Gregg told Murphy he wanted to play, as did fellow Munich survivor Bill Foulkes, and on a solemn night under floodlights at Old Trafford a young and inexperienced Manchester United side beat their opponents 3-0. Gregg wasn't the only player with Irish connections in the United side, for the game marked the debut of Seamus Anthony 'Shay' Brennan. The Sheffield Wednesday players had no chance of winning the game, such was the emotion of the occasion. In the lead-up to the tie, football fans everywhere, regardless of their club affiliation, were so overcome with grief at the terrible loss of so many innocent lives in Munich that it seemed like everyone, including fans from the Steel City, was willing United on to win. Players from both sides, as well as many fans at Old Trafford that night, wore black armbands in memory of those who had died.

For Gregg, the routine of playing football was vital at this time, so he was fortunate that the season did not end there. That summer he played in four of Northern Ireland's six games at the 1958 World Cup finals in Sweden, where he was voted the tournament's best goalkeeper. After drawing 2-2 with West Germany in Malmo on 15 June, Gregg played so magnificently in the game that the Germans, who needed a late equaliser from Uwe Seeler to save the game, lined up and applauded him and his team-mates off the pitch.

However, Gregg twisted an ankle against the Germans and after the game it blew up like a balloon, swelling to three times its normal size. He bathed it for a few hours in the cold sea water near the team's hotel, but it was of no use and he hobbled to the next game, against the Czechs, aided by a stick. When the All-Star team from the tournament was voted on by the journalists covering the finals, Gregg received 478 votes, almost four times more than his closest competitor, the great Russian goalkeeper Lev Yashin, who received only 122 votes. His last appearance in the green of Northern Ireland was on 20 November 1963 at Wembley Stadium. Unfortunately, for him it was an embarrassing 8-3 defeat at the hands of England.

Gregg was a no-nonsense goalkeeper who could more than handle himself in a crowded penalty area at a time when referees offered them very little protection. He used his 6ft frame and weight of 12st 8lb to barge defenders out of his way. Put simply, he was not a man to mess about with, and this was proven when Blackburn Rovers visited Old Trafford on 6 November 1965. The Rovers players tried to bully Gregg at every corner and each time a ball was floated high into the United goalmouth but Harry was having none of it and, to the amazement of most of his team-mates further up the pitch who were totally unaware of what had happened behind them, the referee sent Gregg off for allegedly kicking Rovers defender Mike England.

Gregg played in the first seven league games of 1966-67, but made his 247th and last appearance for United on 7 September 1966 against Stoke City at home. While at United, he kept 48 clean sheets. Busby had just paid Chelsea £55,000 for goalkeeper Alex Stepney, who was immediately handed the No. 1 jersey upon his arrival at Old Trafford, which effectively ended Gregg's career at United.

In December 1966 Gregg moved to Stoke City but he played only two games for them before retiring. And so the career of undoubtedly the greatest Irish goalkeeper in the history of Manchester United came to an end, just before United would go on to win the 1966-67 title, meaning that he yet again missed out on winning a major honour at the club.

In 1968 Gregg moved into management, taking charge of Shrewsbury Town, handing future United centre-half Jim Holton his league debut at the Shrews. After four years with Shrewsbury, he moved on to manage Swansea City (November 1972-January 1975), Crewe Alexandra (1975-78) and Kitan Sports Club, Kuwait (August-November 1978) before returning to United as their goalkeeping coach under Dave Sexton. He left the club in June 1981 soon after the arrival of new manager Ron Atkinson, before taking up a coaching position at Swansea City (1982), then he became Swindon Town assistant manager (July 1984-April 1985) and finally manager of Carlisle United (May 1986-87). When Gregg retired from football for good he owned a hotel in Portstewart on the north Antrim coast which was appropriately called the Windsor Hotel, as he had begun his football journey at Windsor Park, Belfast.

Gregg was awarded an MBE in 1995 and in the summer of 2008 he was made an Honorary Graduate of the University of Ulster and awarded a Doctorate of the University (DUniv) in recognition of his contribution to football. Earlier in the year, he had made a very emotional return to Munich airport for a BBC documentary entitled One Life: Munich Air Disaster, and stood at the scene of the crash that cruelly claimed the lives of eight of his team-mates 50 years earlier. It was the first time he had been back to Munich, and during the filming of the documentary he met the son of Mrs Lukić, who had been in his mother's womb at the time of the disaster. Zoran Lukić said to him: 'I have always wanted this moment, to look into your face and say to you, "Thank you". I was the third passenger you saved, but, at the time, you were not to know that.'

Gregg blushed slightly before responding: 'You've nothing to thank me for. I did what had to be done without thinking about it. I've lived with being called a hero, but I'm not really a hero. Heroes are people who do brave things knowing the consequences of their actions. That day, I had no idea what I was doing.'

In an interview with the BBC prior to the television documentary being shown on the channel, Gregg looked back at Munich and said: 'I don't want my life to be remembered for what happened on a runway. I don't need the sheriff's badge and I don't want to play the hero. The wonderful thing to me about that period of time was the freshness of youth and the free spirit, the manner in which we played. I'm not a poet, but I always think "They laughed, they loved, they played the game together, they played the game and gave it every ounce of life and the crowds – they thronged to see such free, young spirits". To me, that's what I want to remember, that was the wonderful thing.'

Sadly, Harry passed away on 16 February 2020.

Harry Gregg didn't just save shots, he saved lives. He was a real life hero.

Did You Know That?

Harry Gregg was a hero of Sir Alex Ferguson. Your author organised Harry Gregg's Testimonial Match in Belfast on 15 May 2012. I asked Sir Alex if he would like to say anything about Harry in the Testimonial Match Programme and the Boss penned the following tribute.

HARRY GREGG – MY HERO

It was with the greatest pleasure that I immediately accepted an invitation to bring Manchester United to Belfast and play in a Testimonial Match for Harry Gregg. We received the request on 7th January 2012 from The George Best Carryduff Manchester United Supporters Club and 12 days later the Board met and unanimously gave their seal of approval. All too often the word Legend is used in football but more often than not the word is merely used to describe a player who left an indelible mark on the world of football. Harry Gregg's exploits for Manchester United and Northern Ireland, voted the best goalkeeper in the world at the 1958 World Cup Finals in Sweden, are beyond legendary and his place in the illustrious history of Manchester United football Club is enshrined. And so I am absolutely delighted to bring my Manchester United side to Windsor Park, Belfast this evening to honour Harry the footballer but much more importantly than that, to honour Harry the true gentleman and a true hero to many Manchester United fans in word and deed.

I was a 16-year old schoolboy playing for Drumchapel Amateurs, and training every Thursday night with Benburb Juniors, when news of the Munich Air Disaster became known. I made my way to training at Benburb and when I got there I saw the senior players crying. It was at that moment I realised the seriousness of the disaster. When I got home my Dad was staring into the fire, everyone was numb with the shock. My brother, Martin, and I went to our bedroom and it was a quiet place in our house at the time. Over the course of the next two days the full extent of the tragedy unfolded with the local paper listing the names of the people who lost their lives in the disaster including 7 Busby Babes who died instantly: club captain Roger Byrne, Geoff Bent, Eddie Colman, Mark Jones, David Pegg, Tommy Taylor and Ireland's own Liam Whelan. Duncan Edwards became the eighth Busby Babe to die when he lost his brave battle for life 15 days later.

Harry Gregg was on the flight and after regaining consciousness he felt the blood trickling down his face but was too afraid to put his hand up to his head thinking that part of it may be hanging off. Upon seeing a shaft of light he kicked a hole wide enough to crawl through and make his way on the snowy runway. Most mere mortals would have run for their lives but Harry Gregg does not fall into this category of man. Despite his own injuries, and warnings not to go anywhere near the burning fuselage, Harry made his way into the smouldering aircraft time and time again looking for fellow survivors who were in need of help. Harry's unselfish bravery in putting his own life on the line to save others, including a pregnant Mrs Vera Lukic (the wife of a Yugoslavian diplomat) and her daughter, Vesna, his fellow Northern Ireland international and best friend, Jackie Blanchflower, which rightfully earned him the title of "The Hero of Munich."

I first met Harry when I was the manager of Aberdeen. It was near the end of the 1980-81 season and Harry was a coach at Manchester United under manager Dave Sexton. We had invited United to participate in a 1981-82 pre-season Summer Tournament at Pittodrie which also included Southampton and West Ham United. Harry was asked by Martin Edwards, Chairman of Manchester United at the time, to carry out a sort of reconnaissance trip ahead of the tournament. Harry was, and to this day remains, an absolute gentleman and the consummate professional. We had a long chat about numerous subjects with the exception of The Munich Air Disaster which I would have liked to have asked him about but dared not to given the level of respect I had for him. Nowadays Harry will jokingly tell you that he was sent to Aberdeen to suss me out as a replacement for Dave Sexton who regrettably was sacked at the end of the 1980–81 season. However, I still had so much more I wanted to achieve at Aberdeen and very much doubt if it would have been the right time to move south of the border had the opportunity presented itself. Needless to say when Manchester United did approach me in November 1986 I had no hesitation in accepting the job as the manager of the greatest football club in the world.

Harry Gregg has always been a most reluctant hero and the description does not sit comfortably for him on his big broad Irish shoulders. I will forever remember what Harry said when he went back to Munich on the 50th anniversary of the disaster and met Zoran Lukic (the little boy who was in his Mum's womb at the time of the plane crash). Zoran looked at Harry and said: "I have always wanted this moment, to look into your face and say to you, 'thank you'. I was the third passenger you saved, but, at the time, you were not to know that." Typically Harry replied: "You've nothing to thank me for. I did what had to be done without thinking about it. "I've lived with being called a hero but I'm not really a hero. Heroes are people who do brave things knowing the consequences of their actions. That day, I had no idea what I was doing."

Harry once said that the Munich Air Disaster changed Manchester United from a football club into an institution. Few will disagree with Harry's view and even fewer will disagree with the part a young man from Magherafelt played in the aura and mystique which resulted in the worldwide following that Manchester United enjoys today. If I was asked to describe Harry I would call upon the words from a beautiful poem by Nicola Burkett:

A hero thinks of others before they think of themselves
A hero will die to protect
A hero can be of any age, any colour
A hero can be man, woman or child

A hero is courageous, loving and brave
A hero will never complain
A hero can be made in one act of compassion
Or years of tender loving care
Some heroes are remembered, whilst many are left forgotten
Heroes are angels in disguise, saving precious innocent lives

Harry for this 16-year old boy from Govan you were and remain my hero. I wish you and your family a most enjoyable evening and on behalf of Manchester United Football Club, thank you for the part you personally played in making Manchester United the greatest football club in the world."

Sir Alex Ferguson CBE
Manager, Manchester United

GAME NO. 19
BRADFORD CITY 0-0 UNITED
LEAGUE CUP, ROUND 3
VALLEY PARADE, BRADFORD
10 NOVEMBER 1982
ATTENDANCE – 15,568

THE BLACK PEARL OF INCHICORE

"Cinderella Man" is the story of the Irish–American boxer James J. Braddock. He was a supposedly washed–up fighter who came back from obscurity and became Heavyweight Boxing Champion of the World from 13 June 1935 to 22 June 1937. On 10 November 1982, Paul McGrath made his competitive debut for Manchester United, a 0-0 draw away to Bradford City in the 3rd Round of the League Cup but his career would go on to turn him into football's very own Cinderella Man.

Paul was born on 4 December 1959 in Ealing, London to an Irish mother, Betty, and a Nigerian father. Perhaps as a result of feeling guilty about becoming an unmarried mother, Betty had made her way from Ireland to London to give birth to Paul. After she returned to Ireland baby McGrath was passed from orphanage to orphanage in Dublin for the first sixteen years of his young life. Paul began his football career with his school side, Pearse Rovers, before joining junior side Dalkey United. When he was playing for the Hyde Park club he was spotted by Manchester United's chief scout in Dublin, Billy Behan. In 1981, the 21-year old signed as a full-time professional with St. Patrick's Athletic after working as an apprentice sheet metal worker and a security guard in the Irish capital. Paul made his debut for St. Pat's in a home game against Shamrock Rovers in a League of Ireland game at Richmond Park, Inchicore, Dublin. Although spending just one season at St. Pat's the fans took to him instantly and nicknamed him "The Black Pearl of Inchicore". Paul was the rock in the heart of the Irish side's defence; a cool, calm and collected defender, he won the PFAI Player of the Year Award in his only season in League of Ireland football. He played 31 games and scored 4 goals for the Irish club.

In April 1982 Ron Atkinson swooped for the 22-year old McGrath and secured his signature for Manchester United in a bargain £30,000 transfer deal. Prior to the start of the 1982-83 season Paul tasted first team action on 2 August 1982 for the first time in his United career when the club agreed to play Aldershot in a friendly game. The match was in aid of the "South Atlantic Fund" (Britain was at war at the time with Argentina over the Falkland Islands) and was played at Aldershot's Recreation Ground home. However, a niggling injury prevented his senior debut until 10 November 1982 when he played in United's League Cup 3rd Round goalless draw away to Bradford City.

Manchester United: Gary Bailey, Mike Duxbury, Arthur Albiston, Paul McGrath, Gordon McQueen, Remi Moses, Bryan Robson (Capt), Arnold Mühren, Steve Coppell, Frank Stapleton, Norman Whiteside

Three days later Big Ron handed Paul his First Division debut in place of Kevin Moran in a 1-0 win over Tottenham Hotspur at Old Trafford, his assured performance won over the United faithful instantly. However, Atkinson put McGrath back in the Reserve side the following week and he did not reappear again in the first team until 2 March 1983, a 1-0 loss away to Stoke City.

Part of the deal which saw McGrath leave St. Patrick's Athletic for United was an agreement to play the Dublin-based club in a friendly. On 15 March 1983, United were in the Irish capital to honour that commitment and faced St. Patrick's at Dalymount Park before a crowd of 16,000. The game was a dull affair and not even the sight of McGrath back at his old stomping ground was sufficient to help raise the tempo of the game. It wasn't until the 75th minute before the first goal came with Lou Macari scoring a volley from just outside the box. Arnold Mühren added a second for United from a free kick 10 minutes from the end to seal the victory for the visitors. Four Irish players played in the game for United; Northern Ireland's Norman Whiteside (on as a sub for Remi Moses) and the Republic of Ireland's McGrath, Ashley Grimes and Frank Stapleton.

Paul played in 13 League games for United in his first full season at the club, 1982–83, scoring 3 times, his first goal coming in a 3-0 home win over Luton Town on 9 May 1983 (he scored twice in the game with Frank Stapleton scoring the third United goal that day). The latter game was the first in which the famous Irish quartet of McGrath, Moran, Stapleton and Whiteside all played together. However Paul was not selected for United's 1983 FA Cup Final team; Big Ron opting for the centre-half pairing of Kevin Moran and Gordon McQueen instead.

In season 1983–84, Atkinson played Paul in 9 League games (scored once) and often switched him from Paul's preferred defensive role to a combative midfield role. At the start of the 1984–85 season Moran and Graeme Hogg dominated United's No.5 and No.6 jerseys with Paul having to bide his time in the Central League team. However McGrath's strength, speed, stamina and coolness under pressure could not be ignored any longer by Atkinson. When Moran suffered an injury Paul slotted in at centre-half and his consistent Man of the Match displays saw him play in every one of United's last 21 First Division games of the season. When United reached the 1985 FA Cup Final Big Ron had no hesitation in pairing Moran, who had returned to the team in late April 1985, alongside McGrath to face Everton. In the final Paul was a colossus and snuffed out attack after attack from the Merseysiders with Andy Gray and Graeme Sharp barely getting a touch of the ball and all this despite United going down to 10 men after Moran was sent off. Not surprisingly Paul was voted Man of the Match which saw him collect his first and only winners' medal with Manchester United.

When I was writing my book, "*Irish Devils – The Official Story of Manchester United and The Irish*," I interviewed Kevin Moran and I asked him what it was like to play alongside Paul for club and country:

'*My all-time favourite Manchester United footballer has to be without any shadow of a doubt, Paul McGrath. Paul was a magnificent player, courageous in the air and in the tackle, aggressive but not dirty, tremendous stamina, powerful, a great reader of the game and a man you could always rely on to dig you out of trouble if you happened to be having an off day against an opponent. I loved and still cherish every minute of every game I had the honour and privilege of playing alongside Paul in the red of United and the green of Ireland. Paul's dominating presence on the pitch frightened the life out of even the toughest of centre-forwards but off the pitch he was a very quiet and shy man and I should know because I shared a room with him. Paul's place in the history of United's most famous Irishmen is assured as is another one of my good mate's place - Norman Whiteside. What a player Norman was and what a ferocious pair he and Paul made but having said that, they are two of the nicest lads you will ever meet. I remember Paul, Norman and myself going to a Wolfe Tones concert at an Irish Centre located in the Levenshulme area of Manchester during the mid-1980s. To say we had a bit of craic that night would be a gross understatement. I don't think Big Norman had ever heard of the Wolfe Tones prior to that memorable night out but by the time we left the place he knew all about the history of one of Ireland's most famous bands.'*

After making 40 League appearances (3 goals) in season 1985–86 and 34 League appearances (2 goals) in season 1986–87, McGrath's career at Old Trafford went on a downward spiral. Accusations of post training drinking sprees with team–mates, notably Bryan Robson and Norman Whiteside, coupled with chronic knee injuries took their toll on his body and severely restricted his ability to train and reduced his appearances in his favoured No.5 United shirt. During his last two seasons at United he played in 39 First Division games (out of a maximum of 84) and scored 3 goals. In August 1989, Alex Ferguson allowed Paul to leave United after making 198 appearances for the club, scoring 16 goals, and he signed for Aston Villa in a £425,000 transfer.

Ron Atkinson, Sheffield Wednesday manager at the time, attempted to sign Paul for the Owls but United opted instead for Villa. When Paul left United many sports writers at the time were scratching their heads as to why Villa manager Graham Taylor would pay so much money for a player who was just weeks away from his 30th birthday, had dodgy knees, was injury prone, could hardly run let alone train and according to reports brought some social baggage with him.

James J. Corbett, the World Heavyweight Boxing Champion (7 September 1892-17 March 1897) said: "You become a Champion by fighting one more round. When things are tough, you fight one more round." Corbett's words rang so very true with McGrath and he soon had these very same doubters eating their misguided words as he played some of the best football of his career in his 7 years in

Birmingham.

In his award winning book, '*Back From The Brink*,' Paul said that he found the move to Aston Villa a very traumatic one and just 6 weeks into the 1989-90 season he was so depressed that his drinking spiralled out of control and he even attempted suicide. Paul said that his actions were a cry for help and thankfully for all Irish football fans that cry was answered by Taylor. The Villa boss gave Paul all the support he needed and after spending a month at the Priory Clinic recuperating McGrath had only one thing on his mind when he left and that was to repay the faith Taylor had shown in him. When Paul returned to Villa Park he played in every single game of the season as the Villains narrowly missed out on clinching the First Division title finishing runners-up nine points behind Liverpool. Meanwhile, Taylor was persuaded to take charge of the England national team as the successor to Bobby Robson in the summer of 1990 but fortunately for Paul his replacement was also something of a father figure as his former United boss Ron Atkinson accepted the job. Villa pushed United all the way in the race for the inaugural Premier League and while United ended their 26-year wait for that elusive 8th Championship title, United supporters were also delighted that Paul was voted the PFA Player of the Year in deserved recognition of his masterful displays in the centre of the Villain's defence.

The 1994 League Cup Final pitted United against Aston Villa and it was McGrath and Atkinson who were left beaming with smiles when Villa triumphed 3-1 at Wembley. However, United had the consolation of going on to retain their Premier League crown and win the FA Cup to claim the club's first Double. In the summer of 1996 Paul left Villa and to this day is still considered to be one of the greatest players in the club's history. Indeed, the Villa fans nicknamed him '*God*' as a result of the adulation he received in Birmingham. Paul played 252 times for Aston Villa scoring 9 goals in his 7 years with the club. Following brief spells with Derby County (24 games in 1996-97), who he helped to a 12th place finish in their inaugural season in the Premier League, and Sheffield United (11 games in 1997-98), who he helped to the Play-Offs and an FA Cup semi-final, he retired from the game aged 38 with 8 knee operations behind him. His autobiography, *Back From The Brink* (co-written with journalist Vincent Hogan) won the inaugural William Hill Irish Sports Book of the Year.

If his impact on English football was huge, Paul really made his name on the international stage with a series of outstanding performances at the very highest level. He won the first of his 83 international caps for the Republic of Ireland on 5 February 1985 when he came on as a substitute for Mark Lawrenson in a friendly against Italy in Dublin. Interestingly, the Italians would subsequently be the opponents for two major highs in Paul's 12-year international career. During his first year with the Irish national side Paul found himself in competition with Lawrenson, Mick McCarthy, David O'Leary and United team-mate, Kevin Moran for one of the two centre-half spots in the team. However, Paul became an established figure in the Irish side after Jack Charlton took charge of the national team in March 1986 and recognised that Paul was as valuable in the Irish midfield as he was in their back four. Two stand-out performances by Paul in an Irish shirt spring to mind when Irish soccer fans are asked about Paul's greatest matches for his country. The vast majority of Irish fans cite Paul's two magnificent performances against Italy. In the first of these games Ireland faced the host nation in Rome in the quarter-finals of the 1990 World Cup Finals. The Italians were short priced favourites to beat Ireland but McGrath was the star performer in the Republic of Ireland's narrow 1-0 loss when the Juventus striker Salvatore '*Toto*' Schillachi broke Irish hearts.

Yet it was in Ireland's opening Group E match at the 1994 World Cup Finals in the USA that Paul truly made the world sit up and take notice. He was in imperious form as he helped his country to an unlikely 1-0 win over Italy in New York. Back in his favoured position at centre-half, McGrath was simply magnificent. Ireland led through a Ray Houghton goal in the 11th minute and then the Irish defence had to endure long periods of sustained attack from the talented Italians, who reached the final that year. But time and again McGrath repelled Italian attacks, snuffing out danger early, making last ditch tackles and making towering clearing headers. His performance that day in the Giants Stadium had it all including a cameo where he made a number tackles in quick succession before finally taking a shot full in the face from Roberto Baggio before unbelievably getting back to his feet in a flash ready to stop whatever else the Italian attack could throw at him.

Paul was a giant for his country that day. During his international career Jack Charlton acted very much as a father figure to him and there seems to have been a genuine warmth between them. Like Alex Ferguson, Charlton was seen as an authoritarian figure yet when it came to handling Paul, particularly when it came to dealing with his drinking problems, Charlton dealt with him sensitively and compassionately. Paul played his last game for his country on 11 February 1997, a goalless draw with Wales at Lansdowne Road. In the 83 games he proudly represented his country he scored 8 times whilst Ireland won 33, drew 29 and lost 28.

"You will never do anything in this world without courage. It is the greatest quality of the mind next to honour."

Aristotle

Paul McGrath possessed courage in abundance. On 1 November 2006, Ian Clark from *PFA* magazine spoke to Paul McGrath about his brutally honest autobiography, *Back from the Brink.* The following is reproduced by kind permission of *Players' Club* – the official magazine of the PFA.

IC: By the time you left Manchester United you admitted that your life was going downhill but on the pitch you were still able to play without a care in the world – is that fair?

PM: By the age of 26 I knew I was an alcoholic and I had problems with my knees. Graham Taylor was the only manager who put his money where his mouth was. He made a firm offer for me to go to Villa I earned another ten years in the game because of him and I'll always be grateful to him for that. I was told that if I ever left Manchester United I would be on a downward spiral but the supporters took to me at Villa and I had eight seasons there. It was a brilliant move for me. On the pitch, I always had confidence but I lacked it off the pitch. I didn't like doing interviews, for instance. I suppose that I came alive on the pitch.

IC: Would it be fair to say that Villa saw the best of you?

PMcG: It's a difficult one. I felt that I played my best football under Ron Atkinson. He was a brilliant manager, full of fun. He loves the game so much and that transmitted itself throughout the side. We were pushing for the title in Ron's second year. But our main problem was that so many of the lads were young and weren't able to fix on the prize. The older players realised what was at stake but the younger ones weren't focused. Perhaps they couldn't handle it. Yes, I think I played my best football at Villa. At United, even when the team wasn't doing well, there was much more expected of you.

IC: What was the highlight at Villa?

PMcG: For me, the League Cup victory in 1994 against Manchester United – closely followed by the other time Villa won the trophy against Leeds.

IC: Were you bitter at the way it ended under Brian Little?

PMcG: We never fell out. He just didn't see me as playing every week. I thought I could still play but he wanted new blood in, which was fair enough because I was almost 36. If ever I made a mistake, I would be the first to be dragged off. So I asked to go. To be honest, I probably should have stopped playing earlier, but I still needed to make a living. I loved the game. My knees were telling me to go earlier but I needed to earn money because I knew I'd struggle after I retired.

IC: You still found time to play for Derby and Sheffield United though?

PMcG: Actually, one of my fondest memories came with Derby. I went up to Old Trafford with a young team and won 3-2. At the end of the game, the Manchester United supporters clapped us off the pitch which was a lovely gesture.

IC: Your book is called '*Back From The Brink*' – is that how you feel now?

PMcG: I moved back to Ireland when I finished playing. I thought I'd be able to work in the media and I thought there would be more work available for me there. It's proved to be difficult. Writing the book has been brilliant. Reading it back was hard though because I've had such highs and lows. Since I moved back there, I've had long periods when I've been well although it has been a rocky road. And yes, I believe I'm back. I'd be lying if I didn't say I'd been through an up and down time but I genuinely believe I'm back now. You can't put your family and friends through what I've done to them without realising the time has come to stop. I'll never give up the fight though. One of us is going to win and I hope it's going to be me. I know I am blessed because I have good people in my life. I know I was a pretty decent footballer. I know that, despite my worst excesses, I can still be a pretty decent father. I just need to stop running. The past is unchangeable. It's time to stop looking behind.

Did You Know That?

Bradford City's home ground, Valley Parade, was built in 1886 and was the home of Manningham Rugby Football Club until 1903 when Bradford City Association Football Club was formed, the same year the club was elected to the Football League. In 1908 Archibald Leitch, the football architect who designed Old Trafford among a number of other stadia in Great Britain, was given the commission of redeveloping the ground when the club was promoted to the First Division. In season 1907-08, the season Manchester United won their first ever trophy, Bradford City punched above their weight and won the Second Division Championship.

However on Saturday 11 May 1985, Bradford City played Lincoln City at home in their final Third Division game of the season. The afternoon began well for the home side when they were presented with the Third Division Championship trophy before kick-off but at 3.40pm, 40 minutes into the game, a fire broke out in the main stand and within 4 minutes the windy conditions helped the fire to engulf the entire stand which resulted in the tragic loss of 56 fans. The event became known as "The Bradford City Stadium Fire." This tragedy was seen by many as a wake-up call for English football clubs to improve the state of their grounds and implement more stringent safety measures to bring an end to various problems which had been plaguing football in England for many years without any effective action being taken by the game's governing body, the Football Association.

GAME NO. 20
UNITED 1-2 SOUTHAMPTON
SECOND DIVISION
OLD TRAFFORD
25 SEPTEMBER 1937
ATTENDANCE – 22,729

UNITED'S FIRST IRISH CAPTAIN

In 1936, *The Green Hornet* radio show debuted in Detroit. The series detailed the adventures of Britt Reid, a debonair newspaper publisher by day and a crime-fighting masked Superhero by night. In 1936, United signed their own Green Hornet from the Emerald Isle. The signing of Johnny Carey was one of the most significant in the history of the club and unquestionably the bargain buy of the 20th century but it very nearly didn't happen at all.

Frank Colbert, author of 'Gentleman Johnny' in *The Forgotten Legends* takes up the story:

> *Carey's astonishing transfer was initially sparked off by the Reds' legendary Dublin scout and ex-player, Billy Behan, who wrote to Manchester United's manager, Scott Duncan, about a promising Bohemians centre-forward named Benny Gaughan. Duncan went over to Dublin to see for himself and was happy with Gaughan's potential. As a result, arrangements were*

made to sign the player, and Louis Rocca, United's chief scout, was due to go over shortly afterwards to complete the deal. Meanwhile, Scottish giants Celtic had stepped in with a better offer and Gaughan soon went to Glasgow instead while Rocca was on his way to Dublin. When he arrived on Saturday morning to find Gaughan had already left for Celtic, he was naturally disappointed but the persuasive Behan asked him to stay on in the city to have a look at another youngster the next day - the 17-year-old playing for St. James Gate, named Carey.

According to Behan, Rocca agreed to have a look at the lad and thought him a great prospect despite his lack of experience. Carey was playing against Cork Athletic and scored in the first minute – it was only his sixth game for St. James in just two months of League of Ireland football. While describing this same game in Dublin, Rocca states: "It was a poor game but there was something about the inside-right which took my fancy. A meeting of the St James' directors was called there and then. We talked for hours and eventually I got Carey's signature for £200, which was a League of Ireland record fee. No greater Irish player crossed the Irish Sea to make a name in English football". That same evening Carey's father gave Rocca a real homely Irish welcome that lasted well into the early hours of the morning!

When Johnny and his father got off the train at Piccadilly Station in Manchester, Carey Junior spotted a newspaper stand with a poster which read "*United's Big Signing*". Johnny nudged his dad and pushed him in the direction of the newspaper stand to purchase a copy of the paper. However, much to Johnny's disappointment he opened the pages to find he was not reading about himself but about John Ernest "*Ernie*" Thompson, a prolific centre-forward who had just signed for United from Blackburn Rovers in a transfer deal worth £4,500 which was 18 times the fee United paid for young Johnny. Carey Senior just chuckled as his son handed him the newspaper and walked away. Just two lines of the newspaper story touched on the acquisition of Carey and yet it was he, and not Thompson, who played only 3 games for United scoring 1 goal, that went on to become one of the most accomplished footballers in England and Europe.

Born on 23 February 1919 in Dublin Carey played for local side Home Farm whilst still at school, the young Johnny loved playing football but like many of his school friends he also played Gaelic Football and was selected to represent Dublin at minor level before being banned by the Gaelic Athletic Association (GAA) because he also played a "*foreign*" game, association football! After arriving at Old Trafford the young Carey was placed in digs near the ground and captained United's Youth Team. His impressive displays at full back were brought to the attention of Scott Duncan, the United manager who gave the 18-year old Carey his Manchester United debut at inside-left against Southampton in a Second Division game at Old Trafford on 25 September 1937. This was the Manchester United team Duncan selected: Thomas Breen, John "Jack" Griffiths, William Roughton, James Brown (Capt), Walter Winterbottom, William McKay, William Bryant, George Gladwin, John Ernest Thompson, Johnny Carey, William Manley

United lost the game 2-1 but the 18-year old retained his place in the side for United's next League game a week later, a 1-0 home defeat to Sheffield United. On 7 November 1937 Johnny won the first of 29 caps for the Republic of Ireland against Norway at Dalymount Park in a qualifying game for the 1938 World Cup Finals to be held in France, the game ended 3-3 and the Republic of Ireland failed to qualify. Two days later Scott Duncan shocked Manchester United when he resigned leaving Walter Crickmer to take charge of the club for the second time.

Carey did not play again until United visited Nottingham Forest on 28 December 1937. The legendary Stan Pearson, who signed for United as an amateur aged just 15 in December 1935 (signed as a professional in May 1937), was one of a few players who kept Carey out of the first team. Stan made his debut on 13 November 1937 in a 7-1 hammering of Chesterfield at Saltergate. Pearson retained his place for the next four games before Carey replaced him for the trip to Forest. Johnny scored his first goal for the club in United's 3-2 victory and his performance that day was good enough to see him go on a run of 8 consecutive League games and he played in three of United's four FA Cup games in season 1937-38 but it was Pearson who occupied the No.10 shirt for United appearing in the last 4 League games with Crickmer opting to alternate Carey and Pearson in the team depending on the state of the pitch. However, Carey had more than played his part, appearing in 16 League games and scoring 3 goals, in helping Manchester United to runners-up spot in Division Two behind champions, Aston Villa.

United went into the final game of the campaign sitting joint third in the table on 51 points with Coventry City, both clubs trailed

Sheffield United by two points who had completed their fixtures. Aston Villa were already crowned Champions on 55 points with one game still to play. Sheffield United had a goal average of 1.30, Coventry City 1.47 and United's goal average was 1.60. With United possessing the superior goal average a home win over Bury would be good enough to secure promotion. United won the game 2-0 (scorers: William McKay & John Smith) and were promoted back into the First Division. A number of the top clubs in England contacted Walter Crickmer to inquire about Carey's availability but all advances for their star Irishman were rebuffed.

At the start of the 1938–39 season, Manchester United's visionary Chairman James W. Gibson formed Manchester United Junior Athletic Club (MUJAC). MUJAC served as a nursery club to the Manchester United first team and is considered to be the first club of its kind in England. MUJAC played in the Chorlton Amateur League in Manchester and in their first season won the Championship scoring an incredible 223 goals along the way. In season 1938–39 Johnny played in 32 of United's 42 First Division games, scoring 6 times (Pearson played in 9 League games, scoring once) to help United to a respectable 14th place in the table and guarantee top flight football the next season before World War II brought professional football to a halt in early September 1939.

In March of that year the players, management and Board of Directors of Cliftonville Football Club left Belfast for their now annual outing to see the Grand National at Aintree, Liverpool. During this jaunt across the Irish Sea Cliftonville organised a few friendly games against English League opposition. Given the good relationship they enjoyed with Manchester United a friendly game was organised between the teams at Old Trafford on Monday 13 March 1939. Carey played in and scored in the game for a rampant United who hammered their Irish visitors 9-1.

World War II interrupted Carey's Manchester United career from 1939 to 1945 and he could have taken the easy option and returned to neutral Ireland until the end of hostilities. However, despite being a very patriotic Irishman in 1943 he volunteered for service stating at the time: *"A country that gives me my living is worth fighting for."* During the war he served in the Queen's Royal Hussars and was stationed in North Africa and Italy and was nicknamed *"Cario"* by the Italians who quickly took to the affable Irishman. During the war Carey managed to make in excess of 100 Wartime League Football appearances for

United and also made a number of guest appearances for several English League clubs. In addition he also played some football whilst stationed in Italy. When peace was restored in 1945 Johnny was asked to stay in Italy and play his club football there but luckily for United and Ireland he opted to return to his beloved Manchester United, now being managed by a former soldier and ex-Manchester City, Liverpool and Scottish international wing-half, Matt Busby.

On 13 October 1945, much to the delight of the United fans and the fans back home in Ireland, Carey reappeared in a United shirt in a 3-0 Football League North defeat at Everton. Busby knew that in Carey he had a natural leader at his disposal, a player highly respected by his team-mates, a player he could ask to play anywhere and who would never disappoint him but above all else a player who could be his general on the pitch. Unsurprisingly Busby appointed Carey captain of Manchester United succeeding George Roughton as United skipper who had moved on to become manager of Exeter City. Therefore, not only was Carey the club's first post war captain but he was also the first player from outside the United Kingdom to lead Manchester United on the field of play. Busby decided to try Carey out at half-back and played him in this position at home to Blackburn Rovers on 9 March 1946, a game United won 6-2. After five consecutive games at half-back Busby and his assistant, Jimmy Murphy, asked Johnny to play at full-back away to Manchester City on 13 April 1946. At this time United were playing their home games at City's Maine Road ground as Old Trafford had been badly damaged following a bombing raid by the German Luftwaffe on the nearby Trafford Park industrial estate on the evening of 11 March 1941, they wouldn't return 'home' until August 1949. Carey put in an impressive performance in his new full-back role to ensure United won the Manchester Derby 3-1. Both Busby and Murphy had seen enough and from that day he played full-back for the rest of the season, United finishing 4th in the Football League North Championship.

In season 1946-47 Carey captained United to runners-up spot in the First Division, a single point behind Champions Liverpool. United were a formidable attacking force throughout the League campaign and ended the season as the division's second highest goal scorers with 95 goals (Wolverhampton Wanderers scored 98) and with 54 goals conceded they possessed the best goal average, 1.759. Stan Pearson scored 19 League goals whilst Charlie Mitten, later to become famous as *"The Bogota Bandit,"* found the back of the net 26 times. On 28th September 1946, Johnny won the first of his seven caps for Northern Ireland, England running out 7-2 winners at Windsor Park in a British Home International game. Although United had to play Preston North End away on 10 May 1947 in what was their third last League game of the season, Johnny was released by United for the day to travel to Glasgow where he was given the honour of captaining a Rest of Europe side against a Great Britain side in an exhibition match played at Hampden Park. Can you imagine the same thing happening today! A bumper crowd of 137,000 poured into the stadium paying a world record £31,000 in gate receipts (the monies went straight into FIFA's coffers) and were treated to a magnificent game of football which was played to celebrate Great Britain's return to FIFA, an organisation they had left in 1920. The game was quickly dubbed *"The Match of the Century"* by the press with Great Britain easily winning the game 6-1. Another unique honour achieved by Johnny in 1947 was the fact that he captained both the Republic of Ireland and Northern Ireland international sides.

Over the next 5 seasons Carey was captain of the most exciting team in the English game. Busby's free-flowing side was largely made up of graduates of MUJAC. During this post-war era crowds just wanted to be entertained and United more than provided value for money. Their cup run in 1947-48 was typical – United scored 18 goals and conceded 7 on their way to Wembley, including an incredible 6-4 win at Aston Villa before a crowd of 58,683 in round 3 that left scoreboard operators out of breath.

In the final they faced Stanley Matthews' Blackpool. United trailed The Seasiders 2-1 at half-time but when the players returned to the changing rooms it was Carey who spoke words of encouragement to urge his team-mates to express themselves more in the second half. The Irishman's words of wisdom did the trick as United scored three goals in the second half (Rowley, Stan Pearson, John Anderson) to beat Blackpool 4-2. And, so on 24 April 1948, Eire's Johnny Carey became the first Irishman to captain an FA Cup winning team in the illustrious 76-year history of the world's most famous Cup competition.

By the summer of 1948 Carey was an icon known around the British Isles as *"Gentleman John"* and the following season United finished runners-up for the third time in a row under Busby, this time behind Portsmouth, but a measure of Carey's standing in the game saw him voted Football Writers' Association Footballer of the Year, following in the footsteps of Sir Stanley Matthews who was the inaugural winner of this most prestigious award the previous season. In the late 1940s Johnny was the school coach at St. Bede's College, Manchester where his son attended the junior school. The pupils at the school knew he was the captain of Manchester United and although he would not become a manager in the Football League until August 1953, he showed at this early stage how good a manager he would go on to become earning the respect of all of the boys under his charge with his quiet and gentle approach to training. An ex-pupil recalled that Johnny's most famous advice to them was: "*Go to meet the ball*." Matt Busby's son, Sandy, was also at St. Bede's College then and Johnny spent many extra hours at the end of the school day coaching the young Busby to become a centre-half.

In season 1949-50 United ended the campaign in 4th place behind champions Portsmouth and they were runners-up yet again in 1950-51 behind Tottenham Hotspur but in 1951-52, Carey finally led United to the club's third First Division success, to give Matt Busby the first of his 5 Championship crowns. In the process Carey also became the first Irishman to captain a team to the First Division Championship title (and the first non-Englishman to captain an FA Cup winning team and a Division One Championship winning team). He played in 38 of United's 42 League games and scored 3 times. Roger Byrne had made his United debut at left-back in a First Division away game at Liverpool on 24 November 1951 (0-0 draw) and never missed another League game all that season. However, in the last 6 League games of United's 1951-52 Championship winning season Busby played the 23-year old Byrne at outside-left and he scored 7 goals.

At the start of the 1952-53 season Carey played at half-back and it marked the 34-year old Irish international's last full season as captain of Manchester United with the team finishing in a disappointing 8th position in the First Division. After playing in his unfavoured position of outside-left, Roger Byrne did the unthinkable and handed in a transfer request. Byrne was dropped for United's next two League games but realising the talent he had at his disposal, Busby reinstated the youngster into the Manchester United line-up at left-back for their next League game and switched Carey to right-back. Carey went on to play in 20 of United's remaining 23 League games of the 1952-53 season with 19 of them in the half-back role. On 18 February 1953, Matt Busby called upon Carey to help out the team in an hour of need following an injury to goalkeeper, Ray Wood. Faithful as ever he obliged and donned the United No.1 jersey for a tricky First Division away game at Roker Park. United drew the Division One encounter 2-2 with Carey performing admirably as the United custodian. At the end of the 1952-53 season Johnny decided to leave Old Trafford having spent almost 17 years with the club and accepted an offer in August 1953 to become the new manager of Blackburn Rovers. Amazingly, in his 344 appearances for Manchester United, the extremely versatile Johnny played in every position on the pitch except outside-left.

Johnny's 29 Republic of Ireland caps (1937-53) and 7 Northern Ireland caps (1946-49) saw him score 3 goals, all three for the Republic of Ireland. He scored the first of his three international goals for Ireland on 13 November 1938 in a 3-2 victory over Poland in a friendly at Dalymount Park. His other international goals also came in friendly matches; against Hungary and Norway. His last match for the Republic was on 21 March 1953, a 4-0 friendly win over Austria. Uniquely Johnny captained both Irish international teams and without question his greatest ever moment in an Irish jersey came on 21 September 1949 when he captained the Republic of Ireland in a friendly against England at Goodison Park. The Irish won 2-0 to inflict the first ever home defeat on England by a *"foreign"* side. Between 1955 and 1967 he also served as team manager of the Republic of Ireland, however Carey had very little say in the management of the national team as a selection committee decided which players were chosen to play.

In his first managerial role, Carey guided Blackburn to promotion to the First Division at the end of the 1957-58 season (runners-up to West Ham United). Upon leaving Blackburn he accepted Everton's invitation to become their new manager but things did not work out well for him at Goodison although he did guide the Toffees to 5th place in Division One in season 1960-61, two places above United in the table. Before the 1961-62 season could get underway Carey was famously sacked by Everton Chairman John Moores in the back of a London taxi whilst en route to the Annual General Meeting of the Football League. Johnny moved on to Leyton Orient in August 1961 and in a strange twist of fate, Carey then went on to manage Nottingham Forest from July 1963-December 1968, the team he had scored his first ever goal for United against. Gentleman John guided Forest to runners-up place behind United in 1966-67 and in January 1969 he returned to Ewood Park and was made co-manager of Blackburn Rovers with Eddie Quigley before leaving the Lancashire outfit in June 1971.

Cool, calm, collected, committed, courageous, dedicated, genius, loyal, magnificent, powerful and reliable are just some of the words used to describe Johnny Carey but above all else he was a true Gentleman both on and off the pitch but tragically on 22 January 1995, Manchester United and Ireland mourned the passing of one of the greatest ever captains and full-backs the club or country has ever had.

"The most luxurious possession, the richest treasure anybody has, is his personal dignity."

Jackie Robinson

Gentleman Johnny Carey was worthy of the honour and respect he achieved in his life.

Did You Know That?

On their way to FA Cup success in 1948 United met Derby County in the semi-finals at Hillsborough. United beat The Rams 3-1 thanks to a hat-trick from Stan Pearson but before the game all was not well in the United camp. The United players had learned that their opponents would be paid £100 a man to reach the final. It was a staggering sum of money given the fact that Football League rules at the time set the maximum wage at just £8 per week. The heads of the United players were obviously turned. A rift was imminent and it was Carey who helped his manager, Matt Busby, calm tensions in the United dressing room down. Busby may have been the boss but Carey was his calming influence. Carey knew the Old Trafford hierarchy would never break the maximum wage rule and focused his team-mates on winning the cup.

But Carey had to intervene again in pre-season when he was once again asked by his team-mates to ask for more money from the club. This time the United captain argued that the club's hands were tied, only for several players, notably Johnny Morris, Charlie Mitten and Henry Cockburn, to insist that it was his duty as skipper to present their demands to Busby. The United manager refused their request, although Busby tried to broker a compromise by asking club directors to give every player a new set of golf clubs but that offer was also turned down.

In the end the players didn't last much longer at Old Trafford: Johnny Morris departed for Derby in January 1949 and Charlie Mitten followed him out of the door a year later when he was tempted by a big money offer from Independiente Santa Fe in Colombia, neither ever played for the club again.

GAME NO. 21
UNITED 1–0 WEST BROMWICH ALBION
FIRST DIVISION
OLD TRAFFORD
14 SEPTEMBER 1963
ATTENDANCE – 50,453

THE BEST YEARS OF OUR LIVES

On a bright sunny day on Wednesday 22 May 1946 a genius was born in Belfast who would change the face of football forever. In June 1945 Dickie Best had married his sweetheart Anne Withers and eleven months later the couple welcomed their first child and named him George after Anne's father. Dickie was a modest working class man and a hugely respected figure in the local community of Castlereagh in East Belfast where the Best family lived at Burren Way. Dickie worked at an iron turner's lathe at the world famous Harland & Wolff shipyard at Queen's Island, Belfast where the *Titanic* was built. Anne worked on the production line at Gallaher's tobacco factory, the largest tobacco factory in the world, located in North Belfast. Dickie was 26-years old when Geordie, as the family called him, was born and played amateur football until he was 36 whilst George's mum was an outstanding field hockey player. From the moment he could walk all George ever did was play football and it was his Granda George who would kick a ball about all day with his grandson. On the other side of the family it was his Granda James "*Scottie*" Best, who took him to his first football match to see Glentoran play at The Oval in East Belfast, close to James's house. Well there wasn't much else for the kids growing up on the streets of post-war Belfast to do except play football as very few families had a television set at the time and the only "*net*" young boys were concerned about in the early 1950s was a make shift goal made from placing jumpers on the ground.

The young George attended Nettlefield Primary School in Radnor Street, Belfast and on his way to and home from school he would take a tennis ball out of his coat pocket and dribble it along the pavement, throwing his hips from side to side as he weaved in and out of pedestrians. The unsuspecting early morning workers were, in George's mind, defenders he had to snake past en-route to goal. When the bell rang to announce the mid-morning break no one at the school had to go looking for George as he was the first out on the playground waiting for one of the older boys to produce a football for a kick-about. Lunchtime was the same, a game of football with jumpers for goal posts, and after school George played football on a strip of grass near his home. It was no wonder George was a skinny kid with all that running about he did and food was the last thing on his mind when his mum had to go looking for him at tea time. It was usually quite dark by the time George got home, perhaps having played football for 4 hours or more at the end of the school day. When all the other kids had been dragged home by their parents George improvised and kicked his tennis ball against the kerb so as it would bounce back to him when he would control it and passing it against the kerb again. Shooting practice for George was placing the tennis ball on the ground and aiming for the handle of a garage door. George loved Christmas time because that was when he would either receive a brand new football from his parents or a pair of football boots depending on whether his current ball had seen its best days or if his feet had grown too big for the boots he was wearing at the time.

However despite football taking up all of his spare time George was an excellent pupil and a very quick learner. He passed the 11-plus and went to Grosvenor High School on Grosvenor Road. George hated the school but not for academic reasons, none of his mates were at the school and worst of all Grammar Schools in Belfast played rugby, not football. In his first year at Grosvenor George found himself running with an oddly shaped ball in his hands rather than having a football at his feet doing whatever he wanted it to do. But George gave rugby a go and was a half decent fly-half although for George no sport could replace his love for football. George hated going to the school and used to trick his teachers into sending him home ill as the shrewd young Best used to suck on a certain brand of "hot" sweet which made his throat turn red.

When George started to *"go on the beak"* (Belfast slang for playing truant) at Grosvenor his parents, sensing he was unhappy there, managed to get him into Lisnasharragh High School. And whereas other young boys at the time, including Alex *"Hurricane"* Higgins, who were similarly avoiding a school day would make their way to a nearby snooker hall, the young Best made his way to a patch of grass to kick his ball about. Away from school Higgins frequented the Jampot Snooker Club in the Sandy Row area of Belfast whilst George could find a makeshift football pitch almost anywhere. The Hurricane was three years younger than George and in many ways the lives of the two ran parallel with the highs the duo achieved during their careers followed by the unbearable lows. Alex was as mercurial with a snooker cue as George was with a football, and was called the "*George Best of the green baize*" – they were a pair of geniuses.

George's new school was in Stirling Avenue and much closer to his home than Grosvenor but more importantly to George all of his mates attended the school and they played football there, not rugby. Despite rugby being the number one sport at Grosvenor High School their rugby team only ever won the top prize in Northern Ireland Schoolboy Rugby on one occasion, lifting the Ulster Schools Challenge Cup in 1983, when the best days of George's playing career were a distant memory. Goodness only knows how many times Grosvenor High School would have won the Ulster Schools Challenge Cup had George chosen rugby ahead of football. And so when George walked out of the gates at Grosvenor for the last time, little did the school know it at the time but they were effectively giving a free transfer to a teenager who would go on to become the greatest ever footballer in the world; a player who in today's crazy football transfer market would cost well in excess of the world record fee of £198m paid to Barcelona by Paris Saint-Germain for Neymar in August 2017.

Apart from his local team, Glentoran, when George was a young boy he also supported an English League side but it wasn't Manchester United but the Red Devils huge rivals during the 1950s Wolverhampton Wanderers. Managed by the legendary Stan Cullis and captained by England captain Billy Wright, Wolves won the league title three times in the 50s and finished runners-up twice. The contrast between Wolves and United was stark, Cullis was famous for a "*kick and rush*" style of football while Busby's men were drilled in pass and move tactics. In the summer of 1953 Wolves became one of the first clubs to install floodlights at their Molineux ground which enabled them to play some very high profile friendly games against the world's best teams. Clubs such as Real Madrid (Spain), Racing Club (Argentina), First Vienna (Austria), Spartak Moscow (USSR) and Honved (Hungary) all visited the Black Country to take on Cullis's all-conquering side. The Wolves v Honvéd game was televised by the BBC on Monday 13 December 1954 and a 7-year old George Best sat in front of the black and white television set at home cheering his heroes in old gold and black. At the time the national game in England had taken a bit of a battering following two shocking defeats to Hungary, the infamous 6–3 defeat at Wembley and 7–1 in Budapest seven months later. Honved were thought of as the best club team in Europe and included 5 of the Mighty Magyars who had humbled the English on both occasions: József Bozsik, Gyula Lóránt, Sándor Kocsis, Ferenc Puskás and Zoltán Czibor.

From the outset George was captivated by the Hungarian's style of play which centred around their two magnificent strikers, Puskás and Kocsis, and driven on from midfield by the majestic Bozsik. The Hungarians just seemed to be moving that much quicker than their hosts and led 2–0 at half-time with goals from Kocsis and Machos inside the first 15 minutes of play. To slow the Hungarians down Wolves boss Cullis ordered an already damp pitch to be watered at half-time to slow the visitors down and the English champions stormed back using their direct style, Roy Swinbourne scored two following a penalty from Johnny Hancocks and Cullis hailed his team as the "*Champions of the World*". This game is widely believed to have been the inspiration behind the suggestion made by Gabriel Hanot, the French sports journalist and editor of *L'Equipe*, for UEFA to devise a club competition to be competed in by the various League Champions of European countries and the following season UEFA inaugurated the Champions' Club Cup.

When he was 13-years old George played for his local youth club, Cregagh Boys. The team was run by Bud McFarlane, a close friend of George's father, and he was also coach of the Reserve Team at Glentoran. McFarlane knew from day one that this young skinny boy from Burren Way had what it took to become a footballer and mentored the young Best. Bud would constantly offer George advice on all aspects of his game and on one occasion he told George that he felt he was concentrating too much on playing with his right foot and suggested that he practice with his left. George took Bud's advice on board and over the following week he never touched the ball with his right foot; he was still practicing with a tennis ball at the time. When he turned up for Cregagh Boys next match he only brought one football boot with him, his left one. George put the boot on and wore a *guddy* (Belfast slang for a plimsole) on his stronger right foot. Best scored 12 goals in the game and never once used his right foot to kick the ball. Yet incredibly, someone somewhere decided that George was not good enough to represent Northern Ireland at Schoolboy level! And this unbelievable decision was actually taken after George played for his youth club against a Possibles Northern Ireland Schoolboys XI which the kids from the Cregagh won 2-1 and George was the best player on the pitch by a country mile. No one really knows why George was excluded from the Northern Ireland Schoolboys set-up, some claimed it was because Lisnasharragh High School did not play in any competitive games whilst others cite George's frail frame as the main reason. Either way it was the country's loss at this level of football. Even his local side, Glentoran, thought he was too small and too light to make it as a footballer.

Bob Bishop was Manchester United's Chief Scout in Northern Ireland from 1950 to 1987 and in his early years Bishop helped coach the famous Boyland Youth Club football team which earned a reputation as nursery club for many teams in the First Division. Bud McFarlane was a close friend of Bob and he persuaded him to take George away for the weekend to one of the many football training camps Bishop held at Helen's Bay, County Down. Bishop agreed and so George set off from his home making the short journey to the camp which was located just outside Belfast. George was an extremely shy lad, not at all extrovert, but Bishop liked what he had seen and decided to keep a watchful eye on him. Leeds United had a useful scouting system in Northern Ireland at the time but according to their scout George was far too skinny to cope with the demands of life in the English Leagues but McFarlane believed in George and refused to give up on securing his young charge a trial with a major English club. Bud asked Bishop to organise a friendly match between Boyland FC and McFarlane's Cregagh Boys Under-16 team. At McFarlane's request the Boyland team was made up of their best 17-18 year olds. Bishop stood on the sidelines watching the 15-year old Best weave his magic on the pitch scoring twice in a 4-2 win against much bigger and stronger boys. It was at that moment that Bishop realised that McFarlane had been right all the long, the young dark haired skinny kid had what it took to become a professional footballer and he sent his now famous telegram to the Manchester United manager, Matt Busby, with the message reading: "*I think I've found you a Genius.*"

Matt Busby invited George over to Old Trafford for a trial in the summer of 1961 during the school holidays. Best, and another young player who Bishop thought could make the grade at United, Eric McMordie, boarded the Belfast to Liverpool ferry in June 1961. George wore his best clothes for the journey, his school uniform! Speaking shortly after George died in 2005 Eric fondly recalled that journey to Manchester, "*I'd played for a club in East Belfast called Boyland since I was 11. There was a man called Bob Bishop who spent his days watching Boyland and sent kids from there to the big clubs. It was like a nursery for Manchester United. George became one of the first to go to United who didn't play for Boyland. Bob's eye for talent was equal to none - he was a very special man. But a match between us and Cregagh Boys, who George played for, was set up. I've never seen a player with so many bruises on his body as George. He was picked on not just because he was wee but because he was so talented. But he fought back and that's what made George the great player he was.*"

The boys were not accompanied by their parents or a guardian for the trip and were simply told to make their way to Lime Street Train Station in Liverpool and take the train to Manchester where a taxi would be sent to meet them and take them to Old Trafford. The entire journey was a terrifying ordeal for two kids from the streets of Belfast who had never been out of Northern Ireland before. When the boys arrived in Manchester there was nobody holding a sign with either of their names on it and so they jumped in a taxi and asked the driver to take them to Old Trafford. Unknown to George and Eric there were two Old Traffords and the driver took them to Lancashire County Cricket Club as the football season had ended and the cricket season had just begun. The taxi driver thought the boys were just young cricketers hoping to join Lancashire. When the pair finally made it to United's home ground they were met by the club's Chief Scout, Joe Armstrong, who took them to the Cliff training ground. There they met a number of the first team players including Northern Ireland's Harry Gregg and Jimmy Nicholson before being taken on to their digs. Armstrong drove the two bewildered young boys to a terraced house in Chorlton-cum-Hardy, a suburb of Manchester, and introduced them to Mrs Fullaway. Little did George know it at the time but Mrs Fullaway's house would be his home on and off for the next 10 years. The Belfast boys were homesick on their first night away from their families and when Armstrong called at Mrs Fullaway's house early next morning to pick them up George told him that both he and Eric wanted to go home. So the boys made their way back across the Irish Sea.

Sometime later in life McMordie, who went on to play for Middlesbrough (1964–75) winning 21 caps for his country, recalled the journey: "*It was an incredible time. There was George in his Lisnasharragh school uniform with his prefect's badge and me. We were just a pair of kids who had never been out of Belfast. It was like another world. But it all became too much and we ended up back home in less than a couple of days. We were both overawed. A short while later George went back and the rest is history."*

Dickie telephoned Busby to find out what had gone on and persuaded George's Dad to send his boy back over again to see if he possessed the necessary talent and ability to become a professional footballer. George had planned to take-up an apprenticeship as a printer in Belfast when he left school but thankfully Busby persuaded him to sign amateur forms at United in August 1961 and George ended up keeping printers all over the country busy over the following 12 years and more. It took the young Best a while to get over the homesickness and to keep him occupied after training United got him a job as a clerk at the Manchester Ship Canal. George hated the job, having to make countless cups of tea all day long. On 22 May 1963, the day of his 17th birthday, George signed professional forms with Manchester United. Three days after celebrating his birthday and becoming a professional footballer, George was sitting in the stands at Wembley Stadium as a member of United's non-playing party at the 1963 FA Cup Final against Leicester City, a game United won 3-1. Goodness knows how many United fans brushed past George that day without even knowing who the skinny dark-haired kid was however by then the rumour mill had started to hum and Best's name was mentioned in hushed tones by supporters who attended youth team games and had contacts at the club. United trainer Jack Crompton would confide in a supporter and then whisper "we're trying to keep him quiet", the quiet didn't last for long!

United made a disastrous start to the next season; a 4-0 hammering in the Charity Shield by Everton had sent a panic through the club and one of their best young players, Johnny Giles, was dropped. Within days Giles was transferred to Leeds following a clash with Busby which left United short of a winger. They won 4 and drew 2 of their opening 6 games with Bobby Charlton filling in for the departed Giles but Busby knew something wasn't quite right. Charlton's best position was in the middle – then Denis Law took a knock against Blackpool on the Wednesday.

George knew nothing of any of this as he happily arrived as a non-playing member of the United squad at Davyhulme Golf Club before the game against West Brom on 14 September 1963. After lunch Busby beckoned the young Irishman towards him and told him that he was playing that afternoon and George's immediate thought was that he would be turning out for the reserves. "No," the boss said, "at Old Trafford!"

Manchester United: Harry Gregg. Tony Dunne, Noel Cantwell (Capt), Bill Foulkes, Maurice Setters, Paddy Crerand, Nobby Stiles, Philip Chisnall, David Sadler, Bobby Charlton, George Best.

In truth Best's debut was not quite the sensational start which numerous authors have subsequently described. He was up against Welsh international Graham Williams who was a typically combative full-back of the era and gave him no quarter, nevertheless there were flashes of promise and United won the game 1-0 with a goal from George's room-mate David Sadler.

Best had to wait 3 months for his next game and was back in Belfast for Christmas when he was recalled in an emergency following a 6-1 hammering at Turf Moor, Burnley on Boxing Day. Best raced back to Manchester for the game against the same opponents two days later and was sensational, scoring the first of 179 goals for the club as United eased to a 5-1 win. By the end of the season Best was a fixture in the team and even found time to help the youth team out as they won the FA Youth Cup for the first time since the Busby Babes had triumphed in 1957.

Best's subsequent career was unique. His looks and style of play contrasted sharply with other players of his era. Gone were the days of heavy boots and long shorts, gone too were the slow jinking runs favoured by the likes of Matthews and Finney. Best was all-action and the scorer of incredible, audacious goals – the birth of television coverage of the game made him as famous as The Beatles. He helped United to two league titles and starred in the European Cup final win in 1968 that finally laid the ghosts of Munich to rest but rather than it signalling the start of a new era, within months it became obvious to George that United were on the wane. When Matt Busby retired in 1969 he lost a crucial father figure and he became disillusioned with the game.

His subsequent decline was painful to watch as he got in fights with opponents and referees, was accused of turning up drunk to training, went AWOL for a game at Chelsea and retired twice before finally calling it quits for good following a 3-0 loss at Queens Park Rangers in 1974. In the meantime George had become more than a footballer – he advertised everything from aftershave to sausages and at one time employed staff to open his fan mail. At his peak his life was intolerable, the press hounded his every move. True creative geniuses are those who understand that a stage or a paintbrush is not required for making the highest art of all. George Best expressed his art on a football pitch where he painted many masterpieces. But for Best the fame and fortune he had achieved playing football were merely illusions, not the solutions they promised to be. And so, the most gifted player ever to play the beautiful game, decided to bring the curtain down on his glittering, yet so unfulfilled to its full promise, aged just 27.

Over the following eight years George flirted with comebacks including a season in the Second Division when he and another football maverick, Rodney Marsh, along with England's 1966 World Cup winning captain, Bobby Moore, packed Craven Cottage with their entertaining football. Best also played in the North American Soccer League (NASL) for the Fort Lauderdale Strikers, Los Angeles Aztecs and San Jose Earthquakes but his football away from Manchester United never quite touched the same highs.

And of course, George reached some lows: constant battles with alcoholism, marriage splits, a liver transplant and a 12-week jail sentence in 1984 for drink-driving, assaulting a police officer and failing to answer bail. But it is the good times that fans will forever remember George for which was what George himself wanted to be remembered for. His magical performance in 1966 against Benfica in their own backyard when he scored twice in United's 5–1 win, a performance that earned him the nickname *El Beatle*. Or his six goals for United in the FA Cup against Northampton Town, and who will ever forget that night at Wembley on 29 May 1968, when George scored in the European Cup final in their 4–1 win over Benfica. In season 1967-68 George, a member of United's famous triumvirate along with Denis Law (European Player of the Year 1964) and Bobby Charlton (European Player of the Year 1966) scored 28 times in the League, 1 goal in the FA Cup and 3 times in United's successful European Cup campaign. United's Holy Trinity of Law, Charlton and Best had delivered the Holy Grail, the European Cup, for their manager, Matt Busby to help United erase the memory of the Munich Air Disaster some ten years earlier. George was voted European Player of the Year in 1968.

On 20 November 2005, the *News of the World* newspaper published a photograph of a very seriously ill George Best lying in his hospital bed at the request of the Manchester United legend. The caption with the photograph read: "*Don't die like me.*" Sadly George died in Cromwell Hospital, London five days after the photograph was published but the shy Belfast boy will forever have a special place in the hearts of every Manchester United fan. After George passed away his long-time friend and former business partner, Manchester City's Mike Summerbee, was asked to describe George in three words. His responses summed up George's life exquisitely: "A genius but quiet and shy."

Did You Know That?

A 17-year old George Best made his debut for Northern Ireland in the British Home International Championships on 15 April 1964. The Irish travelled to Swansea to play Wales at The Vetch Field, home to Swansea City. Pat Jennings, the legendary goalkeeper, also made his international debut in the game aged 18 which the Irish won 3-2. Pat paid a beautiful tribute to George after the United legend's death: "He was the finest player I ever played with or against. I treasure my memories with him even though on occasions he made me look rather foolish." However, whereas Jennings went on to win a record 119 caps for his country and play at two World Cup final tournaments (1982 and 1986), George only managed 37 caps, scoring 9 times, and football fans around the world never saw him display his skills on the international world stage at any major finals.

GAME NO. 22
UNITED 3-1 WIMBLEDON
PREMIER LEAGUE
OLD TRAFFORD
26 AUGUST 1995
ATTENDANCE – 32,226

MANCHESTER UNITED'S FANTASTIC FOUR

The Fantastic Four are a fictional superhero team who appeared in American comic books published by Marvel. On 15 May 1992 a crowd of 14,681 turned up at Old Trafford to watch the second leg of the 1992 FA Youth Cup final and witnessed the emergence of a new Fantastic Four. Manchester United's Youth Team led Crystal Palace 3-1 on aggregate having won the first leg at Selhurst

Park the night before. Nicky Butt scored twice and David Beckham also scored for the team captained by Gary Neville. The United kids won the second leg 3-2 (scorers: Ben Thornley, Simon Davies and Colin McKee) to give United their first success in the competition since season 1963-64 when a 17-year old kid from Belfast named George Best inspired his team-mates to a 5-2 aggregate victory over two legs against Swindon Town. Best scored in the 1-1 draw at the County Ground with captain Bobby Noble lifting the trophy at Old Trafford in front of 25,563 fans.

For the second leg of the 1992 FA Youth Cup final Manchester United were captained by an 18-year old kid from Cardiff, Ryan Giggs. Like Best before him, Giggs play for both the senior and junior sides that season and by this time had already played 51 times for the first team during the 1991-92 season including 38 in the First Division, scoring 3 goals as United finished runners-up to Leeds United. When Giggs held aloft the FA Youth Cup it wasn't the first piece of silverware he had won with United. A month earlier, 12 April 1992, Giggs won a League Cup winners' medal when United beat Nottingham Forest 1-0 at Wembley.

The Welshman had made his debut for Manchester United on 2 March 1991, a 2-0 loss to Everton at Old Trafford. On 16 September 1992 Gary Neville became the second member of the Fantastic Four to progress to the United first team when he played against Torpedo Moscow in the UEFA Cup, First Round, first leg. The game ended 0-0 at Old Trafford with Neville used as a substitute in the 88th minute for Lee Martin. David Beckham made his debut for Manchester United on 23 September 1992 against Brighton and Hove Albion in the League Cup, Second Round first leg. The tie ended 1-1 at the Goldstone Ground, Beckham came on as a substitute in the 72nd minute for Andrei Kanchelskis. Nicky Butt's maiden appearance in the first team came on 21 November 1992 in a 3-0 victory over Oldham Athletic, he came on for Paul Ince in the 64th minute with Giggs also playing in the game.

On 21 September 1994, Paul Scholes had been given his senior United debut when they beat Port Vale 2-1 at Vale Park in the League Cup Second Round, first leg and he made a sensational start to his United career by scoring both United goals. The United side that evening included Beckham, Butt and Gary Neville as well as three other members of the 1992 FA Youth Cup final winning team, Simon Davies and Keith Gillespie. The sixth member of the 1992 side dubbed

"Fergie's Fledglings" who played in the win over Port Vale was John O'Kane who came on as a substitute for Neville in the 77th minute. Phil Neville was handed the famous first team red shirt for an FA Cup tie. Wrexham visited Old Trafford on 28 January 1995 for a Fourth Round game. United beat the Welsh club 5-2 as the younger Neville walked out of the Old Trafford tunnel alongside Giggs and Scholes. Beckham joined them in the match as a 74th minute replacement for McClair.

So it wasn't until 26 August 1995 that United's Fantastic Four all played in the same Manchester United first team for the first time. It was United's third Premier League game of the season, Wimbledon were the opponents, and Alex Ferguson was tweaking his side following the departures of Mark Hughes, Paul Ince and Andrei Kanchelskis over the summer. On the opening day of the season United had been beaten 3-1 at Villa Park. It was a relatively inexperienced United side which included Butt, Gary and Phil Neville and Paul Scholes. The press hammered United's performance and criticised Ferguson for not strengthening the team by replacing the trio who had left over the summer when he had bought three goalkeepers, Tony Coton, Nick Culkin and Raimond van der Gouw for a collective £750,000 but no replacements for Hughes, Ince and Kanchelskis.

United won their next Premier League game, a 2-1 victory over West Ham United at Old Trafford in which Beckham, Butt and Scholes started the game. In the 84th minute of the match Alex Ferguson did something he did throughout his time as Manchester United manager, he put his faith in his young players. He sent on Ben Thornley, a 1992 FA Youth Cup winner, for McClair. Thornley, who scored against Crystal Palace in the 3-2 Youth Cup final win, had made his first team debut on 26 February 1994 in a 2-2 draw away to West Ham United replacing Denis Irwin in the 79th minute. Surprisingly, none of his classmates from 1992 featured in the game.

Paul Scholes had played in the 1993 FA Youth Cup final which United lost 4-1 to Leeds United over the two legs. Beckham, Butt and Gary Neville (Capt) were also losing finalists in 1993 along with Phil Neville. Scholes scored a penalty in the 2-1 loss at Elland Road.

During the 1990s there was a distinct lack of creativity and originality in giving Manchester United players a nicknames: Becks, Brucey, Butty, Choccy, Gazza, Incey, Pally, Schmeichs, Sharpey and Sparky didn't quite cut it. Mind you, Clayton Blackmore's "Sunbed" monicker was pretty catchy. Even the manager had a less than adventurous monicker, "Fergie," but nowhere near as catchy as Ron Atkinson's "Mr Bojangles," tag. Ryan Giggs was known as "Giggsy," by his United teammates and fans. The title of "Welsh Wizard" had already been given to another Manchester United legend, Billy Meredith in 1909. And comparing like for like the predecessors who played for United before the 1990s enjoyed more than a "Y" at the end of their nickname.

The team which Alex Ferguson selected to play Wimbledon on 26 August 1995 was a testimony to the faith he had in his young players. Three players who had won an FA Youth Cup winners' medal in 1992 started the game and both substitutes were also 1992 FA Youth Cup winners. The Manchester United team that day read: Peter Schmeichel, Gary Neville, Denis Irwin, Steve Bruce (Capt), Gary Pallister, Nicky Butt, Roy Keane, Lee Sharpe, David Beckham, Paul Scholes, Andy Cole. Substitute: Ryan Giggs for Cole 72 mins, Simon Davies for Scholes 83 mins

United beat Wimbledon 3-1 with two goals from Keane (28 & 80 mins) and a goal scored by Andy Cole in the 60th minute. When Ryan Giggs retired at the end of the 2013-14 season having made a club record 963 appearances (1991-2014) he had scored 168 goals for United. He signed for the club as a trainee on 9 July 1990 and as a professional on 29 November 1990. Looking back on Giggs' United career he so could very easily have been dubbed, "Mr Fantastic." Mr Fantastic was the leader of Marvel Comic's "Fantastic Four" but apart from captaining the club's 1992 FA Youth Cup final winning team, Giggs rarely captained Manchester United.

Like Giggs, Neville was a one club career man after signing as a trainee with United on 8 July 1991 and as a professional on 23 January 1993. He represented United 602 times, scoring 7 times from 1992 until he retired at the end of the 2010-11 season. When Beckham left Old Trafford for Real Madrid on 2 July 2003 in a £23 million transfer, he had played 394 times for United, scoring 84 goals (1992-2003). He signed as a trainee with United on 8 July 1991 and as a professional on 23 January 1993. In July 2004, Butt swapped Uniteds and moved to Newcastle for £2.5 million. He had turned out for Manchester United on 387 occasions (1992-2004) and scored 26 goals after signing as a trainee on 8 July 1991 and as a professional on 23 January 1993.

Each member of Marvel's Fantastic Four got their superpowers at the same time. They were test pilots on an experimental rocket ship and when they were in space their ship was bombarded with cosmic radiation. The rocket ship crashed back to earth but all four on-board survived and discovered that they now had superpowers. Manchester United's Fantastic Four of David Beckham, Nicky Butt, Ryan Giggs and Gary Neville acquired their superpowers in the 1992 FA Youth Cup final.

Did You Know That?

Jimmy Glass was the Crystal Palace goalkeeper in both legs of the 1992 FA Youth Cup final. In season 1998-99, United won the Treble to write their name in the football history book. That same season Glass's name was forever enshrined in the same book. Going into their last game of the 1998-99 season Carlisle United needed to beat Plymouth Argyle to avoid dropping out of the Football League. Glass was somewhat of a journeyman goalkeeper and during his Crystal Palace career (1989-96) he was sent out on loan to Dulwich Hamlet, Portsmouth, Gillingham and Burnley and in season 1998-99 he was out on loan to Carlisle United from Swindon Town. On 8 May 1999, it was make or break for Carlisle United when they faced relegation rivals Scarborough at Brunton Park. The Cumbrians were sitting bottom of the entire Football League whilst Scarborough were one point better off so a draw would be good enough for the visitors to stay up.

With 90 minutes gone and the score 1-1 the away fans were celebrating, believing their team had staved off relegation to the Conference. The fourth official held up a plastic board with the No.4 on it indicating that four minutes of added-on time would be played. With the four minutes almost up the home side were awarded a corner kick. They had one last roll of the dice. Glass, who had been signed as an emergency goalkeeper after the transfer deadline, was directed by his manager Nigel Pearson to go up for the corner kick. As the ball came over a header was parried away by the Scarborough goalkeeper and just as it was about to hit the ground, Glass caught it sweetly on the half volley with his right boot and fired it into the back of the net. It was pure "Roy of the Rovers" material which saved Carlisle United from relegation and consigned Scarborough to non-league football and ultimately the club went out of business in 2007.

GAME NO. 23
UNITED 5-0 SUNDERLAND
PREMIER LEAGUE
OLD TRAFFORD
21 DECEMBER 1996
ATTENDANCE – 55,081

ERIC PAINTS HIS MASTERPIECE

A man can be an artist in anything: food, writing and even football. It depends on how good he is at it. Eric Cantona's art was scoring goals and on 21st December he created a masterpiece. The famous Italian artist, Leonardo da Vinci, painted the masterpiece for which he is most famous, the "Mona Lisa," between 1503 and 1506 but it took just seconds for Eric to conceptualise and execute a masterpiece that is still replayed years later and remains perhaps the avatar for his Old Trafford career – it had ambition, skill, was executed to perfection and it was all topped off with Gallic swagger.

United were the reigning league champions and holders of the FA Cup while Sunderland were playing in their maiden Premier League season having won Division One by four points over Derby County in season 1995-96 who were also promoted. Sunderland's style of play was aggressive, but totally committed to winning which reflected the demands and style of their manager, the former Everton midfielder Peter Reid. In season 1984-85 Reid won the PFA Players' Player of the Year Award and came fourth in the World Soccer Player of the Year Award which was won by Juventus's talismanic French captain, Michel Platini.

This was United's 18th Premier League game of the season in defence of their trophy, having won 7, drawn 7 and lost 3 of their previous 17 Premiership games. The three losses all occurred consecutively: 5-0 away to Newcastle United, 6-3 away to Southampton and a 2-1 loss at Old Trafford to Chelsea, as a result of this poor start United were sitting in sixth at kick-off. Sunderland were holding their own among the big boys – in their first 17 outings they had notched-up 5 wins, 5 draws and 7 losses. Six days before they made the trip to Manchester, Reid's side beat Chelsea 3-0 at their famous Roker Park home. Sunderland nicknamed "The Black Cats," did not move to the Stadium of Light until the 1997-98 season.

The team which played Sunderland was: Peter Schmeichel, Gary

Neville, Denis Irwin, David May, Gary Pallister, Paul Scholes, Phil Neville, Ryan Giggs, Nicky Butt, Eric Cantona (Capt), Ole Gunnar Solskjaer. Subs: Brian McClair (for Pallister, 46 mins), Karel Poborsky (for Solskjaer, 54 mins), Ben Thornley (for Giggs, 63 mins)

On paper the match seemed to be a regulation home win for the Reds and when "The Baby Faced Assassin" Ole Gunnar Solskjaer, opened the scoring in the 36th minute and two minutes before half-time Cantona scored from the penalty spot against his former Nîmes teammate, Lionel Pérez, who was in goal for the visitors it was looked like a fairly unmemorable afternoon. Solskjaer made it 3-0 three minutes into the second half and the Black Cats were getting a mauling – it was United who were doing the purring. The visitors' midfield was run ragged by a rampaging United who looked like they would score every time they attacked a beleaguered defence. Alex Ferguson's side were producing the style of play which saw them win the Double the previous season and in Eric Cantona they possessed a player who knew what it took to win a game, and win it in style. Nicky Butt was rewarded for his endeavours in the United midfield when he scored to make it 4-0 in the 58th minute. There was still 30 minutes to go but the game was over. There was no need for any United player to exert themselves any further and they could be forgiven if they took their foot off the pedal knowing they had another game in five days against Nottingham Forest at the City Ground but Cantona wasn't finished with Sunderland.

With 21 minutes of play remaining Cantona collected a pass on the halfway line with his back to the Sunderland goal. Using his strength and sublime skill, he spun around Kevin Ball and Richard Ord and passed the ball to Brian McClair who was making his way into the Sunderland half, Ord kicking thin air when he attempted to tackle Cantona. Ball and Ord had hopelessly failed to pin Eric down throughout the game, both players were fully aware that he was the one player who made United tick but they could get nowhere near him. McClair and Cantona did a quick one-two, the Scot's lay back feeding Cantona who was just inside the penalty area. Cantona composed himself, looked at where Pérez was standing and coolly chipped the ball over his countryman and into the net off the inside of the left post. It was the deftest of touches, a dink which was executed to perfection, a work of art but Eric had one final stroke of the paintbrush left before his Masterpiece was complete. Still standing on the same spot, collar turned up, hands by his side, Cantona slowly rotated 360 degrees to accept the adulation that scoring such a spectacular goal deserves. There was no expression on his face as he slowly raised his arms in the air as if to say "did you expect anything else". It was a theatrical, magnetic performance worthy of the masterpiece he had created. The United fans were instantly aware that they had just witnessed a very special goal from a unique player.

It would have been so appropriate if the stadium announcer had played Carly Simon's "Nobody Does It Better" in recognition of Cantona's extraordinary, but perfectly executed, chip which he celebrated inauspiciously, but with so much impudence. Cantona's celebration after scoring such an iconic goal was voted the Premier League's greatest ever celebration. Eric was 30 at the time and the goalkeeper he beat, Pérez, was wearing No.30 on his back. United won the game 5-0 with Eric giving the United fans an early Christmas present.

In 1935 the second edition of the world famous golf tournament, the US Masters (in 1934 it was known as the Augusta National Invitational Tournament) was held at the Augusta National Golf Club. A moment occurred in the fourth round of the tournament, which became golf's fourth Major, which went down in the annals of sporting history. The American golfer, Gene Sarazen, who had snubbed the inaugural tournament the year before, trailed leader Craig Wood by three shots after 14 holes. At the fifteenth, a Par 5 covering a distance of 530 yards and named "Firethorn" Sarazen found himself 235 yards from the flag. He took out a 4 wood from his golf bag and fired his shot at the hole. Sarazen's shot was hit lower than Cantona's measured chip, it never rose higher than 30 feet off the ground, and it carried the water hazard and skipped its way towards the hole and then dropped into the cup.

Watching the shot, O.B. Keeler, an actor and a writer, described Sarazen's shot, "The ball bounded once, twice and settled to a smooth roll, while the ripple of sound from the big gallery went sweeping into a crescendo, and then the tornado broke." Lovely words but it was the foremost voice of his generation, and a founding member of Augusta National to boot, Grantland Rice, who summed it up best. He called it the "Shot heard round the world" a clever use of words to allude to the start of the American War of Independence in 1775 and which lasted until 1783. Sarazen's albatross (three under par on one hole) could not quite match Cantona's chip towards the Sunderland goal but it did ensure that he pulled on the famous Green Jacket to identify him as the first US Masters Champion.

Eric Cantona's beautifully lobbed dink over Pérez to score may not have reached the ears or eyes of the world as Sarazen's shot some 70 years before did, but it reeked havoc in the Premier League. Cantona's goal send vibrations through the other teams who must have been thinking "Why does the eye see a thing more clearly in dreams than with the imagination being awake?" (Leonardo da Vinci)

Many years after the game Lionel Pérez recalled the moment, "This goal (Cantona's lob) shouldn't exist. We were losing 3-0 after 48 minutes and Eric had stopped playing. He stayed in the middle of the pitch and didn't run any more because the game was over. Then there was one moment, when Ryan Giggs crossed and he had a shot which I saved. It was the only save I think I made in the game. Eric then said to me, just in a funny way, 'Lionel, you should have left it!' But I didn't want to be smiling with him when we were losing. Before the match, one of my friends rang me from France to say he'd seen Eric playing against Chelsea and Frank Leboeuf was very friendly with him on the pitch. I thought, 'I'm not going to be kind with him because I don't want any French cameras seeing that. I don't want to be that man laughing when we are losing 3-0'. So I just blanked him when he was joking with me. And after I blanked him he started to run everywhere because he wanted to f*** me! He started to be mental. He was like, 'F***** hell, he doesn't want to give me an answer. If this guy doesn't want to talk to me, he's going to see what I am made of.' I am very sure that if I answered him, he would have stayed calm until the end of the game but, instead, his attitude really changed."

During a UTD Podcast Cantona was asked about his floated goal over a dumbfounded Pérez. The United Legend said that his goal was an act of revenge and explained why. "I never celebrate a goal in the same way, because every goal is different. The energy is different, everything is different. But maybe I did this celebration, I don't know, it's nice to take the energy of all the fans, you know? And sometimes it's even more. Maybe it's because the goalkeeper, he was French. Before the game, in the tunnel, I came to him to shake his hand and say hello to him because I hadn't seen him since I left (Nîmes). It was the last club I played for in France. And he didn't want to shake my hand. So maybe I scored this goal because of that! That's the biggest humiliation for a goalkeeper, and this kind of celebration too. Because he's angry and you don't run anywhere. I just stand there.

Look at me."

Pérez added: "Even now, every time Eric is on the TV in France, I have phone calls from friends because they show the goal all the time. I'm on TV a lot, but it's not because of me unfortunately! I smile because I always remember all my family were over to see me for Christmas and came to watch the game. My Grandma was there and after the game she said, 'Have you seen all these French flags? They are for you.' It was funny because she didn't realise they were not for me, but for Eric!"

Leonardo da Vinci was also renowned in the fields of chemistry, geometry and mathematics. Cantona's goal against Pérez had the chemistry of his one-two touch move with McClair, the geometry of Cantona knowing the properties of the space around him and a perfectly calculated chip towards goal that even the eminent mathematician, Albert Einstein, would have been proud of.

Did You Know That?

During the COVID-19 pandemic no football was played and so BBC TV's *Match of the Day* programme on a Saturday night decided to get Gary Lineker, Alan Shearer and Ian Wright together via a three way teleconference from their homes to talk about football. A number of shows were produced along with a "Top 10" style theme to them. One such show was "Top Ten European Imports." Each player selected their Top 10.

Shearer's Top 3 were: 1. Roy Keane, 2. Thierry Henry, 3. Eric Cantona (Cristiano Ronaldo was No.7)

Wright's Top 3 were: 1. Roy Keane, 2. Thierry Henry, 3. Cristiano Ronaldo (Eric Cantona was No.4)

During the discussion about Eric Cantona, the following was said:

Ian Wright: "For me. He was the ultimate talisman in a football team."

Shearer: "If you are going to play with your collar up you'll have to be some player. And he was."

Lineker: "He's quite the individual though wasn't he? Quite a personality. On the field and off it."

Wright had nothing but admiration for Cantona and he recalled the goal against Pérez fondly: "It's so majestic. He could have been a Gladiator in Roman Times. That's how he celebrated. He had such an aura about him." Wright then recalled how his Arsenal teammate, Marc Overmars, failed so badly in attempting to copy Cantona after the Dutch winger scored the only goal of the game at Old Trafford on 14 March 1998. Arsenal's 1-0 win effectively sealed the 1997-98 Premier League title for The Gunners. Wright held his hands up in the air and said: "Did you see when Marc Overmars tried it? It was ridiculous. It was like watching an Oompa Loompa doing something." Shearer burst into laughter.

Wright then turned his attention to Cantona's celebration after scoring and said: "You know something? I still feel that the Cantona celebration is the best because only he could do that celebration. He is the only one who could exude that kind of arrogance and confidence (Shearer could be heard agreeing). It was beautiful to watch. It was a beautiful thing to watch. They should do it in slow motion so people could do it in slow motion so people can watch it in slow motion. Just watch the majesty of him."

GAME NO. 24
PORT VALE 0-2 UNITED
LEAGUE CUP, ROUND TWO, FIRST LEG
VALE PARK
21 SEPTEMBER 1994
ATTENDANCE- 18,605

THE GINGER PRINCE

On 21 September 1994, Manchester United visited Vale Park for a League Cup, Round 2, First Leg tie. Their opponents were Port Vale, a First Division side who are one of the few English League clubs not named after a city or town. Nicknamed "The Valiants," a reference to the valley of ports on the Trent and Mersey Canal, the Staffordshire club has never played in the top flight of the English game and hold two unique records: the most number of seasons in the Football League (as at 2019-20) with 108 and the most number of seasons in the second tier of English football (41) without ever reaching the First Division/Premier League.

At the time, Manchester United were reigning Premier League Champions and FA Cup holders and a crowd of 18,605 fans paid their entrance fee into Vale Park to see the game. Alex Ferguson put out a weakened side for the game which lined up as follows: Gary Walsh, Gary Neville, Denis Irwin, Nicky Butt, David May, Roy Keane, Keith Gillespie, Simon Davies, David Beckham, Brian McClair and a

19-year old player who was handed his first team debut. Step up to the plate the Salford born 5 feet, 7 inches tall midfielder, Paul Aaron Scholes.

Scholesy had signed for United as an apprentice on 8 July 1991 aged 16, and then signed professional forms on 23 July 1993, aged 18, technically he wasn't a member of the "Class of '92" but would come to be associated with them. Four days earlier United had beaten Liverpool 2-0 at Old Trafford but when United played Port Vale, Alex Ferguson rested Peter Schmeichel, Denis Irwin, Steve Bruce, Gary Pallister, Lee Sharpe, Andrei Kanchelskis, Paul Ince, Ryan Giggs, Mark Hughes and a player the Port Vale fans were hoping to see, Eric Cantona. Subs: John O'Kane for Neville 78 mins, Sharpe for Butt 82 mins.

On the night, United won 2-1 with both goals scored by Scholes (36 & 53 minutes) who became the first player since Bobby Charlton on 6 October 1956, to score two goals for the club on his debut. The home fans could only look on in awe at the performance put in by the young ginger haired kid from Salford who tortured the home defence. Scholes was quite simply unstoppable on the night, his enthusiasm and his exuberance of youth was just too much for the opposition to handle. Clearly Alex Ferguson was impressed with Scholesy's maiden outing because he selected him for United's trip to Portman Road to play Ipswich Town just three days later. United lost the Premier League game 3-2 with Cantona and Scholes scoring for United. Paul played 25 times (includes 11 as a substitute) in season 1994-95 and scored 7 goals helping United to runners-up spot in the Premier League to Blackburn Rovers. In the 1995 FA Cup final he was given a place on the bench and came on for Lee Sharpe in United's 1-0 loss to Everton.

When Hughes, Ince and Kanchelskis all left Old Trafford in the summer of 1995, Scholes seized his opportunity and continued to impress his manager and he managed to secure a regular starting place in the side. In season 1995-96, Scholes pulled on the United shirt 31 times and scored 14 goals, helping the club win their second Double of Premier League and FA Cup in three seasons.

At first glance Scholes seemed to be at a disadvantage, short and squat midfielders towered above him but what he lacked in physical attributes he more than made up for between the ears. Paul Scholes had one of the greatest football brains of all time, he always seemed to be several steps ahead of everyone else on the pitch. He always made himself available for a teammate to lay the ball off to him if his teammate was being pressed by an opponent then the little magician would twist one way and the other, before firing a pinpoint 50-yard pass on to the toe of a teammate. Scholesy was a Master Passer, and should really have been nicknamed "Ping" because he could ping a long distance pass to a teammate like Tiger Woods could ping an iron shot to within an inch of the hole. More importantly Scholesy never got flustered under pressure and he very rarely gave possession away. He seemed to operate at a different pace to everyone else – he always seemed to have a second longer in which to conjure up the next United move.

Ferguson trusted Paul to do the job he assigned to him and the little dynamo of a midfielder never let his manager down, on or off the pitch. Unlike some of his teammates, Scholes shunned the limelight, rarely gave an interview and was too shy to speak to the TV cameras after a game, even when he was named Man of the Match. He just stuck to what he did best, played the game with his heart on his sleeve for the club he loved. Mind you the young Scholes grew up an Oldham Athletic fan.

Many of Paul's teammates, both at United and when he played for England, knew they had a special player in their team, a player who could win a match with a moment of genius by providing a crisp pass to one of his strikers or by scoring a spectacular goal, the Ginger Prince could do it all. He could score with his left foot, his right foot and his head and he had the ability to strike a ball towards goal with unerring accuracy whether it was on the floor or on the volley. Paul was neat and compact on the ball, possessing an exquisite feather like touch as he caressed the ball with a pass. Somehow he always managed to find space in a crowded midfield which the magnificent Barcelona midfield partnership of Xavi Hernandez and Andrés Iniesta surely modelled their game on. He was a football artist, a genius but every genius has a flaw and the only thing Paul couldn't master was the art of tackling. By the end of his career the two-footed lunge was as much a trademark as the unerring cross–field ball.

At the end of the 2010-11 season he took the decision to retire, aged 36, having played 676 games for United, scoring 150 goals. He had won everything club football had to offer: 10 Premier League titles, 3 FA Cups, 2 League Cups, 5 FA Charity/Community Shields, 2 UEFA Champions Leagues, 1 Intercontinental Cup and 1 FIFA Club World Cup. In 2008, Scholesy was inducted into the English Football

Hall of Fame. He had also played 66 times for England and scored 14 international goals. In 1993, Paul was a member of England's Under-18 team which won the UEFA European Under-18 Championship.

Yet retirement was short-lived. With an injury crisis looming in January 2012 Sir Alex Ferguson persuaded Scholesy to blow the cobwebs off his football boots and return to United. Paul answered his manager's call and added a further 21 games to his appearances tally and another 4 goals in the last five months of the 2011-12 season. Paul got his appetite for the game back and he decided to play one more season for United. In season 2012-13, Paul had a fairytale ending to his Old Trafford career when he helped Manchester United win a record 13th Premier League title, his 11th, playing 21 times, scoring once. When he finally hung up his football boots for good, on the final day of the 2012-13 season when his manager also retired, Paul had made a total of 718 appearances (499 Premier League) for United and scored 155 goals (107 Premier League).

Many players were quick to pay tribute to one of the best ever players to grace the game.

"In the last 15 to 20 years the best central midfielder that I have seen — the most complete — is Scholes. I have spoken with Xabi Alonso about this many times. Scholes is a spectacular player who has everything. He can play the final pass, he can score, he is strong, he never gets knocked off the ball and he doesn't give possession away. If he had been Spanish then maybe he would have been valued more."
Xavi Hernandez

"If he was playing with me, I would have scored so many more."
Pele

"He is the greatest player in Premier League history."
Thierry Henry

"It's only natural to want to select your best players and there is no doubt for me that Paul Scholes is still in a class of his own. He's almost untouchable in what he does. I never tire of watching him play. You rarely come across the complete footballer, but Scholes is as close to it as you can get. One of my regrets is that the opportunity to play alongside him never presented itself during my career."
Zinedine Zidane

"He's always so in control and pinpoint accurate with his passing – a beautiful player to watch."

Sir Bobby Charlton

Did You Know That?

After Liverpool were crowned World Champions in December 2019, Paul was asked by the *Independent* about the time he won the FIFA Club World Cup with Manchester United in 2008. Scholesy's reply was pure genius and he just couldn't resist having a little jibe at United's fiercest rivals.

"Even now if someone said to you 'What trophies did you win over the years?' I don't think we'd mention the World Club Championship. I really don't. I'm not joking, I'm serious! But you know what, it's like anything else, it might take more importance over the years. It looks like Liverpool have enjoyed it, they've celebrated it and probably will mention it and why not – but just when we were playing it wasn't that serious I don't think. But now you look back I suppose you're quite happy but it's not something you set out to do as a player I don't think," said Paul. Then when he was asked which meant more to him – FIFA Club World Cup success or winning a trophy at his local badminton club, Scholes replied: "My badminton trophy!"

GAME NO. 25
RSC ANDERLECHT 0-2 UNITED
EUROPEAN CUP, PRELIMINARY ROUND, FIRST LEG
STADE EMILE VERSE, BRUSSELS
12 SEPTEMBER 1956
ATTENDANCE – 35,000

PIONEERS OF EUROPEAN FOOTBALL

On 12 September 1956, Manchester United did something no other English football club had ever done before: they played a competitive European game and thereby pioneered the way into European football club competition for all English clubs. The United manager, Matt Busby, built his young side, the famous Busby Babes, around a European odyssey when Manchester United accepted an invitation from the French football magazine, *L'Equipe* to participate in the 1956–57 European Champions Cup competition.

The European Cup was only in its second year and the First

Division Champions in season 1954-55, Chelsea, had been ordered by the Football League not to enter the inaugural tournament in 1955-56. The English game's hierarchy regarded the tournament as a distraction to domestic football, with some members of their Executive Board even referring to it as a "Gimmick" and a "Football Circus" but in Busby, Manchester United had a manager who was not a man to listen to orders barked at him from anyone. Busby served in the army during World War II. He joined the Kings Regiment and then became a football coach in the Army Physical Training Corp. It was Busby who was used to giving orders, not taking them, and he defied the Football League by playing his young Manchester United side in the competition. Busby had the full backing of his Chairman, Harold Hardman, and the club's Board of Directors. A good run in the competition would also generate additional funds which would help fund the cost of floodlights being installed at Old Trafford.

United were the dominant force in England during the 1950s having won the First Division title in 1951-52 and 1955-56 (they also went on to win it in 1956-57 and ended runners-up in 1958-59) as well as finishing runners-up in 1950-51 added to the latter Busby's right hand man, Jimmy Murphy, was developing a youth system at Old Trafford that was capable of winning the first four FA Youth Cup finals in 1953, 1954, 1955 and 1956 (they also went on to win it in 1957). Busby knew that he had to pit his young players against the best Europe had to offer if he was to make United a household name in world football. In many ways Busby and Ferguson were quite similar in that they both knew the importance of a successful youth team but more importantly they did what they felt was right for the club regardless of what others thought or dared to tell them to do.

United were drawn against the Champions of Belgium, RSC Anderlecht, and two days before the 1st leg away to Anderlecht, Busby flew to Brussels to spy on them. However he only got to see them play the last 20 minutes of their 5-1 home win over Antwerp as a result of a delayed flight. The Belgian side were in excellent form and hadn't been beaten in nine months and had recently enjoyed a win over Arsenal in a friendly.

The team that made history that evening lined-up as follows: Ray Wood, Bill Foulkes, Roger Byrne (captain), Eddie Colman, Mark Jones, Jackie Blanchflower, Johnny Berry, Liam Whelan, David Pegg, Dennis Viollet, Tommy Taylor. Duncan Edwards had to withdraw from the game the day before it with a toe injury meaning Blanchflower took his place.

United won the tie 2-0 (scorers: Dennis Viollet and Tommy Taylor) at Stade Émile Versé. In truth, while they had reigned supreme in Belgium, the home team were no match for United as the visitors dominated throughout, going ahead in the 25th minute from a Viollet 25 yarder. An improved second half saw Anderlecht awarded a penalty but Martin Lippens' effort struck a post. A cross from David Pegg was headed home by Tommy Taylor late on to secure a 2-0 win in Brussels.

A fortnight later United recorded their biggest ever European win (it is also a record club victory in all competitions) in the return leg at Maine Road, 10-0 (scorers: Viollet 4, Taylor 3, Whelan 2 and Berry). Jeff Mermans, the captain of RSC Anderlecht and capped 57 times by Belgium, was impressed with United saying: "I've never played against a team so adept at the best continental style of football. We have nothing to be ashamed of in being beaten by such a team. They should pick this whole team for England." Well not quite as Billy Whelan was a Republic of Ireland international.

At the time Old Trafford was still without floodlights and as all European Cup games were played on a Wednesday night, United had to rent Manchester City's ground Maine Road to play their home ties in the competition. United reached the semi-finals of the competition at their first attempt, losing 5-3 on aggregate to the inaugural winners and defending champions, Real Madrid. United lost the first leg 3-1 in Estadio Santiago Bernabeu on 11 April 1957 and drew the home leg two weeks later 2-2 this time at Old Trafford, now resplendent with floodlights.

The participating clubs in the first five seasons of the European Cup were selected by French football magazine *L'Equipe* on the basis that they were among the top rated and most prestigious clubs in Europe at the time. Chelsea, the English Champions, were replaced by Gwardia Warszawa from Poland. This was also the only UEFA tournament to include a representative of Saarland, 1. FC Saarbrücken, unified into West Germany in 1957.

But it was in Brussels that United's European odyssey began on 12 September 1956, setting in motion a long, painful and often tragic road that would 12 years later see his third great side do what his Busby Babes would surely have done – win the European Cup.

Did You Know That?

Hibernian Football Club were the first British club to compete in the European Cup. The Champions of Scotland in season 1954–55 were managed by Hugh Shaw and duly accepted *L'Equipe*'s invitation to test their players against the best club sides in Europe. The Scottish Football League's Executive Board were not as staid as their English counterparts and anxious to see how one of their clubs would fare on the continent.

In Round 1 Hibs beat Rot-Weiss Essen from West Germany 4–0 away and drew the home leg 1–1. Round 2 was actually the quarter-final stages and in the first leg Hibs beat Djurgardens IF Fotboll 3–1 in the Swedish capital, Stockholm and won the return leg 1–0. The semi-final draw was kind to Hibs as they avoided the Italian Champions, AC Milan, and the Champions of Spain, Real Madrid but it proved a step too far for Shaw's side losing both legs, 2–0 away and 1–0 at home to the Champions of France, Stade de Reims. In a pulsating final the aristocrats from Spain defeated their flamboyant French opposition 4–3 at Parc des Princes.

GAME NO. 26
NEWCASTLE UNITED 0-1 UNITED
PREMIER LEAGUE
ST JAMES' PARK, NEWCASTLE
4 MARCH 1996
ATTENDANCE – 36,584

TEARS ON THE TYNE

In 1996 the sports documentary *When We Were Kings* was released. It is a film directed by Leon Gast about the famous "Rumble in the Jungle" Heavyweight bout between reigning World Champion George Foreman and the former champion Muhammad Ali. The fight was held in Zaire (now the Democratic Republic of the Congo) on 30 October 1974 and is infamous for Ali's "Rope-A-Dope" tactics in the fight where the former champ allowed Foreman to punch himself out before turning the tables in the eighth round with a stunning counter-attack to win and the 1995-96 season saw a similar turnaround take place.

On 4 March 1996 Manchester United travelled to St James' Park to face Newcastle United in a crunch Premier League encounter. In the minds of all football fans this was the title decider. Whichever team left the pitch victorious would almost certainly win the 1995-96 Premier League title while a draw for the home side would unquestionably mean they would go on to win their first League Championship in 71 years. Newcastle United had last been crowned Champions of England in 1926-27 (Manchester United finished 15th) but under the management of Kevin Keegan Newcastle had been promoted back to the top flight in 1992-93 and never looked back. Keegan had played for the club from 1982-84 and in his final season as a player, 1983-84, he scored 27 times in 41 League games to help them to third place in the Second Division and automatic qualification into the top flight of the English game. He was a cult hero on Tyneside and his team played fast, attacking, Devil-May-Care football and, having finished third in their first season back in the top flight they consolidated in 1994-95 finishing sixth.

Manchester United's season had started poorly and questions were raised after Alex Ferguson sold Mark Hughes, Paul Ince and Andrei Kanchelskis during the summer with no replacements being brought in. Eric Cantona, banned following his kung-fu lunge into the Selhurst Park crowd, was not eligible to play until October 1995 and without him United were knocked out of both the League Cup and UEFA Cup and even after the French talisman returned to the team form was patchy enabling Newcastle to build up a sizeable lead at the top of the table.

By the time United arrived in the North East for the vital game Newcastle were riding high at the top of the Premier League, four points clear of second placed United. They had led by 10 points at Christmas but United beat the Magpies 2-0 on 27 December to keep their title hopes alive and soon Cantona, Keane and Schmeichel had the young lads around them in title winning form. As recently as 20 January Newcastle had been 12 points clear at the top and Keegan's side were bookies' clear favourites to bring the Premier League Championship to Tyneside whilst United could only hope they slipped up. At home The Magpies were clinical and hadn't lost a Premier League game all season. The Newcastle United Chairman Sir John Hall bankrolled Keegan's assault on the Premier League summit and in the summer of 1995 they added England striker Les Ferdinand from Queens Park Rangers, French international winger David Ginola from Paris Saint-Germain, defender Warren Barton from Wimbledon and Shaka Hislop from Reading to their squad for a combined total outlay of £16 million. In February 1996 Keegan persuaded England midfielder David Batty to leave reigning Premier League Champions Blackburn Rovers and Colombia's Faustino Asprilla was purchased from Série A club Parma. The latter two cost a total of £11 million and the media dubbed the team "The Entertainers."

Keegan had one of the best players in the Premier League at his disposal, the impish but hugely influential England midfielder Peter Beardsley, who Keegan had played alongside during his final season at Newcastle United. Beardsley conducted Keegan's attack and along with Ginola he created numerous goal scoring opportunities for the prolific Ferdinand who scored 25 goals league goals. In Asprilla Keegan had acquired a player who was often moody and temperamental but oozed quality. Although he wasn't an out and out goal scorer, the Colombian could play on the wing, in midfield or up front. He was lightning quick, extremely agile, almost rubber-like as he twisted his body around defenders, very powerful, creative, skilful and he scored some spectacular goals which he celebrated with his trademark somersault followed by a double fist pump.

Alex Ferguson's team that day read: Manchester United: Peter Schmeichel, Gary Neville, Denis Irwin, Steve Bruce, Phil Neville, Lee Sharpe, Nicky Butt, Roy Keane, Ryan Giggs, Eric Cantona, Andy Cole. Substitutes: David May, Paul Scholes, David Beckham.

Unlike the corresponding fixture the previous season, former United junior Keith Gillespie was allowed to play for the home side and Andy Cole, a cult hero during his time on Tyneside (68 goals in 84 games, 1992-95), could turn out in the red of United. When the game commenced the atmosphere inside the ground was at fever pitch. With the exception of a pocket of red high up in the stands, the crowd resembled a zebra crossing which wrapped its way around all four sides of St James' Park. It was a sea of black and white. And with Batty and Rob Lee entrenched in a feisty midfield battle with United's Nicky Butt and Roy Keane, it wasn't long before the mercury in the game began to rise.

Newcastle made a superb start, as Les Ferdinand fired shot after shot at Peter Schmeichel but United's Great Dane produced save after save to thwart the England striker. The Geordie's strike force had been lethal all season with Ferdinand and now Asprilla being supplied with goal scoring opportunities by Ginola and Beardsley but United had a player who matched all of them, Eric Cantona. King Eric had not scored in United's three previous games but *Cometh The Hour, Cometh The Player.* After a first half spent largely on the back foot, just like Muhammad Ali United knew when to time the counterattack and in the 51st minute The Reds made a rare foray into their opponents' half. Keane won the ball off David Batty and found Phil Neville who quickly found Cole. The striker beat two defenders with superb shimmies and gave the ball back to Phil Neville who floated a high ball into the penalty area which landed on the right foot of the enigmatic and talismanic French genius, Cantona, who struck it first time. The Frenchman fired his volley into the turf and it bounced upwards and past Pavel Srnicek in the Newcastle United goal. As Eric wheeled away in delight, the United fans celebrated. In stark contrast the home fans screeched with disbelief. A feeling of doom quickly descended on the black and white striped fans. United held on to win to reduce their opponents lead at the top to a single point. Just like Ali the experienced campaigner had done a number on the man acknowledged as a knock-out specialist. The Premier League title race seemed wide open with 9 games left and although the Geordies' had a game in hand the psychological blow of losing such a huge game proved crucial.

The *Newcastle Evening Chronicle* summed up how the Toon Army felt after losing such a crucial game. *"The silence was deafening as thousands of Geordies left their field of dreams with hunched shoulders and nostrils heavy with the scent of defeat. A Premier League lead, once 12 points with a game in hand, is now down to a solitary point and the funeral parade outside of St. James's Park reflected the mood of an area. There was no violence, no clenched fist defiance. This is what TV didn't see – proud Geordies, once used to disappointment but elevated to new ground in the last four years, retaining their dignity. Oh, all is not lost. Newcastle are still top, 30 points are left to play for, and hope beats eternal in a Geordie breast within hours of a setback. But Manchester United are on a roll – so are Liverpool for that matter – and it is now about stout hearts. Newcastle United are right, of course, to point out that they are still league leaders. Still genuine championship contenders. What we need now is for that belief to come pouring through in the 10 cup finals left to play."*

United went on to win 7, draw 1 and lose 1 of their remaining 9 Premiership games with Cantona proving the catalyst in these games which gave United their third Premier League crown in four seasons, finishing the campaign four points clear of Keegan's despondent men who won 5, drew 2 and lost 3 over the same period.

After silencing the Toon Army, Eric Cantona scored United's injury-time equaliser in a 1-1 draw at Queens Park Rangers, scored the only goal of the game in 1-0 wins at Old Trafford over Arsenal, Tottenham Hotspur and Coventry City with Peter Schmeichel in unbeatable form. He also scored in United's 3-2 away win over Manchester City and in the 5-0 thrashing of Nottingham Forest at Old Trafford. The night after the Forest game Newcastle United beat Leeds United 1-0 at Elland Road. When Keegan was interviewed after his team's win it was evident that he had cracked up under the pressure piled on to him and his team by Alex Ferguson and his resurgent United side. The Sky Sports TV cameras screened Keegan's infamous: "*I'd love it if we beat them. Really love it,*" rant. United's only defeat during this run was a 3-1 reversal away to Southampton.

When United beat Liverpool 1-0 in the FA Cup final on 11 May 1996, United claimed their second Double in three seasons. The scorer? Who else but King Eric in the 86th minute of the game.

> *"Genius is about digging yourself out of the hole in which you sometimes find yourself."*

Eric Cantona, 1994

How profound these words became after Eric was handed an 8 month ban following his sending off versus Crystal Palace away in the Premier League on 25 January 1995.

Did You Know That?

Peter Beardsley played one game for Manchester United. On 9 September 1982 United paid Vancouver Whitecaps a £250,000 loan fee for the former Carlisle United player. Ron Atkinson was never known for being frugal with the United cheque book, splashing the cash at will when he felt his side needed freshening up, but he just wasn't ready to fully commit to buying a player who had spent the previous three seasons playing for Carlisle United in the Third Division. On 6 October 1982 he made his United debut in a 2-0 win over Bournemouth in a Round 2, First Leg League Cup tie. Harry Redknapp, the future West Ham United and Tottenham Hotspur manager, scored an own goal with Frank Stapleton scoring United's second goal. During the game Beardsley was replaced by Norman Whiteside. On 1 February 1983 Beardsley returned to the Canadian club with United getting their money back but within a year he was linking up with Keegan and helping Newcastle to promotion and by the end of the decade he was part of a dominant Liverpool team and was capped 59 times for England, scoring 9 goals.

GAME NO. 27
BOLTON WANDERERS 1-1 UNITED
BURNDEN PARK
FIRST DIVISION
1 OCTOBER 1960
ATTENDANCE – 39,197

POETRY IN MOTION

This match was a re-run of the 1958 FA Cup final which had seen United's patched up team defy the odds to reach Wembley following the Munich Air Disaster, the Trotters prevented a fairytale ending to United's season in 1957-58 by defeating United 2-0 at Wembley.

United had got off to a disappointing start to the 1960-61 season winning 2, drawing 1 and losing 6 of their first 9 League games and the seventh place finish they had managed in the previous campaign seemed highly unlikely. Matt Busby, who was still suffering both mentally and physically from the after-effects of the crash, had set about building a third great Manchester United team following the 1948 Cup winners and the Busby Babes but it was proving far harder than first thought and some pundits felt that it was a step too far for the United manager. The club's first season after Munich was remarkable as a team packed with juniors, makeshift signings and the survivors of the disaster finished an incredible second to Wolves but it proved to be a mirage. 1959-60 had revealed defensive frailties as despite scoring 102 goals (Dennis Viollet scoring 32 league goals to set a club record that still stands) they conceded 80 including 7 at Newcastle and 5 at Arsenal and Spurs and things hadn't improved in the new season.

In their previous nine games the opposition had continued to score with ease, United had leaked 21 goals as opponents overran a weak United midfield. Busby had handed half-back Frank Haydock his debut for the opening game of the season alongside tough-tackling Maurice Setters but United won only one (a 4-0 home win over Everton) of their first five games losing the rest. Another junior, Belfast-born Jimmy Nicholson, was tried alongside Setters with slightly more success as United drew a home game with Leicester before hammering West Ham 6-1 at Old Trafford but successive 3-1 defeats at home to Aston Villa and at Wolves left Busby scratching his head. So before the trip to Burnden Park Matt talked to his right hand man Jimmy Murphy who suggested a young half-back in the junior ranks. So that October morning Norbert Peter Stiles was included in the first team squad.

Murphy had overseen Stiles' development at the club as he worked his way through the youth and reserve teams and told Busby that young Norbert was ready to make his senior bow. Born in Collyhurst, North Manchester on 18 May 1942, Nobby had signed for United as an apprentice in September 1957 and was the latest product of United's junior team having graduated from local primary school and church teams, Nobby had attended Saint Patrick's Primary School in the 'Red or Dead' area of North Manchester.

If ever there was a footballer who never really looked liked a footballer, someone who you would look up and down at and then say to yourself: "He's no chance of making a career in the game" then Stiles was it. No doubt many sports writers thought the same when they saw Paul Scholes make his Manchester United debut and Stiles, like the diminutive Scholes, made them eat their words. Nobby stood just 5 foot 6 inches tall and weighed 10 stones, 12 pounds wet through! In boxing terms he was a light middleweight but he could handle a striker like Muhammad Ali could handle a right hook. However not only was Nobby small for the role of midfield enforcer, he was as blind as a bat without his thick-rimmed, milk bottle glasses. His career took a definite upturn when he was fitted for contact lenses. All of a sudden he could see his opponents!

As a junior Nobby was living his boyhood dream and when he turned up for training every day he stood in awe; eyes agog, knees trembling as players he admired and hoped one day he would play alongside, breezed past him on their way to the changing room as Nobby made his way to the reserves for training. As an apprentice Nobby had been delighted to end his day cleaning the boots of United captain Roger Byrne, Tommy Taylor and the player United fans, regardless of their generation, consider to be the club's greatest ever, Duncan Edwards but alas Nobby never got the opportunity to play in the same team as these United Legends.

Then, in June 1959, 17-year old Stiles signed as a professional for the club and it soon became clear that what Nobby lacked in height and weight he made up for in energy and courage. If he had been a figure from the Holy Bible, Nobby would have been David but whereas David had to rely on his stone catapult to bring down Goliath, Nobby relied on his perfect timing to win the ball back from his opponent. Mind you, along the way he did totally wipe out the odd opposing midfielder or two. He was not someone you took lightly because if you did there wasn't a magic wet sponge in the world which would help you carry on playing in the game after it.

So, when Nobby sat in the away dressing room at Burnden Park, his heart was pumping twice as quickly as usual but the increased pulse was nothing to do with nerves, it was all down to the pride the 18-year old Manchester boy had in his heart when he pulled on the famous football jersey for the first time in his Old Trafford career.

The United team lined up: Harry Gregg, Maurice Setters (Capt), Shay Brennan, Nobby Stiles, Bill Foulkes, Jimmy Nicholson, Ian Moir, Johnny Giles, Alex Dawson, Bobby Charlton, Albert Scanlon.

Nobby made an impressive debut in the heart of the United midfield and showed a composure on the ball which belied his age and his lack of experience playing against professionals. He was, as Johnny Tilotson sang in his 1960 no.1 hit, "Poetry In Motion". United went away with a 1-1 draw, Nobby setting up Johnny Giles for United's equaliser in the 75th minute. Munich survivors Harry Gregg, Bill Foulkes and Bobby Charlton also played in the game while Wanderers were managed by Bill Ridding who had played for United from 1931-34, making 44 appearances and scoring 14 goals. Yet it is a game best remembered for the professional debut of the diminutive Stiles who eased seamlessly into the heart of the United midfield and gave Busby's team the steel they had previously lacked. The debutant's play was natural, measured and assured. The thought of a long-term contract was the furthest thing from his mind, Nobby was an 18-year who just wanted to play football for his boyhood club.

Stiles debut impressed the most important person, manager Matt Busby as he played in United's next 7 League games and by the end of the season he had played 26 League games, 2 League Cup games and 3 FA Cup games and to round off a good season he scored his first and second goals for United with his maiden goal arriving in only his fourth appearance, a 3-2 victory over Newcastle United at Old Trafford on 22 October 1960. On 14 January 1961 Nobby scored in a 2-0 league win over Tottenham Hotspur (he opened the scoring in the 14th minute and Mark Pearson added a second in the 78th minute) against the team who went on to win the first league and cup double of the twentieth century at the end of the season. And while United's defence was still leaky (they conceded 76 league goals in 1960-61) the half-back position was no longer quite so problematic as other areas of the United rearguard came under greater scrutiny.

Nobby played in an era when goalkeepers and centre-forwards were regarded as "fair game" for bruising attackers and tank like centre-halfs and when the Rules of the Game may as well have been akin to the Rules which came on the box lid of the famous board game, Monopoly. If a roll of the dice lands you in jail then you lose your turn. Nobby was never a dirty player, but the odd tackle or ten from Nobby resulted in an opponent lying on the deck like he had been shot in the leg from a sniper in one of the stands. In contrast Nobby's fellow pros were lauded for their ability, or in some cases lack of it, to win a tackle. Cases in point being Ron Harris (Chelsea) who was given the nickname "Chopper" for obvious reasons and Leeds United's most feared centre-half, Norman "Bite Yer Legs" Hunter while Dave Mackay of Spurs was not a player to be messed around with. Just ask a very sheepish Billy Bremner, the Leeds United enforcer, and a player who enjoyed a midfield battle or several, when Mackay grabbed his shirt one day just below the throat and told Bremner what he thought about his tackle on him producing the now iconic image and of course there was always "The Anfield Iron" Tommy Smith who wasn't averse to sending that player to the nearest Casualty Unit. Nobby was aggressive in the tackle but he possessed no malice, he just wanted to win the ball back at all costs.

In season 1966-67 Nobby played in 37 of United's 42 First Division games and scored 3 goals and helped a very gifted team, which included the famous trio of Bobby Charlton, Denis Law and George Best, win their second League title in three seasons. If any player deserved to be named the Football Writers' Association Player of the Year then surely it was Stiles. Since Nobby had made the step up into the first team many notable players were recipients of this prestigious award: Danny Blanchflower (Tottenham Hotspur) 1961, Jimmy Adamson (Burnley) 1962, Stanley Matthews (Stoke City) 1963, Bobby Moore (West Ham United) 1964, Bobby Collins (Leeds United) 1965, Bobby Charlton (Manchester United) 1966 but in the end it was Nobby's 1966 World Cup winning teammate, Jack Charlton of Leeds United, who the football journalists selected as their outstanding player of the 1966-67 season. Charlton made 28 League appearances and scored 5 times as

Leeds United finished fourth.

Nobby was always destined to be overlooked for individual awards as he was not a flamboyant player, he just did what Busby asked of him and he did it meticulously and whilst the media never fully appreciated just how good a player Stiles was, his manager and his United and England teammates fully appreciated his worth to the team – namely he could stop the best from playing.

Nobby was a passionate England fan and was overwhelmed when Alf Ramsey handed him his international debut on 10 April 1965, aged 22 years and 327 days. He had already played five times for England Schoolboys in 1957 when he was playing for Manchester United Junior Athletic Club. England's opponents were Scotland and the game ended 2-2 with two of his United teammates scoring, Charlton for England and Law for his beloved Scotland. Nobby impressed Ramsey with his performance and in particular his confrontations with the player he played alongside with at United, the pass-master of the midfield Paddy Crerand. Nobby was cut from the same red cloth as Crerand, they were both fearless warriors when playing for their countries and they gave no quarter that day. As a result Nobby was one of the first players Ramsey selected for his 1966 World Cup final squad.

On 23 July 1966, England faced Argentina in the World Cup quarter-finals of the World Cup at Wembley. The South American side were the most skillful side in the tournament but were well known for their hard style of play which included late challenges, over the top tackles and off the ball scuffles. Few players looked forward to playing against them but Stiles relished the battle. Despite being one of the smallest players on the pitch he, along with Blackpool's Alan Ball, was outstanding. England won the game 1-0 with a Geoff Hurst header and it was the Argentinians who lost their rag as their captain António Ratin was sent off by the German referee in the 35th minute of the game after persistent fouling. Ratin and his teammates set out to be as disruptive as they could to stifle England and his histrionics after being dismissed meant that it took him 10 minutes to leave the field. Ramsey ran on to the pitch at the final whistle and physically stopped his players from exchanging shirts with their opponents who he later described as "Animals". Stiles, more than any other player, gave the Argentinians a taste of their own medicine and they didn't like it. But this wouldn't be the last time Nobby would tango with the Argentines.

In season 1968–69 United, as reigning European Cup holders, met Estudiantes de La Plata, the reigning South American champions, in a two-legged final of the Intercontinental Cup. The first leg was played in Buenos Aires on 25 September 1968. In the days leading up to the game Otto Gloria, the manager of Benfica who United had beaten in the 1968 European Cup final, gave an interview to the local press and described Nobby as an "Assassin". In the official match programme Gloria's interview was reproduced in full and he went on to say that "Stiles was brutal, badly intentioned and a bad sportsman." This was sour grapes indeed and in singling Nobby out it was tantamount to an incitement to assault him. Sure enough during the game Nobby was kicked, punched and head-butted but he refused to retaliate, instead he walked away from any potential trouble. Nobby could do nothing right in the eyes of the match officials with one linesman reporting him to the referee for standing too close to Carlos Bilardo yet it was Bilardo who was the most aggressive player on the pitch and constantly hacked down the United players but wasn't booked. Bobby Charlton received a head wound in the game which required stitches. Even the crowd attacked Nobby, booing and hissing every time he touched the ball. In the 79th minute Nobby's patience had been tested one time too many and he retaliated to a challenge and was instantly dismissed, he would miss the return leg. United lost the game 1–0 with a goal from Marcos Conigliaro in the 27th minute. Three weeks later United drew the home leg 1–1 meaning the South Americans returned home with the trophy following a 2–1 aggregate victory.

Nobby won 2 First Division Championship titles (1964–65 & 1966–67), 2 Charity Shields (both shared in 1965 & 1967) and the European Cup with United in 1967–68. Although Busby knew his value to his team, he sacrificed Nobby in favour of Maurice Setters for the 1963 FA Cup final when United beat Leicester City 3–1. Nobby played for his country 28 times (18 wins, 8 draws, 2 losses), and scored 1 goal. His goal came in what proved to be a dress rehearsal for the 1966 World Cup final, a 1–0 win against West Germany at Wembley on 23 February 1966. Stiles was given the No.9 jersey for the game but contrary to newspaper reports he did not play as a centre-forward, he occupied his usual midfield berth.

With England he won the British Home International Championship three times in seasons 1964-65, 1965-66 and 1969–70 but the greatest moment in his career came on 30 July 1966 when England defeated West Germany 4–2 after extra time in the World

Cup final. It was his 22nd game for his country and Nobby celebrated the victory by dancing a jig on the Wembley turf, the glistening gold Jules Rimet trophy in his left hand and his false teeth in his right. After travelling with England to Mexico in 1970 to defend their title as World Champions he wasn't used by Sir Alf Ramsey and was never selected to play for his country again.

In May 1971 Nobby left Old Trafford in a £20,000 move to Middlesbrough, he had played 397 times for United and scored 19 goals. On 20 November 1991, Nobby was given a huge surprise when he was presented with TV's most famous big red book when he was on the Old Trafford pitch receiving an award. Michael Aspel then interviewed Nobby on the popular ITV show *This Is Your Life*. In May 2016, he was honoured when a street was named after him in his hometown Collyhurst, Nobby Stiles Drive. Sadly Nobby passed away on 20 October 2020 after a battle with dementia, he was truly a United and England legend.

Did You Know That?

On 15 April 1967 England faced arch rivals Scotland in a British Home International Championship game which also served as a qualifying game for the 1968 European Championships. It was the first meeting between the old rivals since Bobby Moore lifted the World Cup. When the teams lined up in the tunnel before the game Bobby Charlton greeted his teammate Denis Law but Stiles refused to even acknowledge that Law was there and fixed his gaze on the sunlight at the end of the tunnel. This summed up Nobby. He didn't care who you were, there were no allegiances in his book; if you weren't wearing the same shirt, then you were fair game, you were the enemy. The Scots won the game 3-2 with Law scoring and after their victory Denis declared Scotland "the best team in the world, the new World Champions" – Nobby was not amused. Another future United player, Jim McCalliog, also played for Scotland and scored in the game.

GAME NO. 28
UNITED 2-1 SHEFFIELD WEDNESDAY
PREMIER LEAGUE
OLD TRAFFORD
10 APRIL 1993
ATTENDANCE- 40,102

FERGIE TIME

In season 1991-92 Manchester United had been neck and neck with Leeds throughout the season but fixture congestion and injuries saw them finish runners-up for the third time since the last time they had last won the First Division Championship with Matt Busby's legendary third great side in 1966-67 during the halcyon days of the magnificent triumvirate of Bobby Charlton, Denis Law and George Best.

For United fans the summer of 1992 was a time for reflection and many believed that they would never actually witness their team lift the league title, such was the angst surrounding the defeat at Anfield which saw Leeds win the last First Division title before the top flight turned into the Premier League.

Yet Alex Ferguson seemed as determined as ever and set out to put the record straight and never gave up on his dream of making Manchester United the Kings of English football once again. But after the opening two games United's dream had quickly become a nightmare, a 2-1 loss at Sheffield United on the opening day (scorer: Mark Hughes) was followed just four days later with a 3-0 defeat by Everton in the Premier League with Duncan Ferguson running amok – United were rock bottom of the Premier League in 22nd place and only won the third game of the season, at Southampton, thanks to a last minute winner from summer signing Dion Dublin. On 21 November 1992, United beat Oldham Athletic 3-0 at home with two goals from Brian McClair and another from Sparky Hughes and moved up to 8th, yet the team still seemed to be some way from emerging as challengers and sat 9 points behind surprise leaders Norwich City with Arsenal tucked in second just a point behind. United had already been dumped out of the League Cup and the UEFA Cup and Ferguson's grip on the Old Trafford throne was beginning to look shaky.

However that week saw one of the most momentous moments in the history of the club. United had been struggling without a regular goalscorer following an abandoned pursuit of Sheffield Wednesday's David Hirst and the crisis reached crisis point following the loss of Dion Dublin for the rest of the season with a broken leg. Eric Cantona had been a pivotal signing for Leeds during the run-in the previous season and when Martin Edwards (at Ferguson's urging) asked Leeds Managing Director Bill Fotherby about the possibility of signing the Frenchman there was surprise when the request wasn't immediately laughed out of court. The deal of the century was on! What Edwards and Ferguson didn't know was the extent to which Eric had fallen out with authoritarian Leeds boss Howard Wilkinson. Within days they had agreed a £1.2 million deal to bring the Frenchman to Old Trafford.

The signing was pivotal, by the turn of the year United had slipped well into top gear and after defeating Coventry City 5-0 at Old Trafford on 28 December 1992 they eased to the top of the table. After beating Liverpool 2-1 at Anfield on 6 March 1993, United topped the Premier League table ahead of Aston Villa, and a chasing Norwich City side. With 11 games remaining United fans lived in hope that the team could put the disappointment of the previous season behind them. Alex Ferguson was, more than anyone, anxious to remove that albatross from his shoulders which Busby's predecessors had found impossible to shift – Wilf McGuinness (1969-70), Frank O'Farrell (1971-72), Tommy Docherty (1972-77), Dave Sexton (1977-81) and Ron Atkinson (1981-86) had all followed in the footsteps of the great man but none of them had been able to step out of the huge shadow the Father of Manchester United had cast over Old Trafford during his 26 years in charge. In the previous 25 seasons, apart from season 1991-92, the closest United came to pinning a Champions' flag on the summit of the English game was a runners-up place under Sexton in season 1979-80 whilst Ferguson had also guided United to a distant runners-up finish in 1987-88.

So could season 1992-93 finally be the season to lay this particular ghost to rest or would United once again be dubbed "Pretenders to the Crown"? The League Championship had become United's Holy Grail, the supporters' obsession.

After the win over Liverpool, United's next four Premiership games didn't go to plan and after losing 1-0 away to Oldham Athletic they had three draws in a row; a 1-1 draw at home with title rivals Aston Villa managed by former boss Ron Atkinson, a 1-1 draw away to Manchester City and a 0-0 draw with Arsenal at Old Trafford.

Ferguson's side looked far from being a Championship winning side. They had slipped to third in the table behind leaders Villa and Norwich City who they had to play next. United's season was on the verge of being derailed when they visited Carrow Road on 5th March 1993 for a Sky Monday Night Football game. The Canaries, managed by Mike Walker, had been the surprise team of the season and had a lethal strike force comprising Efan Ekoku, Chris Sutton and former Red Mark Robins. United had struggled for results at Carrow Road for years and many expected a home win but on that windy night in East Anglia United rose to the occasion and played some beautiful attacking football which put them 3-0 up after just 21 minutes with goals from Giggs, Andrei Kanchelskis and the mercurial Cantona. The home side could not cope with the accuracy of United's pin-point passing despite the blustery conditions and the speed of Giggs and the flying Russian, Kanchelskis, on the wings. United won the game 3-1 and leapfrogged Norwich City into second place but a point behind Villa. Next up United faced Sheffield Wednesday on Easter Saturday 10 April 1993, the sixth last Premier League game of the campaign. The United side which took to the Old Trafford pitch to play Sheffield Wednesday that sunny afternoon was: Peter Schmeichel, Paul Parker, Denis Irwin, Steve Bruce (Capt), Gary Pallister, Paul Ince, Lee Sharpe, Ryan Giggs, Brian McClair, Mark Hughes, Eric Cantona – substitute: Bryan Robson (for Parker 68 mins).

With the Stretford End still being rebuilt the attendance was limited to 40,102 but was nevertheless United's biggest all season. Wednesday were a decent side who had finished third the previous season. They were managed by Trevor Francis who had been an exquisite player who in 1979 became Britain's first £1 million player when he moved from Birmingham City to Nottingham Forest. They were in superb form having only lost twice in their previous 25 games and they had quality throughout their team; England's No.1 goalkeeper, Chris Woods, Roland Nilsson, John Sheridan, Chris Waddle, Mark Bright and United old boy Viv Anderson. Two seasons earlier they had beaten United 1-0 in the League Cup final at Wembley Stadium thanks to a penalty scored by Stretford lad John Sheridan.

Meaning to repeat the start of the Norwich game, United threw everything at The Owls' defence in the first half but the Yorkshire side stood firm but after seeing an hour's worth of United attacks come to nothing Wednesday grew in confidence and it came as little shock to the pessimists in United's support when Paul Ince brought down Chris Waddle in the box and the ref immediately pointed to the spot. Sheridan coolly converted from the spot and United seemed to be repeating the mistakes of the previous season's title run-in.

Fans sat with their head in their hands, others could be seen lighting a consolation cigarette and some seemed close to tears. Throughout Fergie stood in his technical area without a flicker of emotion in his face but deep down he must have feared the worst. What did his team have to do to win the title?

United responded with wave after wave of attacks but Wednesday manned the barricades and repelled the Reds time after time. It was a totally different game to the previous meeting that season, a 3-3 draw at Hillsborough, when United scored a couple of late McClair goals to rescue a point. Now, as time ticked by, it looked more and more like United would not breach the Yorkshire wall and hopes of ending a 26 year wait to call their team "Kings of England," would fizzle out before their very eyes. The late afternoon sun was not the only thing casting a shadow over Old Trafford.

People were checking transistor radios for the score at Villa Park where United's main title rivals faced Tottenham. It was still 0-0 there when, with 22 minutes of the game remaining, Fergie sent on Bryan Robson for Paul Parker for what was only Captain Marvel's ninth game of the season. United continued to push and in the 86th minute Robbo won United a corner and a shot from Hughes was saved by Woods but went behind for another corner. Up went Daisy and Dolly (Fergie's nicknames for centre-halfs Steve Bruce and Gary Pallister) more in hope of being able to win the ball in the air and set up a chance for a team-mate rather than score themselves but Bruce was a goal threat, only two seasons earlier he had bagged 19 goals and had been United's joint top goal scorer in the First Division along with McClair on 13 goals. Mind you, Bruce was United' penalty taker that season and had successfully converted 12 from the spot. Going into the game against Wednesday he had scored twice during the season (Cantona was United's new Penalty King) whilst Pallister was still waiting on his first goal of the campaign to arrive. Giggs swept the ball into the box and Bruce met it on the right hand corner of the area and his bullet like header fired into the net over the hands of Chris Woods – 1-1 and game on. When the ball hit the back of the net the cacophony of noise which erupted inside Old Trafford must have reverberated all the way to Birmingham and back. Could United somehow complete the comeback?

Not satisfied with a point United continued to push for a winner. The full-time whistle had already blown at Villa Park on a goalless draw as the afternoon's second referee (the first had been stretchered off hence the extra added time) played 6 minutes extra.

Then: a weaving run on the left and cross into the box by Giggs was almost turned into his own net by Anderson but went behind. Another corner. Chris Waddle was asking the referee how much longer there was to play when Giggs took it. It was met by Bruce and his skewered header arrived back with Giggs, United's wonder kid then hit a cross which went over everyone's head and was retrieved by Pallister on the right wing. Crossing a ball accurately into the penalty box was not exactly part of Gary's repertoire or among his skills base and his cross was headed back across goal by a defender but Steve Bruce latched on to it and headed his second goal of a dramatic encounter to send United top of the league!

There was delirium in the stands. The United fans went berserk with delight. Immediately Alex Ferguson ran from his seat on the bench to the touch line and raised his clenched fists aloft in sheer relief more than delight. Brian Kidd, his assistant, went one step further and ran on to the pitch and dropped to his knees with his arms in the air waving frantically in celebration of seeing the miracle which had just unfolded before his very eyes. It was Biblical and United, like Lazarus, had come back from the dead.

The Wednesday fans were gutted. With only five minutes of the game to play it had looked like their team would claim a famous scalp yet their defence had imploded conceding two late goals and both from headers following a set piece. And spare a thought for Villa fans getting into cars as they left their game thinking they had stayed top of the league – the seismic effect of the two late goals shifted momentum squarely in United's favour and the legend of 'Fergie Time' was born with the nation united in the (misguided) belief that the substitute referee had added on too much injury time.

It proved to be the turning point in the title as United won their five remaining games and were crowned Champions. Fittingly it was Captain Marvel and Captain Courageous, Robson and Bruce, who together lifted the inaugural Premier League trophy high into the Manchester air after United beat Blackburn Rovers 3-1 at Old Trafford on 3 May 1993 and Gary Pallister finally got his first goal of the season meaning all of United's outfield players had scored in the

Premier League during their title winning campaign.

Did You Know That?

In season 1974–75, United won the English Second Division Championship with Aston Villa finishing runners–up and Norwich City third. In the inaugural Premier League season, 1992–93, the three teams occupied the same places in the table.

GAME NO. 29
UNITED 4-0 BLACKPOOL
SECOND DIVISION
OLD TRAFFORD
26 APRIL 1975
ATTENDANCE- 58,769

BACK UP WHERE WE BELONG

In season 1974–75 United found themselves in the Second Division, their first season in the second tier since season 1937–38 when they finished runners–up and won promotion back into the top flight. You could be forgiven for thinking that supporters would be despondent, after all the glamourous away trips to Anfield, Highbury, Elland Road, Goodison Park, Maine Road, St James' Park, Stamford Bridge or White Hart Lane would be replaced by visits to Bloomfield Road (Blackpool), Eastville Stadium (Bristol Rovers), Boothferry Park (Hull City), and the Manor Ground (Oxford United).

Yet this tour of the Second Division would revitalise a club that had been in the doldrums ever since the 1968 European Cup triumph which effectively marked the end of Sir Matt Busby's reign and the drawn out saga of George Best's retirement. Now the United support would find new heroes to follow and their pied piper was The Doc, wise–cracking Glaswegian Tommy Docherty.

The Board of Directors at Old Trafford have to take credit for not sacking Docherty when United were relegated. A few days after United's fate was sealed The Doc was summoned to Matt Busby's office and he expected the boot. Instead Sir Matt offered him a case of champagne and the board stood by him. It was Docherty's chance of redemption and he took it with both hands to fashion a team in Sir Matt's image based on quick passing and direct wing play.

One of The Doc's signings in the summer of '74 was Stuart

'Pancho' Pearson from Hull City for £200,000 with Paul Fletcher, a Reserve Team player at United, going the other way as a make-weight. It proved to be an inspired signing. The 24-year old had played for The Tigers from 1968-74 and had scored 44 goals in 129 League games, all in the Second Division. It looked like a modest return but then Hull City were a modest team. He had been the club's top league goal scorer in seasons 1971-72 (15 goals) and 1972-73 (17 goals). More importantly Pearson was a player accustomed to the hustle and bustle of a 42 game campaign in the Second Division.

On the opening day of the 1974-75 season United travelled to East London to play Leyton Orient at Brisbane Road. The Three Degrees had just gone to No.1 that very same day in the UK Singles Charts with their song "When Will I See You Again" and many United fans who made the four hour coach trip to the game must have been thinking when they were going to see the glamour venues of English football again because Brisbane Road was a humble ground with uncovered terraces and a modest main stand accustomed to modest crowds. Yet approaching the ground, the players quickly saw something strange was happening, the area was completely mobbed by United fans from all over the country, they had three-quarters of the ground inside and thousands were locked out. It was a trend that would continue for the rest of the season.

United won the game 2-0 with goals from Willie Morgan and Stewart Houston. After the opening day victory United won their next three League games beating Millwall 4-0 (including Pancho's first goal for United) and Portsmouth 2-1 at Old Trafford before a 1-0 win at Ninian Park, Cardiff on 31 August. United were top of the table and were never displaced from topping the Division thereafter.

By mid-season United's support had grown in notoriety to the extent that questions were asked in the House of Commons and all the club's away games were made all-ticket with police forces up and down the land stopping coaches from arriving wherever the club were playing. The grounds at away every game seemed to be dominated by the Red Army and the club seemed to be attracting the kind of hysteria associated with pop acts such as The Bay City Rollers or Mark Bolan.

On 5 April 1975 the table topping Reds visited The Dell to play Southampton in their 39th League game of the season. Lou Macari scored the only goal of the game and secured promotion back into the top flight. The Doc had repaid the trust Louis Edwards and Matt Busby had placed in him. United then beat Fulham 1-0 at Old Trafford with Gerry Daly scoring his 11th League goal of the campaign and a 2-2 draw at Notts County clinched the Second Division Championship title. Houston and Greenhoff were the goal scorers who sent the travelling Red Army away from Meadow Lane in celebratory mood.

After 6 years in the doldrums the buzz around the club was back: The Doc's attacking brand of football, the huge following, the intensity of the crowds who would sing throughout the game and the emergence of star players such as Coppell, Pearson, rugged centre-half Jim Holton and Lou Macari was a seductive recipe for a new generation of fans. The average home attendance for United games in season 1974-75 was 48,388, a figure higher than any club in the country.

On 26 April 1975 Derby County ran out at their Baseball Ground for their last game of the season having already been crowned First Division Champions before a crowd of 36,882 fans who witnessed them lift the First Division trophy following a 0-0 draw versus Carlisle United. That same day Docherty sent his Champions out at Old Trafford to face Blackpool in the last game of the season, and regardless of the result against The Seasiders, Martin Buchan would be holding aloft the Second Division Championship trophy before 58,769 fans.

Docherty's selection for the game was: Alex Stepney, Alex Forsyth, Stewart Houston, Steve James, Martin Buchan (Capt), Brian Greenhoff, Sammy McIlroy, Gerry Daly, Steve Coppell, Lou Macari, Stuart Pearson

United entertained the masses, some of whom even managed to climb onto the main stand roof, with an emphatic 4-0 victory with two goals from Pearson (who finished the season as United's leading goal scorer in the League with 17), Macari and Brian Greenhoff. The loudspeakers inside Old Trafford belted out the No.1 song at the time *Bye Bye Baby* by The Bay City Rollers, it seemed appropriate given the youth of United's following as the club waved goodbye to Second Division football for good.

Did You Know That?

Manchester United's Second Division Championship winning squad included 8 Scottish players from a pool of 24: Arthur Albiston, Martin Buchan (Capt), Alex Forsyth, Jim Holton, Stewart Houston, Lou Macari, Jim McCalliog and Willie Morgan.

GAME NO. 30
EVERTON 0-1 UNITED
1985 FA CUP FINAL
WEMBLEY STADIUM
18 MAY 1985
ATTENDANCE- 100,000

BIG NORM STRIKES AGAIN

In season 1984-85, Manchester United went into battle with Everton on four occasions. Once again the best club side in English football came from Merseyside but this time they were wearing blue and not red. Liverpool had been champions for the previous three seasons and had also lifted the European Cup for the fourth time in their history in season 1983-84. Over the previous three seasons Everton, nicknamed The Toffees, had finished 8th, 7th and 7th in the First Division but won the FA Cup in 1984 defeating Watford 2-0 in the final. It was their first trophy success in 14 years and the Toffees began their 1984-85 campaign by beating rivals Liverpool 1-0 in the Charity Shield.

United's record over the same three seasons was better than Everton's: finishing 3rd, 3rd and 4th in the League and winning the FA Cup in 1983 after beating Brighton and Hove Albion 4-0 in a replay of the final after their first game ended 2-2.

Over the summer of 1984 Everton manager Howard Kendall added Paul Bracewell from Sunderland for £425,000, Pat Van Den Hauwe from Birmingham City for £100,000, Ian Atkins from Sunderland for £100,000 and Paul Wilkinson for £250,000 from Grimsby Town in March 1985. Kendall already had an excellent band of players at his disposal who had yet to fulfil their unquestionable talent including goalkeeper Neville Southall, right back Gary Stevens, a rock solid centre-half partnership of Derek Mountfield and captain Kevin Ratcliffe, a choice of midfielders who would get into any side in Kevin Richardson, Trevor Steven, the tigerish Peter Reid and the extremely classy Republic of Ireland international Kevin Sheedy. Up front he had three strikers who were proven goal scorers in Adrian Heath, Graeme Sharp and Andy Gray.

Ron Atkinson, the United manager, was not shy in spending money either and once again at the end of a season he freshened up his options. Ray Wilkins had left the club in May 1984 in a £1.5

million move to AC Milan and fan favourite, Lou "Skip To My Lou" Macari joined Swindon Town in a free transfer in July 1984. Scott McGarvey was sold to Portsmouth for £85,000 in July 1984 and Peter Barnes' loan spell from Leeds United was due to end in October 1984. Big Ron wasted no time in replacing those who had left and in June 1984 he signed Alan Brazil from Tottenham Hotspur for £625,000 and Jesper Olsen from Ajax Amsterdam for £350,000 and Gordon Strachan from Aberdeen for £600,000. Atkinson's squad contained as much talent as Kendall's with the likes of Arthur Albiston and John Gidman at full-back, one of the best centre-half partnerships that United has ever had, their twin Republic of Ireland jewels Paul McGrath and Kevin Moran, Gordon McQueen was still at Old Trafford, an industrious midfield of Remi Moses, 19-year old Norman Whiteside from Belfast, the exquisitely gifted Dutch international, Arnold Mühren and the England and United captain, Bryan Robson. His lethal front two hitmen were the Republic of Ireland centre-forward Frank Stapleton and a 20-year old Welsh Dragon called Mark Hughes who broke it into the first team during 1984-85. The Irish striker's composure on the ball and in front of goal was complimented by the young Welshman's aggressive, rampaging, fearless style of play. Defenders hated playing against the pair of them.

But on the opening day of the 1984-85 season the Toffees looked far from championship contenders going down 4-1 at home to Tottenham Hotspur before a 2-1 defeat at West Bromwich Albion. When they won their third game, 1-0 away to Chelsea, they only lost three of their next twenty League games which took them to the end of the year. On 27 October 1984 Everton and United met for the first of their four clashes during the season and the visitors were lucky to escape with only a 5-0 hammering, a score which did not flatter the home side. Everton were simply too good for Atkinson's side with goals from Sheedy (2), Heath, Stevens and Sharp. Sheedy was the outstanding player in the game, a player who Liverpool let go to Everton in 1982 for £100,000 after making just three appearances for the Anfield club. United had gone into the game in excellent form having lost just once in their first 12 League games, a 3-0 reversal at Aston Villa, but Everton turned on the style. As if to prove the 5-0 beating of United was no fluke, Everton beat United again just three days later when they knocked them out of the Milk Cup winning 2-1 at Old Trafford.

By the time Everton arrived at Old Trafford for their return league game the visitors were top of the League with 61 points, four points clear of Tottenham Hotspur in second place and 10 ahead of United who were third whilst defending champions Liverpool were fourth on 49 points. Olsen put United 1-0 up in the 30th minute but within six minutes the visitors drew level when Mountfield scored. Gordon Strachan missed a penalty for United and the game ended 1-1, both teams seemed happy enough with a point but more importantly not losing as they both had a European fixture to play four days later. United beat Hungarian side Videoton 1-0 at Old Trafford in the first leg of their UEFA Cup quarter-final tie on 6 March 1985 and the same night Everton defeated Holland's Fortuna Sittard 3-0 at Goodison Park in the first leg of the European Cup Winners' Cup quarter-finals with Gray scoring a hat-trick.

When Everton beat Tottenham Hotspur 2-1 at White Hart Lane on 3 April 1985, they opened up a four point gap on their closest challengers for the title and had games in hand. A 2-0 win over Queens Park Rangers on 6 May 1985 secured the title for Everton even though they still had five League games to play. It was their first title success since 1969-70 when manager Howard Kendall had played for them. With the title already won Everton took their foot off the pedal winning two and losing three of their remaining fixtures. They had bigger fish to fry in the shape of Austrian club Rapid Vienna in the 1985 European Cup Winners' Cup final on 15 May 1985 and a fourth battle against United in the FA Cup final the following Saturday.

On their way to the 1985 FA Cup final showdown with United the Toffees beat Leeds United 2-0 away in Round 3, Doncaster Rovers 2-0 in Round 4, Telford United 3-0 in Round 5, Ipswich Town 1-0 away in a replay in the quarter-finals following a 2-2 draw a Goodison Park and a 2-1 victory after extra-time against Luton Town in the semi-finals.

United's path to Wembley saw them beat Bournemouth, the side which knocked them out of the cup the previous season in the Third Round when United were the holders, 3-0 at Old Trafford, a 2-1 Round 4 home win over Coventry City, a 2-0 win over Blackburn Rovers at Ewood Park in Round 5. In the quarter-finals United beat West Ham United 4-2 at Old Trafford, Norman Whiteside scored a hat-trick which included a penalty and Hughes also scored. United drew Liverpool in the semi-finals in what would prove to be one of the greatest semi-final ties in the history of the competition.

On 13 April 1985, the tie at Goodison Park was typical of clashes between the clubs in this era. The atmosphere was hostile verging on riotous and the venom from both sets of supporters made for an intense, volatile game. United under Ron Atkinson usually got the better of Liverpool in these head-to-head games and when Bryan Robson converted a Gordon Strachan corner to put United ahead midway through the second half it seemed like the pattern would continue until, with time running out Ronnie Whelan scored a spectacular equaliser to send the game into extra time. Frank Stapleton's long range shot restored United's lead but again United were denied victory when Gary Bailey could only parry a header from Ian Rush and Paul Walsh tapped the ball home.

Four days later the replay was staged at Maine Road. Paul McGrath scored the opening goal of the game, an own goal, to put Liverpool 1-0 up in the tie after 39 minutes but United rallied in the second half and two superb goals from Robson, Captain Marvel, in the 47th minute and a superlative strike from Hughes on the hour gave United a 2-1 win and a trip to Wembley.

Both clubs recorded the obligatory FA Cup final song. Everton's "Here We Go" reached No.14 in the UK Singles Charts while United's "We All Follow Man United" peaked at No.10. Both songs were kept off top spot by Paul Hardcastle's "19" with his commentary on the age of US service men in the Vietnam War.

Everton were odds-on favourites to beat United in the 1985 FA cup final after winning the European Cup Winners' Cup three days before the FA Cup final. Their 3-1 win over Rapid Vienna in Rotterdam came courtesy of goals from Gray, Steven and Sheedy.

Prior to the singing of *Abide With Me*, the 100,000 fans in attendance were treated to an array of hit songs from the year's best selling artists including *I Want To Know What Love Is* by Foreigner, Dead or Alive's *You Spin Me Round (Like A Record)*, a collaboration from Phil Collins and Philip Bailey entitled *Easy Lover* which spent four weeks at the top of the UK Singles Charts and *We Are The World* USA For Africa's answer to Band Aid. And perhaps the most apt song of the afternoon, a duet by Barbara Dickson and Elaine Page from the musical *Chess* quite appropriate as Everton and United were meeting each other head-to-head for the fourth time of the season, *I Know Him So Well* which spent four weeks at No.1.

Atkinson, Kendall and the players from both teams wore black armbands out of respect for the 56 people who had lost their lives in the Bradford fire a week earlier. A fire had ripped through Bradford

City's Valley Parade ground during the last league game of their Third Division Championship winning season against Lincoln City. Eight of United's starting 11 players had been members of their 1983 FA Cup success while Arthur Albiston was the only remaining player from United's 1977 FA Cup winning side still in the team.

Manchester United: Gary Bailey, John Gidman, Arthur Albiston, Paul McGrath, Kevin Moran, Bryan Robson (Capt), Norman Whiteside, Gordon Strachan, Jesper Olsen, Mark Hughes, Frank Stapleton. Substitute: Mike Duxbury for Albiston, 91 mins.

Atkinson dare not risk playing Bryan Robson in United's last league game of the season, a 5-1 beating away to Watford, to give his inspirational captain time to recover from a hamstring injury. Robson proved he was ready to face Everton when he scored a hat-trick in a practice match on the Thursday. Danish winger Jesper Olsen was also left out of the trip to Vicarage Road to allow him a much needed rest after playing four games in eight days for United and Denmark. Atkinson was weighing up who to play alongside McGrath against Everton and had to choose between Graeme Hogg and Kevin Moran. Hogg had impressed all season and played in 29 of United's 42 League games but Atkinson wanted to take another look at the McGrath/ Moran partnership so he played Moran with his fellow Irishman against Watford. It was Moran's 19th League start of the campaign and when he scored United's only goal of the game, his fourth of the season, he got the nod over Hogg for the encounter with Everton.

The 1985 World Chess Championships was contested by Anatoly Karpov and Garry Kasparov in Moscow. Aged 22, Kasparov became the 13th and youngest ever World Chess Champion and the action in the first half at Wembley mirrored the action on the chessboard in Moscow, it was slow, ponderous and lacking in any significant action, the closest the teams came to a goal was Peter Reid hitting a post. Both sets of fans expected their sides to raise their game in the second half. Andy Gray wasted a good chance to put The Toffees 1-0 up and when Whiteside was put through on goal by Hughes, the 36-year old Southall raced off his line to smother the young Irishman's effort. At the time Southall, Wales' No.1, was considered to be the best goalkeeper in the world. As the game ebbed and flowed the Everton players looked drained which was hardly surprising as they had just played a European final midweek when United had no such exertions. Then, in the 77th minute, came the moment which made FA Cup final history. A mistake by McGrath was capitalised on by Reid who raced over half way and towards the United goal when he was chopped down by Kevin Moran. It was a cynical trip rather than an over-aggressive challenge which nevertheless sent the diminutive Reid into the air. As referee Peter Willis, a policeman who was officiating his last ever professional game, summoned Moran towards him it seemed to all watching that he was going to book Moran (for a period between the 1980-81 and 1987-88 season the use of red and yellow cards was suspended in the Football League) as the Everton fans were shouting "Off! Off! Off! Off!" Willis took his little black book out of his pocket, the Everton fans wished he had been carrying his handcuffs instead, raised the whistle to his mouth, blew it and pointed towards the dressing rooms.

Brian Moore, who was ITV's commentator for the final, told the viewers that Moran was about to get his name in the referee's notebook before saying: "Oh! He's sent him off. He's sent Moran off." Moore's co-commentator Ian St. John was equally stunned and added: "I really do find that incredible Brian. I think the referee is 100 per cent out of order." Indeed, the referee actually called Moran over to him and asked him to turn around so as he could see the number on his back. In the history of the world's most famous domestic cup competition dating back to 1872, no player had ever been dismissed in the final before. Moran at first remonstrated with Willis, as did Robson, but in the end the inconsolable Irish defender had to be ushered off by his international team-mate Stapleton. FA Cup final history had been made but alas for Moran for the wrong reason.

"What separates the winners from the losers is how a person reacts to each new twist of fate"

Donald Trump

Moran's fate had been sealed but United's fate now rested on how the remaining 10 players would fare against Everton's 11 who must have thought they had the Treble as good as in the bag. The Toffees threw everything at them but Paul McGrath had the game of his life. He was a colossus that afternoon and time after time he kept the Everton attack at bay. Moran's dismissal seemed to be regarded as an injustice by his team-mates as Whiteside had another great chance to score when Hughes fed a pass into the box for him but the ball got tangled at his feet and the Belfast boy wonder spurned the chance. However, it would not be the United No.4's last opportunity to score.

The 90 minutes ended with the score still 0-0 and extra time saw a tactical switch from Big Ron when he took off Albiston in the 91st minute and sent on Mike Duxbury. Everton were still pressing and hoping to avoid a replay against 11 men the following Thursday but they were leaving gaps at the back which a good counter-attack might exploit. In the 110th minute of the tie Mark Hughes, who dropped into a midfield role, collected a pass from Olsen 20 yards inside his own half with his back to goal and there seemed to be no real danger for Everton. The young Welsh striker then swivelled and nonchalantly played a perfectly weighted pass with the outside of his right boot to Norman Whiteside out on the right wing just inside the Everton half. Frank Stapleton was already well forward and Gordon Strachan came bursting up the middle hoping to receive a pass from the Irishman but the teenager from Belfast had other ideas. He backed Pat van den Hauwe towards goal and using the full-back as a shield, he curled the ball around him from outside the box with his magical left foot, round Southall and his shot went into the net off the bottom of the post. The United fans went crazy with delight and Ron Atkinson danced a jig of delight on the touchline, it was one of the greatest goals ever scored at Wembley and ranks as one of the greatest United goal ever scored.

Everton tried to summon up the strength to find a late equaliser and the remaining ten minutes of the game seemed to take an age to pass by but somehow United, with everyone behind the ball, saw time out and they had smashed yet another Merseyside treble.

As Kevin Moran went up with his teammates to collect the FA Cup, the first team to win the famous trophy with a side comprising 11 internationals, he was not permitted to collect a winners' medal. The fearless Irishman, who was famous for sustaining cuts to his head in the United cause, had to await the outcome of a Football Association Committee hearing into his dismissal to determine if he would receive a medal. Willis was asked about his decision the next day and said: "I have no second thoughts about sending off Kevin Moran. I believe I was right at the time and I still believe I was right. But that doesn't stop me feeling terrible about it." Moran later received his winners' medal.

Did You Know That?

The *Daily Mirror* ran a campaign asking their readers to send in a postcard with either "YES" or "NO" written on it asking the question if Moran should receive a winners' medal. More than 1,100 people took part in the vote which was an almost unanimous 93.50% in favour of Moran being given a medal. When the Committee met and voted in favour of Moran being presented with his winners' medal, Big Ron had taken the team to Trinidad & Tobago for a celebratory holiday. When Moran was told that he would get his medal when he returned home to Manchester the delighted defender said: "I'm going to treat the lads to a drink. It's been a traumatic week, but I'm delighted it's turned out this way."

GAME NO. 31
ARSENAL 2-6 UNITED
LEAGUE CUP, ROUND 4
ARSENAL STADIUM, LONDON
28 NOVEMBER 1990
ATTENDANCE – 48,444

TOO SHARPE FOR THE GUNNERS

Season 1990-91 was Alex Ferguson's fifth season in charge of the greatest club in the world but the jury was still out on whether he could end the long wait for a league title. On 13 May 1967 United played out a meaningless goalless draw at Old Trafford with Stoke City and afterwards did a lap of honour with the First Division Championship trophy. All was good at the Theatre of Dreams – United were crowned champions and had a team that looked destined to conquer the English game like the famous Busby Babes side had a decade earlier. Busby had an outstanding array of talent at his disposal and an armoury in attack which could literally blitz any team they faced yet after narrowly finishing runners-up to Manchester City in 1967-68 what followed was a sharp decline that saw them drop into the Second Division before spending the next 15 years watching Liverpool hoover up title after title. How could United bridge the gap?

Alex Ferguson was the latest manager to try and, after winning the FA Cup in 1990, he continued to build towards that goal. In the summer of 1990 United bought Denis Irwin from Oldham Athletic for a bargain £250,000 (8 June 1990) and on 9 July 1990, the United manager signed a 16-year old kid as a trainee who would go on to become a United Legend, Ryan Giggs but he was still too young to take the capital by storm and so on a cold November night it fell to another youthful winger to take centre stage...

United were in North London to play Arsenal in a Fourth Round League Cup tie. The Gunners would go on to win their second First Division title under the management of former United player George Graham at the end of the season while United were seventh in the table going into the game and would end the campaign in sixth, three points behind Manchester City. United's away form was worrying with just one victory from their opening six road trips, a 1-0 win over Luton Town at Kenilworth Road. Arsenal were unbeaten in their opening 14 games of the season, their best start in 43 years, but were still 4 points adrift of Liverpool who had won all but 2 of their games (both drawn). The Gunners were a well-disciplined side with their famed back four of Dixon, Adams, Bould and Winterburn – they would score and then invite opponents to break them down. Their defensive style of play reaped rewards and "1-0 to the Arsenal" became a regular chant by their fans. They went on to win the League by 7 points over Liverpool and in their 42 games they conceded a meagre 18 goals.

Five weeks earlier the sides had met in at Old Trafford, a game that became infamous following an altercation between the players that resulted in a 21-man brawl later dubbed the Battle of Old Trafford by the press. Arsenal won the game 1-0 but an inquiry led to both clubs having points deducted – 2 for Arsenal, 1 for United. There may have been revenge on players' minds but as it turned out one side was just interested in playing football. The United team emerging from the tunnel at Arsenal Stadium wearing their blue and white 'Madchester' kit was: Les Sealey, Denis Irwin, Clayton Blackmore, Steve Bruce (Capt), Gary Pallister, Mike Phelan, Paul Ince, Lee Sharpe, Danny Wallace, Brian McClair, Mark Hughes. Substitutes: Mal Donaghy (for Bruce), Neil Webb

In the previous rounds United had beaten Halifax Town 5-1 on aggregate and then hammered reigning First Division Champions Liverpool 3-1 at Old Trafford with a superb performance. Yet in drawing Arsenal many pundits felt that United would go no further in the competition. This was a time when teams would play their full strength teams in the League Cup so Arsenal's famous back-line were all present and correct but the home support were left stunned by half time as United came racing out of the blocks and led 3-0. Clayton Blackmore got the ball rolling after just two minutes, hitting a daisy cutter of a free kick from distance which beat Seaman at his near post and Hughes added a second in the 44th minute but the third goal by Lee Sharpe sent the away fans in the Clock End delirious; within seconds of Arsenal restarting the game Sharpe broke forward at pace, shifted the ball from left foot to right before curling the ball into the top corner of the net from outside the box. David Seaman could do nothing but admire a superb strike.

Sharpe was unplayable on the night and the normally rock solid Gunners' defence, captained by Tony Adams, couldn't contain him. Yet Arsenal roared back after half-time - Alan Smith scored for the home side in the 48th minute and the gangly striker made it 2-3 with 22 minutes still to play, suddenly the comeback was on and the home fans sensed it, the noise inside the stadium was deafening as they urged their team to attack United at every opportunity. But within minutes their bubble of enthusiasm burst when Sharpe made it 4-2 to United with a flying header and slid on his knees towards the United fans behind the goal. Three minutes later the 19-year old winger had bagged a hat-trick; a coolly taken right foot shot which cut across Seaman into the left hand side of his net. Sharpe celebrated his first and only hat-trick for United by doing an acrobatic front roll before leaping and punching the air with a clenched right fist. The Arsenal team were completely deflated, their shoulders were slumped and some stood drooped over with their hands on their knees. Cries of "This is so f***ing easy" from United's travelling army filled the night air - the sky had fallen in on Arsenal! A late Danny Wallace goal meant the final score read Arsenal 2-6 Manchester United – it was United's finest away performance in years.

Sharpe stole the show but Wallace had more than played his part on the right wing, assisting in four of United's goals to send them into the quarter-finals of the League Cup. Sharpe was quite rightly named Man of the Match and was on his way to the sort of pop star status which George Best attracted in the 1960s and which later was bestowed upon future United pin-ups Ryan Giggs, David Beckham and a player who was better known around the world than any pop star, Cristiano Ronaldo. The fanzine *United We Stand* later paid tribute to Lee by emblazoning "RAVE ON SHARPEY" on their front cover.

The reference captured the music scene in Manchester which was bursting with life in the early 1990s and was as much a thank you to Lee for helping United demolish The Gunners as it was an ode to him being a regular visitor, much to his manager's disdain, to the nightclubs of the city.

After shaking the hand of Arsenal boss George Graham, there was no masking Fergie's delight with his team's display in the capital. "That was Danny Wallace's finest display for us and Lee Sharpe was irresistible. This was the most amazing performance in my time at Manchester United," said the United boss. United made it all the way to the final but lost 1–0 to Sheffield Wednesday. However, there was a silver lining to the season when they lifted the European Cup Winners' Cup after defeating Barcelona 2-1 in the final.

One of the songs being played on the PA system at Arsenal Stadium that evening was a song which had went to No.1 in the UK Music Singles chart on 29 September 1990. The song was *Show Me Heaven* by the Californian rock singer Maria McKee which was the soundtrack of the Tom Cruise movie *Days of Thunder*. United's demolition of The Gunners gave Ferguson glimpses of what Heaven looked like on a football pitch whilst his players would go on to produce more Days of Thunder.

At the end of the season Mark Hughes won the PFA Player of the Year Award whilst 19-year old Lee Sharpe won the PFA Young Player of the Year Award. Hughes was the first United player to win this coveted award when he lifted it in season 1988–89 and the first player to win the award twice. No player has won the award more whilst United players have won the accolade more times than any other club, 11, with Liverpool on 8 and the London duo of Arsenal and Tottenham Hotspur both on 5 wins.

Did You Know That?

Alex Ferguson brought Danny Wallace to Old Trafford from Southampton on 18 September 1989 in a £1.3 million transfer. The 25-year old was just 5 feet, 5 inches tall but he was built like, and had the electric pace of, a 100 metre athlete. His rapid sprint from a standing start left defenders in his slipstream and he could cross the ball with accuracy. Danny took a while to settle in at United but against Arsenal he reproduced the form which had persuaded Fergie to buy him. He was sold to Birmingham City for £400,000 on 15

October 1993 having made 71 appearances for United scoring 11 times. When Danny was once asked about his move to United he said: "I was delighted that Manchester United wanted to sign me. I moved into the Ramada Hotel in the city alongside two other signings, Gary Pallister and Paul Ince. I moved with my family and my dog, a Rottweiler. The hotel weren't too impressed with the dog, especially when I walked him in the car park."

GAME NO. 32
CRYSTAL PALACE 5-0 UNITED
FIRST DIVISION
SELHURST PARK
16 DECEMBER 1972
ATTENDANCE – 39,484

CALL THE DOC!

Soft-spoken Frank O'Farrell had been the surprise choice to succeed Matt Busby for a second time following Wilf McGuinness's departure at Christmas 1970. In truth O'Farrell wasn't Busby's first choice but having come to an agreement with Jock Stein, the legendary Celtic boss changed his mind. Not that this seemed to matter as O'Farrell made an incredible start – by Christmas 1971 United led the First Division by 4 points from Manchester City and George Best had scored 14 league goals including hat-tricks against West Ham and Southampton. Georgie seemed back to his very best but at the very start of 1972 it all went wrong. Following a 3-0 drubbing at Upton Park on New Years Day, United wouldn't win a league game again until March by which time Bestie's focus had permanently shifted from football life to night life and by season's end the Irishman had disappeared off to Spain and announced his retirement.

Having ridden on the coat-tails of the genius Best, O'Farrell now seemed lost without him. To many the highlight of his reign was the signing of future captain Martin Buchan in February 1972 for £120,000. The signing of Ian Storey-Moore (after Derby County's Brian Clough had announced his transfer and even paraded the player at the Baseball Ground) represented something of a coup but the classy former Forest striker was dogged by injury. Wyn Davies and Ted MacDougall were also signed as United continued to struggle in front of goal but neither were United class.

On the opening day of the 1972-73 season all three of United's European Footballers of the Year – Denis Law, Bobby Charlton and George Best – started the first game of the season but a 2-1 loss at home to Ipswich Town set the tone. It was clear all three were living on borrowed time but it was also clear that mild-mannered Frank was not the man who would take the necessary action and begin United's re-birth.

On 16 December 1972 United visited Selhurst Park for a game against Crystal Palace. United were third from bottom and defeat to Palace would see The Glaziers (as they were then known) leapfrog them leaving only Leicester beneath them. The Manchester United team was: Alex Stepney, Thomas O'Neil, Tony Dunne, Terence Young, Martin Buchan (Capt), David Sadler, Willie Morgan, Ted MacDougall, Brian Kidd, Ronald "Wyn" Davies, Ian Storey-Moore. Subs: Denis Law (for Dunne 25 mins)

Up in the stands sat Frank O'Farrell's close friend, Scotland manager Tommy Docherty, and he was as shocked as anyone as by half-time United were 2-0 down, they were abysmal. As The Doc made his way up the stairs for a cup of tea he spotted Matt Busby who wanted a word with him in the Director's Lounge. The conversation quickly turned on how he would turn things around and The Doc told Busby he could turn the ship around with a few basic changes and a substantial transfer kitty – Sir Matt offered Tommy the job on the spot. The second half saw United go down 5-0 in what is arguably the worst defeat in the post-war era – Palace went on to finish second from bottom that season and scored a fifth of their home goals in this game! None of the United Trinity started the game, although Denis Law came on as a substitute, the glory years were well and truly over.

Four days later Frank O'Farrell was sacked and The Doc replaced him and within a few weeks of arriving at Old Trafford Tommy bought two new players, Alex Forsyth from Partick Thistle and George Graham from Arsenal, both fellow Scots. Docherty managed to stave off relegation that season and that April the first of the Trinity retired as Bobby Charlton bowed out to take over as manager of Preston. The second member of the famous triumvirate, Denis Law, was given a free transfer to rivals Manchester City in July 1973 much to the annoyance of The King himself who only found out about it on the television news whilst he was visiting his family in Aberdeen. It only seemed a matter of time before George Best would hang up his boots which he duly did in somewhat controversial circumstances in January 1974 when Docherty accused George of turning up drunk to a cup-tie against Plymouth Argyle. Best denied the charge but George would never play for United again. The Doc may have rubbed a few up the wrong way, and there's no doubt that he was seen as anathema among the 1968 European Cup winning team, but there's also little doubt that this abrasive Glaswegian was the right man at the right time to lead United into a new era and that had to start by cutting ties with former greats who had gone to seed.

Thomas Henderson Doherty was born on 24 April 1928 in the Gorbals area of Glasgow. After a playing career that took in Celtic, Preston and Arsenal, Tommy accepted a job as player/coach at Chelsea under Ted Drake in February 1961. When Drake was sacked Tommy was promoted to manager but inherited a team in deep trouble and he could not prevent them from being relegated at the end of the 1961-62 season. Docherty decided that a shake-up was needed and out went several of the older players to be replaced with younger players including Peter Bonetti, Barry Bridges, Bobby Tambling and Terry Venables.

Chelsea made an immediate return to the top flight at the end of the 1962-63 season finishing runners-up to Stoke City in the Second Division and back in the top flight The Blues made steady progress finishing 5th, 3rd, 5th and 9th in the First Division. In season 1964-65 they beat Leicester City 3-2 over two legs in the League Cup final and in season 1966-67 they lost 2-1 to Tottenham Hotspur in the FA Cup final. In October 1967 Docherty resigned as manager but had left behind a squad of talented players for new manager Dave Sexton, who would also later succeed him as manager of Manchester United. Under Sexton Chelsea won the FA Cup in 1970 and the European Cup Winners' Cup in 1971 with the nucleus of the team that had been blooded by Docherty. Tommy's subsequent managerial career seemed to be faltering as he spent a year at Rotherham, a short spell at QPR (before he was sacked), two seasons at Aston Villa and another at FC Porto before being appointed Scotland boss in 1971.

When he was offered the United job The Doc told the press that he would 'walk from Glasgow' to accept it and he quickly had the United fans and press eating out of his hand. Tommy had a turn of phrase that chimed with public and media yet by 1974 it was clear that United were headed for relegation. However this set-back only enabled Tommy to re-invent the club in the lower tier and they returned to the top flight stronger the following season. Their brand of fast, frenetic football inspired huge devotion and turned United into football's equivalent of the pop groups of the time such as Slade and The Bay City Rollers as young fans mobbed town centres all over the country to follow their heroes.

After winning the FA Cup in 1977 The Doc was sacked following revelations that he had been having an affair with the club physio's wife. The fact he later married Mary Brown and they were still together when he died at the age of 92 in 2021 would indicate that this wasn't just a fling. The question of how far The Doc could have taken the club had he not been sacked in 1977 remains one of the most tantalising questions for supporters.

Did You Know That?

When Willie Morgan appeared on Granada TV's *Kick Off* programme and claimed that Tommy Docherty was 'the worst manager there had ever been', the Scot sued for libel. The libel case gathered together 29 statements from former players and colleagues of the former United boss and when the matter went to trial Docherty collapsed under cross-examination, admitting that he'd lied throughout his testimony. Far from justifying himself, Docherty's career now lay in tatters.

After managing Derby County, The Doc moved back to QPR, where he narrowly failed to gain promotion, before a spell in Australia. He returned to manage Wolves in 1984 where he could not stop the Midlands club's slide down the division. His last managerial position was at Altrincham FC.

Docherty became a popular radio pundit in Manchester, co-hosting Piccadilly Radio's Saturday afternoon football coverage where his wisecracks, such as "OXO have three flavours of stock cube – yellow is chicken, red is beef and sky blue is laughing" infuriated City fans and delighted Reds.

GAME NO. 33
CRYSTAL PALACE 1-2 UNITED (AET)
2016 FA CUP FINAL
WEMBLEY STADIUM, LONDON
21 MAY 2016
ATTENDANCE- 88,610

MANCHESTER UNITED's PRINCE OF ORANGE

Louis van Gaal exploded on to the European football scene in the early 1990s as manager of Ajax winning the UEFA Cup in 1992 and the Champions League in 1995 plus two Dutch league titles, a Dutch Cup and the Intercontinental Cup with a style of football that was the forerunner of the modern game. Van Gaal's Ajax employed precise passing and movement to dominate possession, his total football was a revelation and his young side, composed almost entirely of graduates from Ajax's famed academy, were briefly the greatest club side in the world and regularly defeated clubs with vast wealth from the Spanish and Italian leagues.

Soon Louis was in high demand and it came as little surprise when he succeeded Bobby Robson as Barcelona manager in 1997. Despite winning two La Liga titles during his time in the Catalan capital he quickly fell out with media, fans and star player Rivaldo and left in 2000 to take over the Dutch national team but failed to qualify for the 2002 World Cup and returned to Barcelona but that lasted less than 6 months. Louis then returned to Ajax as Technical Director before moving to AZ Alkmaar where he led the unfancied Dutch team to their second Eredivisie title in 2008-09. The performance was made all the more remarkable because van Gaal had tendered his resignation the previous summer but the players requested he stay on.

Louis was then offered the manager's position at Bayern Munich where he won a league and cup double in Germany but lost the 2009-10 Champions League final 3-1 to Jose Mourinho's Internazionale. The following season he was sacked and so returned to coach the Dutch national team, this time gaining qualification for the 2014 World Cup where the Netherlands made it all the way to the semi-finals, losing to Argentina on penalties and beating Brazil 3-0 in the third place play-off.

During the build-up to the 2014 World Cup, Louis's name was

mentioned in connection with the job of Manchester United manager following the sacking of David Moyes and Reds were pleased to see the revitalised performances of striker Robin van Persie during the tournament, notably in a 5-1 win against World Champions Spain in the opening group game. Despite leading the Dutch to the semis, Louis remained a controversial figure in Holland and United hoped he would at least steady the ship after a disastrous season under Moyes that had seen the 2012-13 champions trail home in 7th and that is exactly what Louis did, United finishing a creditable fourth to qualify for the following season's Champions League and for one glorious spell in April that included spectacular victories over Liverpool at Anfield and Manchester City at Old Trafford, the club threatened to put pressure on runaway leaders Chelsea but despite dominating the opening half hour at Stamford Bridge, United squandered numerous chances and lost 1-0.

Nevertheless hopes were high going into the next season and after seven games United led the Premier League by a point having won 5 out of 7 games but a heavy 3-0 defeat at Arsenal and a shocking run during December soon pushed United out of contention and there were rumours in the press of discontent among the players about Van Gaal's training methods. It was all the more galling because this was the season when the Premier League's 'ugly ducklings', Leicester City, won the league title with just 81 points. So, having exited the League Cup to Middlesbrough in October and finished bottom of their Champions League group, all hopes were pinned on the FA Cup.

In Round 3 United almost fell at the first hurdle and in the end were very lucky to beat Sheffield United 1-0 at Old Trafford when Wayne Rooney scored a penalty in the third minute of added time, his 25th successful conversion for the club. Derby County were their Round 4 opponents but thankfully the cobwebs of the previous round's performance were blown away when United beat The Rams 3-1 at Pride Park with 5,000 travelling Reds in attendance. The draw for Round 5 handed United another road trip this time to Shrewsbury Town. United saw off the League One side winning 3-0 with goals from Chris Smalling, Juan Mata and Jesse Lingard. This was the first ever game played between the clubs which saw Joe Riley make his debut for the club when he came on as a substitute at half-time for Cameron Borthwick-Jackson. Former United player Larnell Cole played for the home side. In the sixth round West Ham United arrived at Old Trafford on 13 March 2016 looking to end United's hopes of winning a trophy in the season and they almost did, taking the lead with a spectacular Dmitri Payet free-kick only to see Anthony Martial bundle home an equaliser in the 83rd minute. The replay took place a month later, 13 April 2016, and United booked their place in the draw for the semi-finals with a 2-1 victory – teenage striker Marcus Rashford, who van Gaal had promoted to stunning effect following an injury crisis in March, arrowing home the opener on 54 minutes before a Martial shot hit Fellaini and deflected into the net. A late rally from the Hammers saw Tompkins pull one back and De Gea was forced into several spectacular saves before Kouyate had a goal disallowed for offside but somehow United held on.

Whoever United faced in the semis they were favourites for the cup with Crystal Palace, Everton and Watford still left in the competition. On 23 April 2016, United met Everton at Wembley (the sides had met in the 1985 and 1995 finals) in what proved to be an old fashioned type of United game during the days Sir Alex was in charge. Early in the game Rooney cleared off the line in his Man of the Match performance against his old club, then Fellaini scored against his former employer in the 34th minute and when David de Gea saved a penalty in the 57th minute from future United striker Romelu Lukaku it seemed United were almost there but when Chris Smalling deflected a Deulofeu shot into his own goal with 15 minutes remaining it was anyone's game. The winner came from Anthony Martial, the unknown 20 year-old French striker who Van Gaal had signed in the summer for £36m. Picking up the ball on the left wing in injury time, the French wonderkid played a one-two with Rashford and another with Ander Herrera before coolly slotting past Everton keep Joel Robles. It was a Fergie Time winner that sent the United end into ecstasy. The next day Crystal Palace defeated Watford by the same score to set up a repeat of the 1990 FA Cup final between the two sides.

It was United's 18th appearance in the showpiece event and Crystal Palace's second after losing 1-0 to United in 1990 in a replay after the first game ended 3-3 after extra-time. On their way to the The Eagles had beaten Southampton 3-1 away in Round 3, a 1-0 home win over Stoke City 1-0 in Round 4, Tottenham Hotspur 1-0 away in Round 5 and Reading 2-1 away in Round 6 of the competition.

Manchester United: David de Gea, Antonio Valencia, Marcus Rojo, Chris Smalling, Daley Blind, Michael Carrick, Marouane Fellaini, Juan Mata, Wayne Rooney (Capt), Anthony Martial, Marcus

Rashford. Substitutes: Sergio Romero, Phil Jones, Darmian Matteo for Rojo 66 mins, Ander Herrera, Ashley Young for Rashford 72 mins, Morgan Schneiderlin, Jesse Lingard for Mata 90 mins

It was a final of few chances but the game came to life in the 78th when a ball was only half-cleared by United, a quick cross picked out Jason Puncheon on the left who beat De Gea to put Crystal Palace in front. Alan Pardew, manager of The Eagles, did a little dance in his technical area much to the bemusement of all watching except the celebrating Crystal Palace fans. Perhaps someone should have reminded him that Palace were twice in the lead in the 1990 final, in which he played, only for United to draw level both times. Time was against United but minutes later a weaving Wayne Rooney run and cross found Fellaini at the back post and Juan Mata steered home the knockdown to send the game into extra time.

The extra half hour was edgy but Yannick Bolasie produced a fantastic save from De Gea but when Chris Smalling was sent off for wrestling the Congolese striker to the floor to prevent a Palace break at the start of the second period it seemed United would have to try and hang on for penalties. The Eagles were suddenly favourites and Dwight Gayle forced De Gea into another save but then United broke down the other end, Valencia crossed and the ball spun back to Jesse Lingard who hit a first time volley clean as a whistle past Palace keeper Wayne Hennessy to give United the lead with just 10 minutes to go. United held on and had claimed a record 12th FA Cup.

Two days after he guided United to FA Cup glory, Louis was on his way out of Old Trafford, sacked to make way for Jose Mourinho as he paid for failing to qualify the club for the following season's Champions League. He had taken charge of Manchester United 103 times with 54 wins, 25 draws and 24 defeats for a win ratio of 52.50%. It was a bitter end to what should have been a triumphant week in the Dutchman's long and illustrious career.

Did You Know That?

Six of Louis van Gaal's Ajax players who won the 1995 UEFA Champions League later played for AC Milan such was the impression they made when the Dutch club beat the Italians in the 1995 Champions League final: Reizeger, Seedorf, Davids, Winston Bogarde (an unused sub in the game) and Kluivert who became the youngest player to score in a European Cup final aged 18 years and 327 days (born on 1 July 1976). Franck Rijkaard having already played for the club winning two European Cup finals in 1989 and 1990 and returned to the Dutch club to win a third in Vienna against his former club. When United won the 2016 FA Cup final it marked a unique double for van Gaal. His 1995 side was captained by Danny Blind and in 2016 Danny's son, Daley, played under van Gaal in the 2016 FA Cup final. Danny won four KNVB Cups with the Dutch club.

GAME NO. 34
UNITED 1-1 ESTUDIANTES DE LA PLATA
INTERCONTINENTAL CUP FINAL, SECOND LEG
OLD TRAFFORD
16 OCTOBER 1968
ATTENDANCE – 63,500

THE GOOD, THE BAD AND THE UGLY

Manchester United went into this game seeking to overturn a 1-0 deficit from the first leg. On 25 September 1968, United faced South American Champions, Estudiantes de La Plata, in the first of the Intercontinental Cup at their home stadium, Estadio Jorge Luis Hirschi, La Plata, Buenos Aires. The ground was opened on Christmas Day 1907 and is named after the man who served as the club's President from 1927-32.

The Intercontinental Cup was an annual contest from 1960 to 1979 endorsed by both UEFA and Confederacion Sudamerica de Futbol (CONMEBOL) featuring the champion clubs of both continents. From 1980 to 2004 it became known as The Toyota Cup in recognition of its sponsor, the Japanese car manufacturer. The winners of the competition could justifiably call themselves the best football club in the world. The Intercontinental Cup was succeeded by the FIFA Club World Cup.

Estudiantes won the first of their four Copa Libertadores crowns in 1968 by defeating Brazil's Palmeiras 2-0 in a playoff. They retained the title for the following two years and won their last title in 2009. Whereas United were one of the favourites to win the European Cup in 1967-68, no sports writers outside of La Plata gave Estudiantes any chance of winning the Copa Libertadores in 1968. A total of 31 teams entered the competition and on their way to being crowned winners, they beat two of Argentina's biggest and successful clubs, Independiente (winners in 1973 & 1984) and Racing Club de Avellaneda who were the reigning champions.

On 16 October 1968, United welcomed Estudiantes to Old Trafford although the word 'welcome' was not perhaps appropriate. The first leg had been more like a boxing bout with the home players laying into the United players at every opportunity, the performance of the South American Champions was nothing short of shameful. Nobby Stiles was singled out for preferential treatment and ended up being sent off after retaliating to one late and dangerous tackle too many. Bobby Charlton left the pitch with stitches in his head. In the 1960s many South American national teams, particularly those from Argentina and Uruguay, and their club sides, were renowned as spoilers who employed dirty tactics and a win at all costs approach. Many teams that faced them effectively lost the game when they lined up alongside them in the tunnel, they were completely intimidated. They were the archetypal bad boys and would not have looked out of place in Sergio Leone's 1966 Spaghetti Western *The Good, The Bad and The Ugly*. No doubt even Clint Eastwood would have flinched facing this band of gunslingers. The theme title from Leone's movie, performed by the Hugo Montenegro Orchestra, spent four weeks at No.1 spot in the UK Singles Chart after reaching No.1 on 13 November 1968.

However not all teams from South America could be tarred with the same brush – Brazil had won the World Cup in 1958 and 1962 while Santos had lifted the Intercontinental Cup in 1962 and 1963 playing superb football but then again Pele and his team-mates were hailed as the greatest team of all time by football writers of that era. Since then Argentinian teams had dominated the tournament after beating Santos in the semi-finals in 1964.

After beating Benfica in the 1968 European Cup final to book their place in the Intercontinental Cup, United had considered not participating. Sir Matt Busby had seen what had happened to Glasgow Celtic who as European champions had travelled to Argentina for the second leg of the 1967 Intercontinental Cup. The Scots had won the first leg 1–0 at Hampden Park but several of their players were on the receiving end of brutal tackling and physical confrontations. After the game Stein said that: "almost every player needs treatment for knocks" while the French sports paper, *L'Equipe* described the game as a "furious battle". In the second leg in Buenos Aires the volatile atmosphere in the stadium was matched by the volatile actions of the Argentinian side who won the game 2–1. A replay was required which became known as "The Battle of Montevideo" with Celtic going down 1-0 at the Estadio Centenario. The news agency Reuters described the match as "a bar room brawl with soccer skills abandoned for swinging fists, flying boots and blatant body checking." In the end Busby and his players agreed that they wanted to test themselves against the best team in South America but the 1-0 defeat over there had tested the manager's faith in football and nothing in the second leg would reinvigorate that faith.

The United team lined up for the second leg: Alex Stepney, Shay Brennan, Tony Dunne, Bill Foulkes, Pat Crerand, David Sadler, Willie Morgan, Brian Kidd, Bobby Charlton (Capt), Denis Law, George Best. Sub: Carlo Sartori for Law (44 minutes)

The home leg proved to be another kicking match with foul after foul committed, the majority of which came from the visitors. Despite early pressure from United the visitors took an early lead through Juan Ramón Verón (father of future United midfielder Juan Sebastian Verón) and from then on the game descended into a kicking match. Needless to say it did not end with 22 players on the pitch as George Best was sent off for punching Jose Hugo Medina in the face before pushing Néstor Togneri to the ground. The referee also sent off Medina who couldn't even return to the dressing room as he was pelted with coins by angry United fans. Willie Morgan equalised in the 90th minute on the night and Brian Kidd put the ball in the net in injury time but the referee claimed that he had already blown the final whistle to end the game. United lost 2-1 on aggregate.

When Estudiantes decided to do a lap of honour around the Old Trafford pitch the United fans pelted them with various objects resulting in the victors deciding it was not such a good idea and they ran back down the tunnel to the safety of their dressing room.

Did You Know That?

When Nottingham Forest won the first of their two European Cups in 1979 they refused to play in the Intercontinental Cup final against Club Olimpia from Asuncion, Paraguay, their place was taken by the team they beat 1-0 in the final, Sweden's FF Malmo, who lost 3-1 to Club Olimpia over two legs. Forest manager Brian Clough took the decision due to the brutality and physicality of the South American game. His decision paid off as Forest went on to retain the European Cup the following year. This time Clough decided to contest the 1980

Intercontinental Cup final as it was now a one-off game to be played in Tokyo. Forest lost the game 1-0 to Nacional from Uruguay.

GAME NO. 35
UNITED 4-0 WIGAN ATHLETIC
2006 LEAGUE CUP FINAL
MILLENNIUM STADIUM, CARDIFF
26 FEBRUARY 2006
ATTENDANCE- 66,866

FERGIE 'LOSES THE PLOT'

Manchester United went into the 2005-06 season looking to be crowned Premier League Champions for the ninth time having finished the two previous Premier League seasons in third place. Arsene Wenger's 'Invincibles' won the title in 2003-04 and "The Special One," Jose Mourinho, had guided Chelsea to their first top flight League title success in 50 years in 2004-05. And just as he did in nearly every pre-season in charge of Manchester United, Sir Alex Ferguson freshened-up his squad. Phil Neville joined Everton in a fee exceeding £3 million and United's 2002 World Cup winner, Brazilian midfielder Kleberson, was transferred to Turkish club Besiktas for £2.5 million after a disappointing Old Trafford career. In came Dutch international goalkeeper Edwin van der Sar from Fulham for an undisclosed fee and South Korean international midfielder Park Ji-sung joined from PSV Eindhoven for £4 million.

United won their first three Premier League games beating Everton 2-0 away, Aston Villa 1-0 at Old Trafford, with Dutch front-man Ruud van Nistelrooy scoring and a 2-0 win over Newcastle United at St James' Park but when United drew 0-0 with Liverpool at Anfield on 18 September 2005 it would be the last time United fans saw Roy Keane play for the club. Keano was forced to leave the field in the 88th minute having broken the metatarsal bone in his left foot and was replaced by Ryan Giggs. On 18 November 2005 the shock news emerged that Keano had left the club and signed for his boyhood heroes Celtic, after his United contract was cancelled with mutual consent following a controversial appearance on MUTV (which was never broadcast) in which the United captain laid into his team-mates following a 4-1 defeat at Middlesbrough. According to reports Keane left no stone unturned in his criticism of everyone connected with the shocking defeat that seemed to epitomise the end of United's period of dominance and that included manager Sir Alex Ferguson. The pair have been on frosty terms ever since.

Keane was a hugely inspirational leader who pulled on the United shirt 480 times (scoring 51 goals) winning 7 Premier League titles, 4 FA Cups, 4 FA Community Shields, the UEFA Champions League and the Intercontinental Cup, scoring the only goal of the game in the 1-0 win over Brazilian club Palmeiras, since arriving at Old Trafford from Nottingham Forest on 19 July 1993 for £3.75 million but his departure left something of a vacuum at the club. Keane's captain's armband was handed to Gary Neville but many doubted that he could inspire his team-mates to the same level as the Irishman.

Most United supporters at the time agreed with Keane's assessment which emerged in tabloid newspapers in the days following his outburst. Defeat at Boro meant that Chelsea were already 13 points ahead of United and there seemed little chance of reeling them in with the current players. Meanwhile the European campaign had been a disaster, having reached the knock-outs in each of the last eight seasons United eventually went out at the group stages following a 2-1 defeat at Benfica in December. In the week following the early exit, newspaper headlines claimed that Fergie had 'lost the plot', yet the seeds of revival were there if anyone cared to look.

The League Cup provided solace; United had taken care of Barnet, West Bromwich Albion and Birmingham City to reach the semi-finals. Then in January 2006 Sir Alex signed two new players - on 5 January Nemanja Vidic arrived from Spartak Moscow for £7 million and five days later Patrice Evra was purchased for £5.5 million from AS Monaco – both signings went somewhat under the radar until a helter-skelter 4-3 defeat at Ewood Park, Blackburn in which the new signings made their debuts. The critics immediately dismissed United's new acquisitions as inadequate.

Back in the League Cup United had drawn Blackburn Rovers in the semis and after a 1-1 draw at Ewood Park, United won 2-1 at Old Trafford. Wigan would provide the opposition in the final having shocked the football world – they beat Arsenal 1-0 at the JJB Stadium and were losing 2-1 deep in extra-time at Highbury and heading out when Jason Roberts scored a dramatic last minute equaliser for the visitors to send them through.

By then changes were afoot at Old Trafford – as Evra and Vidic settled in beside Rio Ferdinand, Gary Neville and Edwin van der Sar in United's back-line, further forward French international Louis Saha had supplanted Ruud van Nistlerooy at the point of the attack and he was flanked by wonderkids Wayne Rooney and Cristiano Ronaldo in a fast, interchangeable attack. The evergreen Ryan Giggs moved into midfield alongside Ji-Sung Park, who was deputising for the injured Paul Scholes, while John O'Shea had reverted to a defensive midfield role replacing Keane, a placeholder for Michael Carrick who would arrive that summer. It was a blueprint for United's forthcoming domination that would begin at the 2006 League Cup final and last well into the next decade.

Wigan chairman Dave Whelan had bankrolled the Latics climb up the leagues and this was their big day – their first ever appearance in a major Cup final and they were huge underdogs. The United team which stood in their way was: Edwin van der Sar, Gary Neville (Capt), Mikael Silvestre, Wes Brown, Rio Ferdinand, John O'Shea, Park Ji-sung, Ryan Giggs, Cristiano Ronaldo, Wayne Rooney, Louis Saha. Substitutes: Tim Howard, Patrice Evra (for Silvestre 83 mins), Nemanja Vidic (for Brown 83 mins), Kieran Richardson (for Ronaldo 73 mins), Ruud van Nistelrooy.

The final was notable more for the sub-plot in the build-up to the game than the action on the pitch. By now it was clear that United's prolific striker Ruud van Nistelrooy, who had scored 148 goals in 209 appearances for the club, was no longer first choice. There were rumours of a training ground bust-up with Cristiano Ronaldo and by the summer the Dutchman would be off to Real Madrid in a £10.3m move. Poignantly, Van Nistlerooy was warming up behind the Wigan goal as Rooney, Saha and Ronaldo capped a dominant 4-0 win in Cardiff to signal the start of another period of dominance by Alex Ferguson's Manchester United. The Dutchman never got on the pitch and looked rueful at the trophy presentation.

United's league form continued to improve in the second half of the season and from trailing by 15 points at the start of February they narrowed the gap to Chelsea down to just 7 points with 5 games to play by mid-April but a disappointing goalless draw against Sunderland, in which van Nistlerooy missed a penalty, let the London side off the hook and a 3-1 defeat at Stamford Bridge meant Chelsea retained their title. Nevertheless United would be back the following season – Fergie had not so much lost the plot as written a brand new one.

Did You Know That?

The JJB stadium was completed in 1999 (known as the DW Stadium since 2009) and the stadium's official opening was celebrated with a friendly against Manchester United on 4 August 1999. United were reigning Premier League Champions, FA Cup holders and UEFA Champions League winners and won the game 2-0 with goals from Ole Gunnar Solskjaer and Paul Scholes. Sir Alex Ferguson was given the honour of officially opening the stadium. Its current capacity is 25,138 and its record attendance was set on 11 May 2008 when 25,133 people watched Wigan Athletic play Manchester United in the final game of the 2007-08 season. United won 2-0 to clinch the Premier League title for the tenth time and just sometimes the underdogs do come out on top as they did in the 1973 FA Cup final when Sunderland beat Leeds United 1-0; in the 1976 FA Cup final when Southampton beat Manchester United 1-0 and in the 1988 FA Cup final when Wimbledon beat Liverpool 1-0. On 11 May 2013 Wigan Athletic were playing in their second major Cup final but whereas in 2006 they were underdogs against United, on this occasion they were beyond being considered as rank outsiders to win the FA Cup. Bookmakers were expecting to take a loss on the outcome of the game but it depended on how many goals Manchester City would score past The Latics. Bookmakers would probably have sent a free taxi to your door to take you to their shop if you were "silly" enough to bet against the Sky Blues. Before the 2012-13 season started champions Manchester City had spent lavishly in the transfer market: £12 million on Jack Rodwell from Everton, £6.2 million on Scott Sinclair from Swansea City, £5 million on Maicon Douglas Sisenando from Inter Milan, £12 million on Matija Nastasić from Fiorentina plus Stefan Savić who cost City £6 million a year earlier and £17 million on Javier Garcia from Benfica. In the same period, Wigan Athletic signed Frasier Fyvie from Aberdeen for an undisclosed fee (around £500,000), Ivan Ramis from Real Mallorca (undisclosed fee), Arouna Koné from Levante for a reported £3 million and Ryo Miyaichi on loan from Arsenal. City went into the game as Premier League runners-up to Manchester United, whereas Wigan Athletic had just been relegated to The Championship after eight consecutive seasons in the Premier League.

Wigan Athletic's record transfer fee paid for a player at the time was £7 million which they parted with to get Charles N'Zogbia from

Newcastle United in January 2009. Quite amazingly Wigan Athletic gave the bookmakers a happy day thanks to a goal from Ben Watson in the first minute of added-on time. Against all odds, Wigan Athletic created arguably the biggest upset in the history of the FA Cup which dates back to 1872 and to quote a line from the song "Against All Odds" the Wigan Athletic players could smile and say "Take a look at me now."

GAME NO. 36
UNITED 2-2 REAL MADRID
EUROPEAN CUP SEMI-FINAL, SECOND LEG
OLD TRAFFORD
25 APRIL 1957
ATTENDANCE- 65,000

LET THERE BE LIGHT

*"In the beginning God created the heaven and the earth. And the
earth was without form, and void; and darkness was upon the face of
the deep. And the Spirit of God moved upon the face of the waters.
And God said, Let there be light: and there was light. And God
saw the light, and it was good; and God divided the light from the
darkness."*

Genesis 1:3

On the evening of 22nd December 1940 Old Trafford was damaged following a bombing raid aimed at Trafford Park, then the central manufacturer of engines for the Spitfire and Hurricane aircraft that had defeated Hitler's planes in the Battle of Britain that summer. The ground was slightly damaged and was repaired in time for football to resume on 8 March 1941. Three days later, on the evening of the 11th, another raid decimated most of the ground and all of the main stand. United wouldn't play a game at the ground until 1949.

One of the reasons the ground took so long to repair was the shortage of materials which were being used to repair existing housing, hospitals and other vital infrastructure vital to economic recovery. So United played at Maine Road and the change of scene served them very well. By the mid 1950s they had stripped their neighbours in terms of attendances and thanks to Matt Busby's management they were the biggest draw in the land. Meanwhile City had yo-yoed between the top two divisions. So when United returned to Old Trafford in August 1949 they played the opening game against Bolton in front of 42,515. Their previous league game against Liverpool in May 1939 had attracted just 12,073.

United's standing in post-war era football went up another notch in July 1956. Harold Hardman, the Chairman of Manchester United, received an invitation from *L'Equipe* to participate in the 1956-57 European Cup. Hardman did not have to ask Matt Busby what he thought as the United manager had already made it quite clear to his Chairman that in order for his young side to achieve their full potential they had to test themselves against the best teams Europe had to offer. Busby was not interested in what a hostile Football League thought about the competition, he had the foresight to see that the European Cup would be the premier trophy in European club football. The Manchester United Board of Directors met and agreed to accept the invitation regardless of stern opposition from the Football League who threatened to deduct United points if they failed to adhere to their First Division fixture commitments.

As European Cup matches were played on a Wednesday night it meant that United had to hire their Manchester City's home ground Maine Road as Old Trafford's floodlights were still under construction. The European Cup games under the Maine Road floodlights were magical and it is still a remarkable fact that United won more European Cup games there than Manchester City! The magic started on 26th September 1956 with a 10-0 win over Anderlecht before 43,635 Mancunians in the Preliminary round of the competition. Round 1 saw tougher opposition as United edged out German Champions Borussia Dortmund 3-2 in front of a remarkable crowd of 75,598. A goalless draw in Germany set up a quarter-final with Athletic Bilbao. After losing 5-3 in Bilbao in the first leg, United had it all to do in the return and the atmosphere at Maine Road on 6th February 1957 was remarkable. Four days earlier United had won at the same ground, beating Manchester City 4-2 in the season's second Derby.

They needed to beat Athletic by at least two clear goals which would be no mean feat against hardened opponents who had run United ragged over in the Basque country, they were a formidable and tough side. After a tense opening Dennis Viollet opened the scoring but the Spaniards pushed hard at the start of the second half forcing Ray Wood into several sharp saves. Then a free-kick in the 70th minute found Tommy Taylor in space and he scored with a fine cross shot before Johnny Berry grabbed the winner with only 5 minutes remaining – United winning 6-5 on aggregate.

No matter who United were drawn to play in the semi–finals would prove to be a huge obstacle in their path to reach the final at the first time of asking. Along with United, the last three teams standing in the competition were the holders, Real Madrid who beat the Champions of France Olympique Nice, 6-2 over two legs in the quarter-finals; Fiorentina the Champions of Italy who beat Grasshopper Club Zurich, 5-3 on aggregate and Yugoslav First League Champions Red Star Belgrade, who won the "Battle of the Iron Curtain" against their Eastern European neighbours, CDNA Sofia (now known as CSKA Sofia 4-3 over their two legs.

For the second successive tie in a row United drew Spanish opponents in Real Madrid. The first leg was played in the impressive Estadio Santiago Bernabeu, Madrid on 11 April 1957 before a crowd of 120,000, the largest audience United had ever played before. If United wanted to play in the final on 30 May 1957, which was being hosted by Real Madrid, Busby knew his team needed to register a win in the Spanish capital, a draw would be an excellent result and if United were to lose then at least score to have a chance in the second leg with an away goal in the bag. Busby made only one change to the team he selected versus Athletic Bilbao and replaced Colman with Jackie Blanchflower yet it wasn't enough to prevent Real from storming into a 2-0 lead with less than half an hour left to play (scorers: Rial & Di Stéfano) they looked like they were cruising into the final for the second consecutive year. But with eight minutes remaining marauding centre-forward Tommy Taylor turned the game on its head when he powered home a header to make it 2-1. The United players barely had time to discuss how to defend the remaining minutes when Enrique Matteos scored past Wood to make it 3-1 on the night. Busby and his team flew back to Manchester to play Luton Town that weekend away in their next First Division (they won 2-0 with Taylor scoring both) match knowing that they had to beat Real Madrid at home by at least two clear goals to face Fiorentina or Red Star Belgrade in the final.

The *Manchester Guardian* reported on the game in the Spanish capital and were gushing with praise, tinged with some criticism, for Alfredo Di Stéfano which was fully justified as he was the outstanding player in the match. "This man Di Stéfano now. Yes he showed why he is the idol of the Latin races, the paragon of Continental footballers. His qualities are feline rather than tigerish, his ball control sleek and furtive, and his sudden, daring accelerations from a standing start something to behold. But this master of the side-step with the spring and agility that makes the matador did not dominate the proceedings in the manner he is accustomed. He executed some exquisite dummies and tricks, it is true, and scored Madrid's second goal cleverly when Wood advanced from goal rather inadvisedly it seemed, but he lost his head, and made on Blanchflower of all people, the most squalid foul one remembers in either representative or cup-tie football. The pretence of a reproof conveyed to Di Stéfano at the referee's instance by his captain almost made one vomit at its cynicism. It seemed incredible that such an artist could trail his wings in the gutter in this way."

By the time the second leg came around Old Trafford had a new structure in the shape of four huge floodlight pylons which were completed on 25 March 1957. But with United due to welcome the Kings of Europe at Old Trafford on 25 April 1957, the club decided to try out the new floodlights in a league game first and played Bolton Wanderers on the day the new lighting system was finished. A crowd of 60,862 (United's biggest at Old Trafford that season) turned up to see how the famous red shirts looked under the glare of four massive lighting towers, each one stretching 160 feet high up into the sky with 54 powerfully bright floodlights in each, constructed by the General Electric Company at a cost of £38,000. United failed in their debut performance under the home spotlight losing the game 2-0.

On 25 April 1957 Real Madrid stood in the way of Manchester United reaching the European Cup final. The Spanish giants were in excellent form and well on their way to securing their fifth La Liga title at the end of the season when they arrived in Manchester but United too were in excellent form having secured back-to-back First Division titles a few weeks earlier with several League games still to play and the Babes were firing on all fronts having also made it all the way to Wembley Stadium to play Aston Villa in the FA Cup final. An unprecedented Treble was on the cards and at the first time of Busby asking his young players to create history.

As Real Madrid ran out at Old Trafford their famous all white kit as the glare shone back at the capacity crowd for this was a team of talents: goalkeeper Juan Alonso, full-backs Manuel Torres and Rafael Lesmes, their centre-half duo of Marquitos and Miguel Munoz (Capt), their superb attacking French international midfielder Raymond Kopa who would go on to win the Ballon d'Or in 1958, Enrique Mateos, Jose Maria Zarraga and their lethal front two of Hector Rial and their second permitted overseas born player, Argentinean Alfredo Di Stéfano who won the Ballon d'Or in 1957 and won it again in 1959. The legendary Ferenc Puskás did not arrive in Madrid until 1958. Los Blancos were coached by José "Pepe"Villalonga Llorente who had not played at professional level but carved out a highly successful career as a football coach. He managed Real Madrid from 1955-57 and guided them to 2 La Liga titles, 2 European Cups and 2 Copa Latina victories. The Copa Latina (The Latin Cup) was contested by club sides from the Latin European nations of France, Italy, Portugal and Spain. As the coach of Atletico Madrid (1959-62) he won 2 Copa del Reys and the European Cup Winners' Cup. In 1962 he was appointed the manager of the Spanish national team and steered them to European Championship glory in 1964.

Busby's young team, with an average age of 22 compared to Real Madrid's average age of 29, stood on the verge of greatness and he placed his faith in: Ray Wood, Bill Foulkes, Roger Byrne (Capt), Jackie Blanchflower, Duncan Edwards, Eddie Colman, Johnny Berry, Liam Whelan, Bobby Charlton, Tommy Taylor, David Pegg

The night before the game Busby asked the Head Groundsman to soak the pitch. The canny Scot had watched how Real Madrid's lethal front five had practically played his team off the pitch in the first leg with their silky, first touch, precise, slick passing on a smooth bed of dry grass. Busby's idea was to see how the Spanish side could play in muddy conditions, something his players were used to during the winter months of a season. However, unknown to ground staff, a newspaper photographer took a photograph of the sprinklers soaking the grass and when the Real Madrid manager woke the next morning and sat down to eat breakfast, he saw a photograph of the Old Trafford pitch covered in pools of water which had not properly soaked into the surface. The Spanish contingent threatened to pull the plug on United's big night under lights by refusing to play the game unless the water was removed.

The game went ahead and the aristocrats of Europe's wealthiest club took the lead when a through-ball in the 25th minute caught United napping and Kopa scored. United had found their way past the Bilbao defence three times but this was Real Madrid and when Rial steered home a cross in the 33rd minute to send the visitors in at half-time leading 2-0, it looked to be the end of Busby's dream. Not much has ever been written about Busby's half-time team talks, and it is doubtful he ever used the "hair dryer" treatment on his players, but whatever he said to his players that evening almost paid off. His team were a different proposition in the second half and with United in the ascendency the Real Madrid players, as gifted as they were, began to feign injury and go down much easier in the tackle than they had in the opening 45 minutes. Taylor pulled a goal back in the 62nd minute before 19-year old Bobby Charlton, who was making his European debut, scored with five minutes to go to make it 2-2 which is how the tie ended. Real were in their second successive final with a 5-3 aggregate victory and went on to defeat Fiorentina 2-0 (scorers: Di Stéfano & Gento) in the final in their own backyard.

The *Daily Express* was scathing of United's performance and ran the headline: "Arrogant Busby Babes Laze and Lose." A little unfair on a United side who had just played three League games in the space of six days prior to the game and who were playing one of the greatest ever club sides Europe has ever witnessed. The *Manchester Guardian* once again turned their attention to Real Madrid's 30-year old striker, Di Stéfano. "That Di Stéfano's colleagues should play instinctively up to him is no more surprising than that an orchestra should play up to Beecham or Barbirolli. He preserves the balance and dictates the tempo in the same way. His rewards are said to be fabulous." Thomas Beecham and John Barbirolli were world famous orchestra conductors at the time.

On a sad note, exactly a year to the day after United overturned a two goal deficit at Maine Road to beat Athletic Bilbao 3-0, seven of the players who starred in the game lost their lives in the Munich Air Disaster on 6 February 1958. Although they were beaten, the games against Real showed that United were ready to climb to the summit of European football and Madrid president Santiago Bernabeu was so stunned at the events of Munich that he offered to help in anyway he could, even offering Alfredo Di Stefano on loan to United for a season but the FA refused to allow it. Following the crash, with United facing a long absence from Europe, Matt Busby arranged numerous friendlies with European opposition and when he approached Bernabeu the Real president waived the club's usual £25,000 fee (the equivalent of £600,000 today) and sent his European Champions to Old Trafford to play the first of a series of matches on 1st October 1959. The Spanish sent their best team over for the game and they overran their Mancunian hosts 6-1 on the night including one outrageous Di Stefano backheel flick from a corner but over the following years the scorelines got tighter until United finally won in Madrid in 1964. It is to Madrid's eternal credit that they were helped the club in their hour of greatest need.

Did You Know That?

Alfredo Di Stéfano (nicknamed "The Blond Arrow") was born in Buenos Airies, Argentina on 4 July 1926. He scored in the first five European Cup finals and during his Real Madrid career, 1953-64, he was the top goal scorer in La Liga every season but one from 1953 to 1959. He played for Los Blancos 624 times and scored 405 goals. Di Stéfano was also one of the few footballers to represent three countries at international level. He was capped seven times for Argentina in 1947, three times by Colombia (1951-52) before obtaining Spanish citizenship in 1956. On 30 January 1957, he made his debut for Spain and scored a hat-trick in a 5-1 win over the Netherlands in a friendly at Estadio Santiago Bernabeu, Madrid. In 31 appearances for Spain he scored 23 goals but never graced the world stage for his adopted country at a World Cup finals.

GAME NO. 37
TOTTENHAM HOTSPUR 3-5 UNITED
PREMIER LEAGUE
WHITE HART LANE, LONDON
29 SEPTEMBER 2001
ATTENDANCE - 36,049

THE GREAT ESCAPE

In 1963, the year Manchester United won the FA Cup for the third time in the club's history, the movie *The Great Escape* was released to a worldwide audience. The film was based on real events but it deviated significantly from the historical event, depicting a heavily fictionalised version of the escape. By way of example, the movie included several compromises such as Steve McQueen's character, Captain Virgil Hilts, nicknamed "The Cooler King" who was one of three Americans in the camp. In reality no Americans were encamped as Prisoners of War in the German POW camp, Stalag Luft III which was located in Sagan (now known as Zagan, Poland) in the province of Lower Silesia. On 29 September 2001, Manchester United's coach arrived in London N17 to play Tottenham Hotspur in the Premier League at White Hart Lane and little did they realise that they would perform the footballing equivalent of the Great Escape that very afternoon.

United were reigning Premier League Champions having won their seventh Premier League crown in season 2000-01 and were playing their seventh Premier League game in defence of their title as Champions of England. When Alex Ferguson's side arrived in North London they had won 3, drawn 2 and lost 1 (a 4-3 defeat away to Newcastle United). United were in third place in the Premier League table but Spurs, under new manager Glenn Hoddle, were in some disarray, with 2 wins, 2 draws and 2 defeats from their opening six games. The United cast for the trip to North London didn't include any Americans, Tim Howard didn't arrive at Old Trafford until the summer of 2003, although they did have a South America in their ranks, Argentina's Juan Sebastian Verón. The Argentine midfielder was one of three players who played against Tottenham Hotspur who had joined United for £29.1 million from SS Lazio, Laurent Blanc was a £2.5 million signing from Inter Milan and a year after Sir Alex Ferguson first tried to sign him, Ruud van Nistelrooy finally arrived from PSV Eindhoven in a £19 million deal. United's other summer signing, Roy Carroll who was signed from Wigan Athletic for an undisclosed fee, was on the bench. The Spurs team included a former fans' favourite Teddy Sheringham who left United over the summer after his four year contract at Old Trafford expired. He was offered a 12 month contract to stay but the 35-year old striker refused it and rejoined Tottenham Hotspur (1992-1997) in a free transfer as one of Hoddle's first signings.

Despite winning three league titles in a row, United's start to the new season had been unusually frantic. After playing in the first game of the season at home to Fulham which United won 3-2, Jaap Stam was dropped for the next two games and then sold to Lazio for £16.5m. It was a decision that rocked the football world and Ferguson later admitted that it was one of the worst decisions of his career.

United hadn't won in their four previous visits to White Hart Lane and lined-up as follows: Fabien Barthez, Gary Neville, Denis Irwin, Ronny Johnsen, Laurent Blanc, Nicky Butt, David Beckham, Juan Sebastian Verón, Paul Scholes, Andy Cole, Ruud van Nistelrooy. Substitutes: Roy Carroll, Mikaël Silvestre (for Irwin 46 mins), Luke

Chadwick, Ole Gunnar Solskjaer (for Butt 40 mins).

The game kicked off in bright sunshine and it was the home side who made a bright start taking the lead after 15 minutes through their new £8.1 million signing Dean Richards who powerfully headed home. Les Ferdinand made it 2-0 ten minutes later when he spun around Blanc and fired a low shot past Barthez. Blanc had attempted to play the England striker offside but Ferdinand was just too quick for the 35-year old defender. The Spurs fans were in a celebratory mood and cheered every touch of the ball by one of their players with shouts of "Olé". The five-man Spurs midfield was completely swamping United's four in midfield and by half-time the home side were 3-0 up after Christian Ziege scored a low diving header in the 45th minute. Spurs were scintillating, United were embarrassing.

Pundits were focussing on United's new Stam-less defence which had leaked 13 Premier League goals since the season kicked off. When United took to the pitch for the second half they were a completely different team, both in terms of their set-up and how they played. Silvestre came on for Irwin and Ferguson decided to go all out in attack by taking off Butt and playing three up front with Solskjaer joining Cole and van Nistelrooy. Whatever Ferguson said at the interval worked immediately when Cole scored within a minute of the restart, heading in a cross from Beckham. Blanc made it 3-2 after 58 minutes when he out jumped Spurs' captain Ledley King from a pinpoint Beckham corner, it was Blanc's only Premier League goal. The home crowd weren't cheering now: their midfield, which had been so dominant in the first 45 minutes, looked decidedly nervous as United's three-pronged attack tested them time and again with decisive runs in behind. King and his fellow defenders looked anxious every time David Beckham had the ball.

United's Dutch frontman, van Nistelrooy, scored the fifth headed goal of the game to draw United level at 3-3 in the 72nd minute and now the Spurs fans could see the writing on the wall. United were simply overrunning Spurs and completely outplaying their hosts. Much to the amazement of Spurs boss Glenn Hoddle, who must have already been thinking of the next day's glowing newspaper headlines, his side conceded a fourth in the 76th minute when Scholes and Solskjaer linked-up and played Verón in whose left foot shot beat goalkeeper Neil Sullivan. The Spurs manager put his right hand up to his face and closed his eyes. It was turning into a horror show for his team at White Hart Lane. Beckham, the England captain, had a magnificent game and added the icing to the cake when he scored a superb right footed shot in the 87th minute to make it 5-3. The unthinkable at half-time, a United comeback, had happened.

At this time Beckham was still Public Enemy No.1 in England and was booed every time he played. The level of vitriol he received during United's games in London was ridiculous and England fans had still not forgiven him for being sent off against Argentina during the 1998 World Cup finals or for his gesture towards the crowd when he was walking off the pitch after England lost 1-0 to Germany at Wembley, the last under the old twin towers. Before United's first away game of the 1998-99 season at West Ham United, an effigy of Beckham was photographed dangling from a hangman's noose outside the Boleyn Ground. The player was verbally abused and whilst his red card against Argentina wasn't an act of treason, some fans chanted "You let your country down". It didn't help that the then England manager, now Spurs boss, Glenn Hoddle had hung the young midfielder out to dry in his post-match comments. So this win must have been very satisfying for Becks as his man of the match display consigned Hoddle and Spurs to a miserable Saturday night.

Did You Know That?

Tottenham Hotspur are the only non-League club to win the FA Cup since the creation of the Football League in 1888. On 20 April 1901, Spurs met Sheffield United at the old Crystal Palace ground in the FA Cup final. A crowd of 110,820 fans turned out to see the game which remains the biggest ever attendance at a football match played in London. Sheffield United were firm favourites to lift the trophy for the second time in three years having beaten Derby County 4-1 in the 1899 final at the same venue. They were a professional club whilst Spurs were an amateur side. Sheffield United had also been crowned First Division Champions in season 1897-98 and were runners–up in 1899-1900. Spurs, then playing in the Southern League, had won the title the previous season. The 1901 FA Cup final ended 2-2 and the replay took place a week later at Burnden Park, Bolton which Spurs won 3-1 before a crowd of 20,470. The 1901 FA Cup final was the first to be shown by Pathé News.

GAME NO. 38
WEST HAM UNITED 1-6 UNITED
FIRST DIVISION
BOLEYN GROUND, LONDON
6 MAY 1967
ATTENDANCE - 38,424

MANCHESTER UNITED's SUMMER OF LOVE

It may well have been the Summer of Love, but in May 1967 Manchester United fans were not sticking a flower in their hair and boarding a plane for San Francisco because that month they were wrapping a red, white and black scarf around their necks, pinning a badge to the lapel of their denim jacket which read "Stretford Enders RULE OK!" and making their way to Stratford, East London.

Going into the last few games of the 1966-67 season three teams stood a chance of being crowned Champions of England. For their penultimate First Division game United had an away trip to West Ham United having played 40, won 23, drawn 11 and lost 6. The teams on their coat tails, Nottingham Forest and Tottenham Hotspur, had two and three League games respectively still to play. Forest, managed by the former Manchester United and Republic of Ireland captain, "Gentleman" Johnny Carey, were chasing their first ever First Division Championship. Tottenham Hotspur, managed by Bill Nicholson, were chasing their second domestic double in six years after winning the First Division title in 1960-61 and the 1961 FA Cup final under Nicholson. Forest's second last game of the season was an away fixture at Southampton. They were three points behind United on 54, but with 2 points for a win and 1 point for a draw, they were very much still in the running with 22 wins, 10 draws and 8 defeats. Spurs were 6 point adrift of United on 51 and their faint hopes of winning their third League crown relied on them winning their last three fixtures, hoping United and Forest would trip up, and Spurs needed to score a bucketful of goals as they had a goal difference of +19. Spurs had won 22, drawn 7 and lost 10 of their 39 League games and a week after the season was due to end they would play Chelsea in the FA Cup final. But the omens for the London side were not favourable side as the club tended to win trophies when the year ended in 1. They won the FA Cup in 1901, 1921 and 1961 as well as the First Division Championship in 1961 and the 1961 FA Charity Shield. They went on to lift the League Cup in 1971 followed by two more FA Cup final victories in 1981 and 1991.

So when United arrived at West Ham United's home ground on 6 May 1967, they knew a win would secure the title, regardless of what happened to Forest at The Dell and even a draw would almost certainly be good enough to give Matt Busby his fifth League Championship as United manager. Manchester United's superior goal average over Carey's talented side looked insurmountable whose Forest side included a former United player, Jeff Whitefoot, and a future one, Ian Storey-Moore.

United had looked like champions from the opening game of the season when they smacked five goals past West Bromwich Albion in a 5-3 win at Old Trafford but it was reigning champions Liverpool who made all of the early running and had a strong squad which would test any opponent. Liverpool had three players who were members of England's victorious 1966 World Cup winning squad: Gerry Byrne, Ian Callaghan and in Roger Hunt, they had a prolific striker who scored goals for fun. Hunt, nicknamed "Sir Roger" by The Kopites, had scored 29 goals in 37 League games during Liverpool's Championship winning season in 1965-66 but United had a trio of players who every side in the League coveted and feared: Messrs Best, Law and Charlton.

Liverpool topped the First Division table on New Years Day 1967 but after United lost 1-0 at Sheffield United on Boxing Day 1966, they went on an unbeaten 20 game run up until the end of the season. United had gone top of the table on 11 March 1967 following a goalless draw against Newcastle United at St James' Park and had not been off top spot since. United were in top form that season beating Everton 3-0, Burnley 4-1, Sunderland 5-0, Blackpool 4-0, Leicester City 5-2 and Aston Villa 3-0 at Fortress Old Trafford. Every side which visited Old Trafford faced a Theatre of Nightmares. Just 36 days before United arrived at the Boleyn Ground, West Ham United visited Old Trafford on 1 April 1967. The visitors were captained by England's 1966 World Cup winning captain Bobby Moore and had two other notable players on display who helped England defeat West Germany 4-2 after extra-time in the 1966 World Cup final, Geoff Hurst and Martin Peters. It may have been April's Fool Day 1967 but it was West Ham United who were made fools of on the day when United won the game 3-0.

Matt Busby's team were on the verge of winning the club's

seventh First Division title, Matt's fifth since he accepted the job in 1945 but Matt's mind was not cast back to United's last First Division Championship winning side under his stewardship two years earlier, 1964–65, he reflected on his First Division Championship winning side of 1956–57, his famous Busby Babes side, which saw 8 of his players perish in the Munich Air Disaster on 6 February 1958. And, one day, one game, one performance, one result would surely define Manchester United's 1966–67 season but would his players once again deliver the goods for him? The team Matt selected for the all important game was: Alex Stepney, Shay Brennan, Tony Dunne, Paddy Crerand, Bill Foulkes, Nobby Stiles, John Aston Jr, George Best, Bobby Charlton, David Sadler, Denis Law (Capt).

In season 1965–66 Busby had selected three goalkeepers throughout the season: Pat Dunne, David Gaskell and Harry Gregg and they conceded 59 League goals between them from the 42 games played. Gregg was the No.1 choice but his time at Old Trafford was fast coming to an end through injury. Busby did not have the faith in Dunne or Gaskell, who was injury-prone, to help United reclaim the First Division title in 1966–67 and so he had dipped into United's war chest and purchased Alex Stepney for £55,000 from Chelsea in August 1966, a record fee for a goalkeeper.

It was a beautiful Spring day in London's East End and the game kicked-off in bright sunshine. The red half of Manchester had invaded London, the attendance of 38,424 was a post-war record for the Boleyn Ground. The home side had lost their last five games starting with that 3-0 defeat at Old Trafford and during this losing streak they flew to Houston, Texas to play a friendly against reigning European Champions Real Madrid. The game was staged as part of several exhibition games to promote soccer in the USA in advance of the United Soccer Association domestic League commencing that summer. The match was played in Houston's Astrodome which was known as the "Eighth Wonder of the World," the first ever football match played indoors and on artificial turf. The Hammers lost 3-2 to Los Blancos.

When West Ham faced United they knew they weren't going to be relegated and so their manager, Ron Greenwood, decided to give two of their Academy graduates a game, 20-year old goalkeeper Colin Mackleworth for what was only his third senior game and 20-year old winger Harry Redknapp. United were missing two players who had played key roles in getting United to within touching distance of winning the title. David Herd was still out after breaking a leg six weeks earlier and left-back Bobby Noble, who had played 29 times in the League that season, was involved in a horrific car crash on his way home from United's 0-0 draw at Sunderland on 22 April 1967. Noble's injuries were so serious he never played again, a career cut cruelly short at just 21 years of age.

United took to the pitch in a gleaming all white kit and by the end of the game the West Ham United players who had played against Real Madrid must have thought The Red Devils had been renamed El Diablos Blanco (Spanish for "The White Devils"). United were a goal up straight away through Charlton, 2-0 up after seven minutes with a headed goal by Paddy Crerand and 3-0 up after ten minutes when Bill Foulkes scored his sixth goal for the club. By half-time the Football League's engraver could start etching the name of the world's most famous club on the base of the First Division Championship trophy as they led a mesmerised home side 4-0 as George Best scored his tenth League goal of the campaign in the 25th minute. The travelling army of United fans were in party mood. After the interval West Ham pulled a goal back when full-back John Charles scored in the 46th minute. Charles won 5 caps for the England Youth Team and was the first black player to represent England at any level. Even the United fans cheered when Charles scored hoping that United would be stirred back into action and reproduce the kind of football they had been drooling over in the first half. The visitors then turned on the style with the mercurial Best goading the Hammers' back four to try and get the ball off him as he turned one way, twisted another and spun around his opponents like a spinning top. No wonder Pat Crerand once described one of George's opponents of wandering from the pitch at full time with "twisted blood". A penalty from Law in the 63rd minute was followed by his twenty-fifth goal of the season in the 79th minute which sealed an emphatic 6-1 victory for the new Champions of England. The United fans invaded the pitch and some of them dug out pieces of turf to remember the occasion.

The Hammers were proud of their Academy which produced players such as Moore, Hurst and Peters but in Law, Best and Charlton United had three University graduates. Manchester United's 6 Star performance was fit enough to be played across the capital in London's Royal Albert Hall it was that commanding.

Did You Know That?

Bobby Moore holds the unique distinction of captaining three Cup winning teams at Wembley Stadium in three consecutive years. In 1964 23-year old Moore was the captain of his club, West Ham United when they beat Preston North End 3-2 in the FA Cup final. Winning that competition meant they qualified for the 1964–65 European Cup Winners' Cup and the Hammers reached the 1965 European Cup Winners' Cup final at Wembley once again where they defeated 1860 Munich 2-0, and Moore proudly held aloft the club's first, and only, European trophy. A year later Bobby was back at Wembley for yet another final but this time captaining his country in the World Cup final. England defeated West Germany 4-2 after extra time and Moore was carried around the pitch on his team-mates' shoulders as he held the famous Jules Rimet trophy in the air.

GAME NO. 39
PRESTON NORTH END 0-2 UNITED
FIRST DIVISION
DEEPDALE, PRESTON
26 MARCH 1955
ATTENDANCE – 13,327

WHEN IRISH EYES WERE SMILING

Although one Irishman, Jackie Blanchflower, survived the horrific Munich Air Disaster on 6 February 1958, another, Liam Whelan, lost his young life. William Augustine Whelan was born on 1 April 1935 in Cabra on the north side of Dublin. He was a devout Roman Catholic who came from a very large family and when he was only 8-years old his father died. Better known as "*Billy*" or "*Liam*" to his teammates, the young Whelan was a prodigious talent and this was evident from the moment he kicked a football in the playground of St Peter's School in Phibsboro, Dublin. From the window of his classroom Liam could see Dalymount Park, the home of Bohemians FC but also the ground where the Republic of Ireland played their home international matches. Teachers at his school would often find the young Whelan staring out the window dreaming that one day he would follow in the footsteps of his hero United and Ireland captain Johnny Carey, and run out in front of a huge crowd of Irish fans wearing the famous green national jersey. Liam started his football career at Dublin's famous football nursery, Home Farm.

Like so many wonderfully gifted players over the years, the teenage Whelan was first spotted by Billy Behan, Manchester United's scout in the Dublin area. Liam was the star performer in an Eire Schoolboys side which defeated an English Schoolboys side 8-4 in Dublin and Behan sent a telegram to Matt Busby in which he raved about the young Irish kid he has just seen tear the English side apart. Busby was intrigued and sent first team coach Bert Whalley to Dublin for a closer look at the kid from Cabra. Four days after Whalley arrived in Dublin the 18-year old Whelan was put on a boat and sent to Old Trafford to sign as an amateur and play in Matt Busby's young Manchester United team. At first Liam's family had refused to allow young Billy to travel to Manchester but the youngster pleaded "Don't stop me Mammy. Let me go," and she reluctantly relented. Within two weeks of his arrival in Manchester and after watching him play several times Jimmy Murphy told Busby: "If this fella doesn't come to me, I'll die." Despite some initial homesickness Liam agreed professional terms with Manchester United. Although he was not blessed with lightning pace for an inside-right he possessed other skills in abundance; he was athletic, a quick thinker, a magnificent dribbler with close ball control despite his tall and ungainly appearance, he had a powerful shot and he could ghost past defenders with a deft shimmy.

Three days after he arrived in Manchester Busby was so impressed with the young Irishman in training that he handed him a place in the Manchester United Youth Team which played Wolverhampton Wanderers' Youth Team in the 1st leg of the inaugural FA Youth Cup at Old Trafford on 4 May 1953. Liam replaced the injured John Doherty and scored in United's 7-1 win and became an instant hit with his team-mates including fellow Irishmen Pat Kennedy and Neil McFarlane. Whelan scored again in the 2nd leg in a 2-2 draw which was good enough to win the competition 9-3 on aggregate. Few players can lay claim to making their first ever appearance for their club in a cup final and scoring in it to help win the trophy. Not a bad start to what promised to be a glittering career for this affable yet very shy young Dubliner. When he arrived at Old Trafford Johnny Carey told the young Whelan that whatever he did try and hold on to his Irish name as the people in Manchester were unaccustomed to Irish names such as Augustine or Liam. However, in the end Liam had no say in it as his teammates started to call him Billy and it stuck with him until he went home for the occasional visit when his family and friends called him Liam.

After retaining the FA Youth Cup the following year by defeating Wolves 5-4 on aggregate, the United Youth Team was rewarded with a trip to Zurich to compete in what was quickly becoming Europe's premier youth tournament, *The Zurich Blue Star Tournament*. Billy was in mesmerising form and helped United win the trophy. After Busby's kids beat Bienne 9-2 (Billy scoring 5) Busby gave an interview to the *Manchester Evening Chronicle* and said: "*I wish you could have been there to see some of Whelan's five goals at our 9-2 win over Bienne on Saturday. For three of his goals he dribbled through the entire defence and rounded the goalkeeper too!*" Unknown to Busby the Brazilian national team were in the crowd watching the game on a day off from preparing for the 1954 World Cup Finals which were being hosted by the Swiss. The South American masters were so impressed with the skinny kid from Dublin that United received enquiries from the famous Santos Football Club as to whether they would release him and allow him to play for them.

The young Irishman was flattered but politely declined the invitation much to the relief of Matt Busby who held high hopes for his yet uncut Irish diamond. Everyone from the first team right down to the third team was fighting for a place in the United team but such was the camaraderie instilled in the players by Busby and Murphy that not a single ounce of animosity or jealousy was displayed among them. They were all in it together, showing happiness for a friend who broke into the first team yet quietly concealing their own bitter disappointment at missing out. They were as tight a group of players that could be found anywhere in Britain or Europe.

After establishing himself in the United Reserve team, Matt Busby decided it was time for Billy to make the step up to the first team to see what he could do. On 26 March 1955 he made his senior debut for Manchester United in their First Division game against Preston North End at Deepdale. Manchester United: Ray Wood, Bill Foulkes, Roger Byrne (Capt), Thomas Gibson, Mark Jones, Jeff Whitefoot, Johnny Berry, Liam Whelan, Tommy Taylor, Duncan Edwards, Albert Scanlon.

Whelan was handed the No.8 shirt for the game which Jackie Blanchflower had worn 26 times before him that season, scoring 8 goals. The young man from Dublin knew he had to seize the moment and impress his manager or he may not get another chance to prove how good he was. hings went well for him on his debut he helped the team to a 2-0 victory and Busby saw enough to merit Liam's inclusion in the side for the following Saturday's visit to Sheffield United. Whelan was magnificent at Bramall Lane scoring in the game and helping his strikers to four more goals for an impressive 5-0 win. He kept his place in the team for the next five League games but after just 1 win, 1 draw and 3 defeats Busby reinstated Blanchflower for the remaining three League fixtures of the season. Jackie repaid his manager's faith in him by scoring twice in a 3-1 away win over Arsenal and then helped the team to a 1-1 draw at Charlton Athletic before rounding of the campaign with a 2-1 home win over Chelsea on the final day of the season. Manchester United finished 5th in the table.

Blanchflower was still Busby's first choice at inside-right at the start of the 1955-56 season although Billy did play in 13 League games and scored 4 League goals to help United to the title and his first senior winners' medal. His form for United impressed the Republic of Ireland selectors and Billy was awarded his first cap for his country on 10 May 1956. The Irish travelled to Feyenoord to play Holland in an international friendly and won 4-1.

In season 1956-57, Liam's career at Old Trafford really took off when he was told by Busby that the No.8 shirt was his to lose. He played in 39 of United's 42 League games, including the first 36 in succession, and scored 26 times in the League to ensure United retained the First Division Championship. In September and October 1956 he was in sensational form scoring in 8 consecutive League games. Billy also played in every round of the FA Cup for United scoring 4 in 6 games including the final where they lost 2-1 to Aston Villa (scorer: Tommy Taylor) and also played in United's first ever game in European competition as well as all the tie in the 1956-57 European Cup finding the net 3 times.

A snapshot of just how well he played this season came in the European Cup quarter-finals against the reigning Spanish Champions Athletic Bilbao. United visited Bilbao on 16 January 1957 for their 1st leg tie. The game was played before 60,000 boisterous Basques at Spain's oldest stadium, Estadio San Mamés, also known as *La Catedral* (The Cathedral). The pitch was rock hard and covered in snow with the match played in wintry. conditions. The partisan home crowd were baying for United's blood and were calling on their team, *Los Leones* (The Lions) to maul the English invaders. The Spanish Champions started the game well and powered their way to a 3-0 half-time lead; Ignacio Uribe Echevarría scoring in the 3rd and 28th minute, Felix Marcaida Aurrecoechea adding the third in the 43rd minute. Talk among the fans on the terraces was of yet more goals in the second half. How right the fans were with first Tommy Taylor (48 mins) and then Dennis Viollet (54 mins) netting for the visitors. Suddenly the Cathedral took on an eerie, almost spooky, silence as the parishioners stood high up on the terraces and prayed to the heavens desperately hoping that their team could stop attack after attack reigning down on the Spanish goal from the Champions of England. These were the nights Busby and Murphy longed for, a chance to show Europe just how good the Busby Babes were. Fear spread throughout the ground before the home fans prayers were finally answered. Armando Merodio Pesquera scored the fourth for Bilbao in the 73rd minute and when José Luis Arteche Muguire netted a fifth in the 78th minute even Busby and Murphy knew that United would have a mountain to climb to turn around a three goal deficit in the home leg at Maine Road (Old Trafford did not have any floodlights at the time). With just 5 minutes to go and United desperately in need of a goal to give themselves a chance in the second leg, up stepped Whelan. The Irishman collected the ball deep in his own half, dribbled his way up the pitch leaving five defenders in his wake and scored with a shot so precise it looked like an arrow released from the bow of Robin Hood.

In the days following the tie the Savoy Cinema in Dublin showed Whelan's goal on *Pathe News* and the whole audience erupted, clapping with delight as they got to their feet. Liam was a local boy and all of Dublin was proud of his achievements in the famous red jersey of Manchester United. Very few people had television sets at the time and back then little football was shown on television. Those who were lucky enough to own a TV sat at home would gather around it to watch Sports Report on RTE Television on a Saturday evening at 5.00pm. Liam used to write home and tell his family how good a player the teenage Bobby Charlton was and it would not be long before Charlton himself would have the football world at his young feet. On his rare trips back home to Dublin Whelan would sit with his family for hours on end and tell them about the famous Busby Babes and the superb skills the likes of Roger Byrne, Charlton, Eddie Colman and Duncan Edwards had, he was in awe of their ability but he had a rare ability himself. Charlton once remarked that he always wanted to be the best player in the world but admitted that as long as

Billy Whelan was at United that particular dream would never come true. This was high praise indeed from one of the greatest footballers that has ever graced the beautiful game.

Having scored 33 goals in 53 games during the 1956-57 season, a ratio of better than a goal every two games, Whelan was on his way to becoming a superstar. His 26 goals in the First Division, 4 more than the prolific Tommy Taylor, made him the club's leading league goal scorer. Every boy in Dublin wanted to be the next Liam Whelan. During the season Liam also won 3 more caps for his country; 3 October 1956 versus Denmark at Dalymount Park, Dublin in a qualifying game for the 1958 World Cup (Ireland won 2-1); 8 May 1957 versus England at Wembley, another qualifying game for the World Cup (Ireland lost 5-1) and finally his fourth and final cap for Ireland versus England at Dalymount Park on 19 May 1957 in yet another qualifying game for the World Cup (Ireland drew 1-1). Whelan's Manchester United teammates, Byrne, Edwards and Taylor, were all in the England team for the game in Dublin.

The following season, 1957-58, Whelan faced his sternest of tests yet at United when he vied with Bobby Charlton for the inside-right jersey. Bobby had made his debut on 6 October 1956 at centre-forward and impressed Busby, scoring twice in a 4-2 First Division home win over Charlton Athletic just five days before he celebrated his 19th birthday. However, not to be outdone and to show the new kid on the block that he had a fight on his hands, Billy also scored in the game. The season could not have started any better for Billy, scoring a hat-trick on the opening day of the season when United beat Leicester City 3-0 away at Filbert Street. On 25 September 1957 Liam returned home to Dublin but the reason for the trip was not to visit his family. Manchester United had been drawn against the League of Ireland Champions, Shamrock Rovers, in the Preliminary Round of the 1957-58 European Cup. It was only the third season of the elite European competition and the first time teams from Ireland were permitted to take part in it. Glenavon from Belfast represented the north of the country as Irish League Champions and Rovers went into the competition as the defending League of Ireland Champions. In the weeks before the match in Dublin the city was buzzing with excitement. The Whelan family were inundated with requests for tickets for the game whilst the kids in Cabra had already played the match on the streets a dozen times before the two teams even met. Everyone wanted to be Liam in those kick-a-bouts but in reality only one boy could be him for the game, with that lucky boy probably the best player among the lads going home afterwards daydreaming that maybe just one day Billy Behan or another United scout would see him play and send a telegram to Matt Busby suggesting that he should be invited over to Old Trafford for a trial with United.

The 1st leg saw United win 6-0 at Dalymount Park (Jackie Blanchflower also played).The vast majority of the 45,000 in attendance that day just turned up to see their fellow Dubliner and he did not disappoint them scoring twice in the game. Taylor also scored twice with Johnny Berry and David Pegg also on the scoresheet.The victory was all the sweeter for Liam because Shamrock Rovers were bitter rivals in the Irish capital to his former club Home Farm. Standing on the terraces that day were hundreds of young Irish boys who were all sharing the same wish that one day they too could pull on the famous red jersey of Manchester United. One 12-year old boy in particular that evening watched in awe as Whelan cast his magical spell around the ground and was transfixed by the magnificent Irish winger. His name was Eamonn Dunphy, a highly promising young midfielder, who grew up in Drumcondra on the northside of Dublin. Within 5 years Dunphy found himself at Old Trafford as an apprentice but the competition at United at the time was phenomenal and he left in May 1965 to join Millwall without ever fulfilling his dream of playing for Manchester United.

Liam missed the return leg two weeks later at Old Trafford which United won 3-2 for a convincing 9-2 aggregate victory (meanwhile Glenavon were beaten 3-0 on aggregate by Danish Champions, Aarhus). Is this the moment when Ireland, well Dublin anyway, became Manchester United mad and adopted the team from across the Irish Sea as their own? Or would it be shortly after another game in which Liam played less than five months later? One of the Shamrock Rovers players who scored that day was a former Manchester United trainee,Thomas "*Tommy*" Hamilton, a native from Bray, County Wicklow. Tommy never made a first team appearance for United and left Old Trafford in November 1955 to join Shamrock Rovers. He also played for Cork, Hibernian and Limerick in the League of Ireland. He was a midfielder and won two caps for the Republic of Ireland, making his debut on 5 April 1959 in a European Championships qualifier against Czechoslovakia at Dalymount Park. The Irish won 2-0. His second and last cap was the return group game versus Czechoslovakia, a 4-0 defeat on 10 May 1959.

Jimmy "*Maxie*" McCann played for Shamrock Rovers in both games (he too scored in Rovers' 3-2 loss at Old Trafford) and when he was once asked what memories he had of them he said: "*I can remember the crowds trying to get up the lane at Dalymount to get into the changing rooms. You had to almost beat your way up. The whole country went bananas when Shamrock Rovers were drawn to play Manchester United. They had lots of great players such as David Pegg, Johnny Berry, and, of course, Duncan Edwards and Liam.*" McCann added that all of the Shamrock Rovers players would have personally known Liam from his Home Farm days and how sad they were when they heard the devastating news that Liam had died in the Munich Air Disaster: "*Liam used to come up to train at Milltown because he was a friend of Tommy Hamilton (Hamilton also played in both games for Shamrock Rovers). He became a friend of all the Shamrock Rovers players then. They had a TV in the bar at Milltown and most of the squad went up to watch the news on the BBC. It was a terrible blow. It was like losing one of your own family. Liam was a really lovely guy.*" Liam played in United's opening 9 League games of the 1957-58 season in defence of their First Division Championship crown (and hoping to win three in a row), scoring 8 times, before missing the trip to Wolves on 28 October 1957 which United lost 3-1. John Doherty, who replaced Whelan in the Wolves game, scored the United goal. Whelan then played in United's next 11 League games, scoring 4 more goals, before eventually losing his place in the team to the ever-improving Charlton. Liam's final League game for Manchester United was played on 14 December 1957, a 1-0 home defeat to Chelsea. Charlton replaced Liam for United's next game, a 4-0 win over Leicester City at Old Trafford on 22 December 1957 with Charlton scoring in the match. The game also marked the debut of Northern Ireland's international goalkeeper Harry Gregg, a recent acquisition from Doncaster Rovers. Billy never wore the United shirt again and was only on the plane to Yugoslavia for United's European Cup quarter-final 2nd leg tie versus Red Star Belgrade as a back-up to Charlton. And so, one of the most talented of all of the famous Busby Babes was tragically killed in the Munich Air Disaster on 6 February 1958 along with seven of his teammates. It has been claimed that Liam, like his manager, a regular church goer, said "*If the worst happens I am ready for death. I hope we all are,*' as the plane sped down the runway for a third and final time.

Manchester United's loss was also the Republic of Ireland's loss and just like Duncan Edwards, who also perished in the disaster, the football world was deprived of seeing just how good these two young men would have become. Both were nowhere near their peak with Duncan aged just 21 and Billy just 22 when his life came to an end. Billy played in 98 games for Manchester United, scoring 52 times, a quite astonishing goals-to-games ratio when you consider that Billy was not even an out-and-out striker.

When his body returned home from Munich it was placed in the gymnasium at Old Trafford and lay alongside six of his team-mates whose lives were also so cruelly ended when the plane crashed. Seven Busby Babes side by side again for one last time. Duncan Edwards lost his brave battle for life 15 days after the crash, 21 February 1958.

Liam's funeral took place at Glasnevin Cemetery in Dublin and was one of the biggest in the history of the cemetery. His cortège left the Christ the King Church on Offaly Road, Cabra close to his parents' home and slowly made its way through the streets of the north side of Dublin with thousands of fans lining the route to pay tribute to one of their own. As the funeral procession passed St Peter's School hundreds of pupils stood with their heads bowed. His coffin was covered in wreaths including one sent by his former team-mates and the management and Board of Directors of Manchester United which was a miniature Old Trafford. At one point the hearse carrying his coffin had to wait until the Garda moved mourners off the road who had spilled off the crammed pavements and on to the path of the funeral route. Many Irish fans still visit his grave today placing red, white and black flowers on the grave as a mark of respect, to a footballer who could have rivalled George Best for the title of Ireland's greatest ever player. The vast majority of visitors to his grave never saw Billy play yet because of the ever lasting legacy he left behind, still regard him as one of the best ever footballers to play for Home Farm, Manchester United and Ireland.

On 8 December 2006 the railway bridge on Faussagh Road/ Dowth Avenue junction in the place of his birth, Cabra, Dublin, was renamed in his honour. Fittingly the unveiling ceremony was performed by Billy's close friend and Manchester United team-mate Sir Bobby Charlton. Speaking about Billy, Sir Bobby said: "*Billy had brilliant close control and was a natural goal scorer. His forte was to scheme, to shape possibilities with his skill and excellent vision. He scored so many goals from midfield he would be a wonder of today's game.*" Nice words from the Manchester United legend who dubbed Old Trafford "*The Theatre of Dreams.*"

When he was a young boy Liam had to cross the bridge to go to school, cross it to attend practice at Home Farm FC and cross if to visit Dalymount Park to watch the Republic of Ireland play. Even today the people of Cabra, quite rightly, speak with enormous pride about Liam whilst the plaque serves as a lasting memory to the people of the area and reminds the children growing up that their area was home to one of the greatest players Manchester United ever had, Liam Whelan a Busby Babe. And who knows maybe one day Cabra may present Manchester United with another William Augustine Whelan. The inscription on the plaque on the Liam Whelan Bridge reads:

"To honour the memory of Liam Whelan
A Cabra boy who played for Ireland and Manchester United
A Busby Babe who died in the Munich Air Disaster in 1958 aged
22 years."

The then Taoiseach Bertie Ahern led a memorial service on Saturday 2 February 2008 at Liam Whelan Bridge and two days later the Irish national postal body "An Post" issued a 55 cent postage stamp to commemorate the 50th anniversary of the Munich Air Disaster which showed a photo of Liam wearing his red United jersey. On 6 February 2008, exactly 50 years to the day the disaster occurred, the Republic of Ireland played an international friendly against Brazil at Croke Park in memory of those who lost their lives in the Munich Air Disaster. Manchester United's John O'Shea played in the game as did former United player Liam Miller, who sadly passed away on 9 February 2018 aged just 36. The Irish lost 1-0 with Robinho scoring for the Brazilians. Many sports writers likened Whelan's style of play as being relaxed, a player who shuffled along the pitch with ball skills a conjuror would have been proud of possessing, a dummy salesman, as it were, to his unsuspecting customers, defenders. He was put quite simply, pure poetry in motion.

Father David McGarry (Parish Priest of The Roman Catholic Parish of St Catherine of Siena, Didsbury, Manchester) who was coached at St. Bede's College, Manchester by Johnny Carey during the late 1940s remembers the artistry of Liam Whelan: *"Billy Whelan was a very unusual player. One day I was watching him from the Scoreboard End at Old Trafford and I saw him walk up to a full-back with his knees in a high step with the ball at his feet. He mesmerised the poor chap as he walked along the dead ball line. In many games there are certain magic moments which capture the beauty of football. I'll never forget the grace of Billy Whelan and I bet those standing beside me in the Scoreboard End that afternoon will never forget him either."*

William Augustine Whelan, thank you for the 994 days you played for Manchester United. You will always be remembered.

Did You Know That?

Some years after Liam passed away, Harry Gregg spoke to RTE in Dublin about his former team-mate: "There were three of us, Gregg, Blanchflower and Whelan and we were all Paddies whether we liked it or not! In those days you were allowed two stand seats, and two terrace tickets for your family and friends. But I didn't know you were allowed to purchase ten tickets. So I'm training with Liam Whelan and he said: 'What did you do with your tickets?' I said: 'I gave them to the family.' He said: 'What about the other ten?' I said: ' I let the lads...' he said: 'Jesus, you don't do that, you could live off them for a year!' Don't let anybody kid you that Liam Whelan couldn't take care of himself!"

GAME NO. 40
CHARLTON ATHLETIC 1-5 UNITED
FIRST DIVISION
THE VALLEY, LONDON
18 FEBRUARY 1957
ATTENDANCE – 16,308

THE YOUNG ONES

"Football has to be fun for kids or it doesn't make sense."
Johann Cruyff

Matt Busby preferred to have a player make his way into United's first team via their youth system than make a signing. Busby didn't sign many players when he was United boss, that was partly because of the talent-spotting ability of his right hand man Jimmy Murphy and partly because for the most part United were strapped for cash, particularly in the ten years following the war.

On Monday 18 February 1957, Matt Busby fielded a team which contained 8 players who had progressed to the first team having played for United's famous Manchester United Junior Athletic Club (MUJAC) or Reserve Team. Busby sent out this young team to play Charlton Athletic at The Valley, in the First Division: Ray Wood, Roger Byrne (Capt), Geoff Bent, Wilf McGuinness, Mark Jones, Eddie Colman, Johnny Berry, Liam Whelan, David Pegg, Tommy Taylor, Bobby Charlton.

Of that team Ray Wood was acquired from Darlington in November 1949 in a £5000 deal, Johnny Berry cost £15,000 from Birmingham City in August 1951 and Tommy Taylor was a £29,999 acquisition from Barnsley on 5 March 1951, the remainder were all MUJAC graduates. Geoff Bent replaced an injured Duncan Edwards in the side, another graduate from MUJAC. At the time it was the most number of young players any English top flight club had ever played in their senior side for a competitive match.

United's young side were scintillating and swept the home side away with an emphatic 5-1 win. Bobby Charlton bagged a hat-trick, his seventh for the club, against his namesake and Taylor scored twice. Less than a year later six of the MUJAC players who played in the game tragically lost their young lives in the Munich Air Disaster on 6 February 1958. Byrne, Bent, Jones, Colman, Whelan and Pegg all died instantly as did Tommy Taylor. Duncan Edwards who played in the 3-3 draw away to Red Star Belgrade the night before died 15 days later in his hospital bed in Munich. Berry and Charlton survived the air crash although Berry's injuries were so severe he never played again, whilst McGuinness was not on the flight home from Munich to Manchester as he was out injured at the time. Harry Gregg had replaced Wood in the United goal after he joined from Doncaster Rovers in December 1957.

The 5-1 victory over Charlton Athletic was only the third and last, game in which 7 of the 8 Busby Babes who lost their lives in the Munich Air Disaster played in the same Manchester United side. The first occasion was an away league game versus Aston Villa on 8 December 1956, a match United won 3-1 with two goals from Taylor and one from Dennis Viollet. In the match, Bent replaced an injured Byrne at left-back. A week later, 15 December 1956, Bent kept his place in the team, Byrne was out injured, when United lost 3-1 away to Birmingham City in the First Division (scorer: Whelan).

It is easy in hindsight to view the Busby Babes through the prism of modern day academies when in fact what Busby and Murphy were doing was radical. The famed academies of Ajax and Barcelona were decades away from producing talent in significant numbers for the club's first team while the rest of English football's reaction to United's revolution was summed up by Manchester City manager Les McDowell who answered a question about his club's youth system by saying "we won't be getting involved in any of that nonsense".

What Busby and Murphy were doing wasn't unique – Major Frank Buckley had developed Wolves youth system before the war, albeit with a more direct playing style – but the scale of it shook British football. By the mid-1950s United had the best young player from every part of the British Isles bar Scotland (and Busby tried to sign Denis Law). Before the decade was out all professional clubs would invest in their academies and United's monopoly would be over.

Over the decades United's youth system has become very much a part of the club's DNA and the club can boast the proud record of having at least one youth player involved in every first team squad since Thomas Hanley was selected on 30th October 1937 (a 1–0 defeat at Fulham) – that's over 4,000 first team matches and counting. Yet across the ten decades that United's youth team has been honing talented youngsters for promotion to the first team, the team of the 1950s is regarded as the zenith.

GEOFF BENT

Geoffrey "Geoff" Bent was born on 27 September 1932 in Irlams o' th' Height, in Pendleton, Salford. Aged 15, he signed as a trainee for United in August 1948 after leaving school and in May 1949 he signed professional terms. He made his debut on 11 February 1954 aged 21 in a 4–2 victory over Burnley at Turf Moor in the First Division. He only made 12 appearances for United without ever scoring. He played twice in season 1954-55, 4 games in 1955-56 when United were crowned Champions and 6 games during season 1956-57 when United retained the First Division Championship. His low number of games meant he did not qualify for a League Championship winners' medal. Geoff was a full-back and was used by Matt Busby as cover for Roger Byrne (right-back) and Bill Foulkes (left-back). In season 1957-58 he broke a foot and was only included in the squad to play Red Star Belgrade as emergency cover for Byrne who himself had just recovered from injury but his fitness was a slight doubt. Byrne captained the team on the night in the Yugoslav capital.

ROGER BYRNE

Roger William Byrne was born in Gorton, Manchester on 8 September 1929. Aged 18 he signed as a trainee for United. He made his debut on 24 November 1951 in a 0-0 draw away to Liverpool in the First Division. Byrne almost became a Rugby League player as he was not considered good enough to become a professional footballer. He signed up for two years National Service with the Royal Air Force and played rugby and boxed for his Unit. He was also a very good gymnast but Byrne wanted to be a professional footballer and he was playing for his local side Ryder Brow when he was spotted by legendary United Scout Joe Armstrong. He made 280 appearances for the club and scored 20 goals. When Johnny Carey left United at the end of the 1952-53 season, Matt Busby handed the 24-year old Byrne the captain's armband. Byrne also won 33 consecutive caps for England from his debut on 3 April 1954 and scored one own goal. He also missed two penalties for England against Brazil and Yugoslavia in 1956. At United Byrne won 3 First Division Championship winners medals in 1951-52, 1955-56 and 1956-57 and an FA Cup runners-up medal in 1957. In season 1956-57, Byrne was named fourth in the Football Writers' Association Player of the Year Award which went to Tom Finney of Preston North End. Byrne helped United win the First Division Championship title in 1956-57 and narrowly missed out on becoming a Double winner when United lost the 1957 FA Cup final 2-1 against Aston Villa. There is a street named "Roger Byrne Close" in memory of him and in May 2019 a plaque dedicated to him was unveiled at Abbey Hey Primary School, Gorton which he attended from 1935-41.

EDDIE COLMAN

Eddie Colman was born on 1 November 1936 in Ordsall, Salford. When he left school aged 15, he signed as a trainee for United and on his 17th birthday he signed professional terms. He made his debut on 12 November 1955 aged 19 in a 3-1 loss to Bolton Wanderers at Burnden Park. He made 108 appearances for the club and scored 2 goals. Colman never played for England at full international level. During his United career, he won 2 First Division Championship winners medals in 1955-56 and 1956-57 and an FA Cup runners-up medal in 1957. Colman won 3 FA Youth Cup winners' medals with United in 1953, 1954 and 1955 scoring two goals in the 1955 final. At the University of Salford there is a block of flats on the campus named in his memory, "Eddie Colman Court" and a street in Manchester is named "Eddie Colman Close."

DUNCAN EDWARDS

Duncan Edwards was born in Dudley on 1 October 1936. Aged 15, he signed as a trainee for United and on his 17th birthday he signed professional terms. He made his debut on 4 April 1953 aged just 16 in a 4-1 loss at Old Trafford to Cardiff City. He made 108 appearances for the club and scored 2 goals. Edwards also won 18 caps for England, scoring 8 goals, from his debut on 2 April 1955, a 7-2 win over Scotland at Wembley Stadium. Aged 18 years and 183 days Edwards became the youngest England player of the 20th century, Roger Byrne also played in the game. During his United career Edwards won 2 First Division Championship winners medals in 1955-56 and 1956-57 and an FA Cup runners-up medal in 1957. Edwards won 3 FA Youth Cup winners' medals with United in 1953, 1954 and 1955 scoring two goals in the 1954 final and one goal in the 1955 final. There is a street in Manchester named "Duncan Edwards Court" in memory of him. In his hometown of Dudley two stained glass windows in St Francis Church were unveiled by Matt Busby in 1961 in Edwards' memory, one depicting him in his red Manchester United kit and the other in his white England kit. In October 1999, a statue of Duncan Edwards was unveiled in the Market Place, Dudley by his mother, Sarah, and his former Manchester United team-mate, Sir Bobby Charlton.

MARK JONES

Mark Jones was born on 15 June 1933 in Wombwell, Barnsley. He joined United as a trainee on his 15th birthday when he left school. He made his debut on 7 October 1950 aged 17 in a 3-1 win over Sheffield Wednesday in the First Division at Old Trafford. Jones made 121 appearances for the club and scored 1 goal. He never played for England at full international level although he came close when he was on the substitutes' bench. During his United career he won 2 First Division Championship winners medals in 1955-56 and 1956-57 but missed the 1957 FA Cup final defeat to Aston Villa with an eye injury. Jones won 2 FA Youth Cup winners' medals with United in 1956 and 1957. There is a street in Manchester named "Mark Jones Walk" in his memory.

DAVID PEGG

David Pegg was born on 20 September 1935 in Ardwick-le-Street,

Doncaster. He joined United as a trainee on his 15th birthday when he left school. Pegg made his debut on 6 December 1952 aged 17 in a 3-2 victory versus Middlesbrough at Old Trafford. He made 150 appearances for the club and scored 21 goals. He was capped once by England at full international level in 1957. During his United career he won 2 First Division Championship winners medals in 1955-56 and 1956-57 and an FA Cup runners–up medal in 1957. Pegg won 2 FA Youth Cup winners' medals with United in 1953 and 1954 scoring three goals in the 1954 final. There is a street in Manchester named "David Pegg Walk" in his memory.

TOMMY TAYLOR

Tommy Taylor was born on 29 January 1932 at 4 Quarry Street, Smithies, Barnsley, England. He signed for Manchester United from his hometown club, Barnsley, on 5 March 1955 for a fee of £29,999. He made his debut for Manchester United just two days later on 7 March 1955, in a 5-2 victory over Preston North End at Old Trafford and scored twice. It only took him 17 minutes to score the first of his 131 goals for United in a career total of 191 games. No wonder he was nicknamed "The Smiling Executioner"! Taylor played 19 times for England, they won 11, drew 6 and lost twice and he scored an incredible 16 goals. With United, Taylor won 2 First Division Championship winners medals in 1955-56 and 1956-57 and an FA Cup runners–up medal in 1957. There is a street in Manchester named "Tommy Taylor Close" in his memory and a plaque to his memory on the house he shared with his wife on Greatstone Road, Stretford less than a mile away from Old Trafford.

LIAM WHELAN

William "Liam" or "Billy" Augustine Whelan was born on 1 April 1935 in Cabra, Dublin. He joined United as a trainee on 1 May 1953 after he was spotted playing for his local club, Home Farm by Billy Behan, United's Scout in the Republic of Ireland. Whelan made his debut on 26 March 1955 aged 21 in a 2-0 win over Preston North End at Deepdale. He made 98 appearances for the club and scored 52 goals. He was capped four times by his country. During his United career, he won a First Division Championship winners medal in 1956-57 but Busby opted to play Bobby Charlton instead of Whelan in the 1957 FA Cup final. Whelan won an FA Youth Cup winners medal with United in 1953 scoring two goals. On 8 December 2006, the railway bridge on Fassaugh Road/Dowth Avenue junction in Cabra was named in his honour. On 4 February 2008, the Irish national postal body, An Post, issued a 55c postage stamp to commemorate the 50th anniversary of the Munich Air Disaster showing a head and shoulders photo of Whelan wearing the red Manchester United jersey with the Munich Clock at Old Trafford also featured. There is a street in Manchester named "Billy Whelan Walk" in his memory.

The Busby Babes dominated English football, they had a swagger, they had style, they were admired by all football fans but whereas other teams attempted to copy them, they simply failed. The Busby Babes were a truly unique collection of gifted and talented young footballers.

When the bodies of Byrne, Bent, Jones, Colman, Whelan, Pegg and Taylor were brought home from Munich their coffins were laid out in the gymnasium at Old Trafford, seven team-mates side-by-side for one last time. These eight young men who had played football for fun were now gone but will never be forgotten.

Did You Know That?

On 8 February 1958, Manchester United's home First Division game versus Wolverhampton Wanderers was postponed as a mark of respect to the 22 people who lost their lives in the Munich Air Disaster (Duncan Edwards was the twenty-third and last to die). All across Great Britain a two minutes silence was observed at every sports ground as the British spotting public paid homage to the dead.

GAME NO. 41
DERBY COUNTY 0-2 UNITED
FA CUP SEMI-FINAL
HILLSBOROUGH STADIUM, SHEFFIELD
3 APRIL 1976
ATTENDANCE- 55,000

"Never let inexperience get in the way of ambition."

Terry Josephson

In 1975 Tommy Docherty transformed Manchester United with the signing of two relative unknowns – wingers Steve Coppell and Gordon Hill. Liverpool-born Economics degree student Coppell was an unlikely figure in Manchester United's re-birth. Arriving in March 1975 for £60,000 from Tranmere to displace Matt Busby's last signing, Willie Morgan, on the right wing, Coppell quickly became a firm fan favourite during an eight-year Old Trafford career that brought 70 goals in 396 appearances. In contrast to the studious scouser, left-winger Gordon Hill, who arrived in November 1975 following a £70,000 transfer from Millwall, was a street-wise cockney with a lethal shot and an attitude that chimed with the young United supporters that followed the club around the country in droves. Together the pair would terrorise the best teams in the country following United's return to the top flight.

Rather than switch to something more staid against the better teams of the First Division, The Doc persisted with the 4-2-4 formation that had seen United return to the top flight at the first time of asking. Following Morgan's departure Alex Stepney was the last member of the Class of '68 remaining at the club; at full back were tough-tackling Scots Alex Forsyth and Stewart Houston who attempted to cover the flanks (wingers were not encouraged to track back); at centre-half captain Martin Buchan provided calm command amid the storm while alongside him ball-playing defender Brian Greenhoff was encouraged to join in the mayhem further forward. Diminutive midfielders Gerry Daly and Sammy McIlroy were full of energy and invention and in front of them were Lou Macari and Stuart Pearson, surely the smallest front pairing in the history of the club who nevertheless fed off superb crosses from Hill and Coppell. Many have since described Docherty's team as 'punk football' – an apt description given the era, even if Johnny Rotten was as yet unknown to the British public!

Tommy Docherty's exciting young side were a breath of fresh air in the top flight, like a bunch of kids invading an adult dinner party. Perhaps it was the exuberance of youth in the side and the lack of top flight football experience, or maybe it was down to their manager's Glaswegian swagger which reflected on the players' performances, but United settled in seamlessly among the big boys. They were undefeated in their opening six games which produced 5 wins and a draw and against all odds they sat at the top of the table. However with the combination of a dip in form and injuries to key players, they simply could not sustain their title challenge despite not having been outside the top 5 all season. United eventually finished a respectable third in their first year back behind Queens Park Rangers and champions Liverpool. It was United's highest place finish since season 1967-68 when they so narrowly missed out on winning a then unique double of First Division and European Cup.

So all hopes on glory were pinned on that season's FA Cup. In Round 3 United's inexperienced but hugely ambitious side beat Oxford United 2-1 at Old Trafford with both goals scored by United's classy Republic of Ireland midfielder Gerry Daly. There were very few players who were as calm taking a penalty as Daly, he seemed to have the knack of sending the goalkeeper the wrong way. In the next round United's name was drawn first again and Peterborough United provided the opposition. Goals from Forsyth, McIlroy and Hill eased them past The Posh into Round 5 with a 3-1 victory. That brought about a trip to Filbert Street to face Leicester City, a rematch of the 1963 FA Cup final and on this occasion United defeated The Foxes 2-1, Macari and Daly the goal scorers. In the Sixth Round United were handed another home tie. Wolverhampton Wanderers were the visitors and earned a home replay following a 1-1 draw (scorer: Daly). Three days later United faced Wolves at Molineux in what proved to be a classic cup-tie – Wolves went two up after just 20 minutes before goals from Pearson just before half-time and Greenhoff midway through the second half took the game into extra time. It took a spectacular volley from Sammy McIlroy to decide the tie and United somehow held on to make the semis.

The other three teams left in the competition were Crystal Palace, Derby County and Southampton. Palace were a Third Division side (finished fifth), Southampton were in Division Two (finished sixth), whilst 1974-75 champions Derby County would end the season in fourth place in the First Division, one place and three points behind United. The top flight sides were drawn together and pundits assumed that whoever won this game would see off either lower division side in the showpiece final.

On 3 April 1976, Tommy Docherty's Red Army travelled to Hillsborough, the home of Sheffield Wednesday, to see if United could reach their first FA Cup final since their victory at Wembley in 1963. The Brotherhood of Man were at No.1 in the UK Singles Chart with their 1976 Eurovision Contest winning song, "Save All Your Kisses For Me" but the question on the fans' lips was, "Who would be kissing goodbye to their dreams of lifting the FA Cup?

It was a bright sunny afternoon in South Yorkshire and three quarters of the ground were steeped in red. Hillsborough, along with Villa Park, home to Aston Villa, were among the favoured venues to host FA Cup semi-final games as the grounds were easily reached by motorway. In many ways it proved to be a hoodoo for both clubs as Villa had not reached the last four of the competition since 1959-60 when they were beaten 1-0 by Wolverhampton Wanderers at The Hawthorns while Sheffield Wednesday had last made it all of the way to the final in 1966 but lost 3-2 to Everton after being 2-0 up after 57 minutes.

The United side that day was: Alex Stepney, Alex Forsyth, Stewart Houston, Martin Buchan (Capt), Brian Greenhoff, Steve Coppell, Gerry Daly, David McCreery, Gordon Hill, Sammy McIlroy, Stuart Pearson.

Reigning champions Derby County, managed by Dave Mackay, included Roy McFarland, David Nish, Colin Todd, Archie Gemmell, Kevin Hector, Bruce Rioch, ex-Manchester City forward Francis Lee, and the player whose goal in extra-time of the 1971 FA Cup final gave Arsenal the Double, Charlie George and were marginal favourites to win.

Yet on the day United were too good for The Rams. Derby's defence were never given a moment's rest with the two Northern Ireland internationals, McCreery and McIlroy, a Green Dynamic Duo, bossing the midfield. McCreery in particular was a constant thorn in their side with his ferocious, take no prisoners style of tackling. Pancho never allowed a defender to take his time on the ball, while wingers Coppell and Hill made non-stop raids all afternoon as captain Buchan marshalled his defence and led his team like a Field Marshall commanding his troops.

The mercurial Hill, who always looked like he had the ball tied to the tip of his left boot with an invisible piece of string, was the game's outstanding player. The man the fans had nicknamed "Merlin" produced a goal in each half – the first came after a Derby attack broke down, Greenhoff found Hill who played a one-two with Daly before setting himself and curling a superb shot into the top left hand corner. United continue to dominate but several times Derby forced Stepney into action. Then with time running out and just as Derby were beginning to throw men forward in desperation United won a free kick 30 yards out. The quick-thinking Hill surprised the Derby defence by hammering it at goal before they were set and the ball took a slight deflection to put United 2-0 up.

United would face Southampton at Wembley after The Saints had beaten Crystal Palace by the same score at Stamford Bridge but alas despite the predictions of a straightforward win for United, Southampton pulled off one of the biggest shocks in the history of the tournament. A controversial Bobby Stokes goal (which many United fans felt was offside) proved the difference on an afternoon when United just couldn't find their rhythm. The following day at the team's open top bus tour in Manchester The Doc promised fans that they would be back in the final the following May and win the FA Cup...

Did You Know That?

At the end of the 1976–77 season, Gerry Daly left United and teamed-up with his old boss Tommy Docherty. Not long after his arrival at The Baseball Ground, Daly scored a penalty versus Manchester City in a home First Division game but the referee made him take the spot kick again following complaints from the City players who claimed that the ball was not on the penalty spot! In fact no one knew where the penalty spot was as the box was a mud bath. So the referee had the penalty spot repainted and Daly placed the ball on it. Daly retook the penalty and sent Joe Corrigan the wrong way again!

GAME NO. 42
FC BARCELONA 1–2 UNITED
1991 EUROPEAN CUP WINNERS' CUP FINAL
STADION FEIIJENOORD, ROTTERDAM
15 MAY 1991
ATTENDANCE – 45,000

DREAMS

Before the 1990–91 season the 5-year ban imposed on English clubs competing in European club football's three major cup competitions following the Heysel Stadium disaster was lifted. On 29 May 1985, Juventus faced Liverpool in the European Cup final in Brussels. About an hour before kick–off a crowd of Liverpool fans charged towards a group of Juventus fans which resulted in a wall collapsing. A total of 39 people, mostly Italian fans, lost their lives. UEFA acted swiftly and banned all English clubs for five years but gave Liverpool an additional three years reduced to a year on appeal.

The ban meant that United, FA Cup winners in 1985, were denied the opportunity of competing in the 1985–86 European Cup Winners' Cup which was won by Dynamo Kiev (their second victory in the tournament after winning it in 1974–75). Similarly Everton, the 1984–

85 League Champions, were not permitted to enter the European Cup, a competition ultimately won by Steaua Bucharest. However, the Toffees did win the 1984-85 European Cup Winners' Cup three days before the Wembley loss to United. The loss of European football over the next five years had a negative impact on the English game and many pundits felt that it would be years before English clubs would win one of the three European trophies.

Manchester United fans have always had a close had a special relationship with European competition. As the first English club to enter European competition and the tragedy of Munich, the relationship with the continent's finest is woven into the fabric of the club and the loss of European action was never felt more keenly during those 5 years than at Old Trafford. UEFA introduced the European Cup Winners' Cup in season 1960-61 as a secondary competition to run in tandem with the European Cup which was first contested in season 1955-56 and the Inter-Cities Fairs Cup, although this competition was not organised by UEFA and continues to be overlooked as a proper European trophy as a result. Qualification for the Cup Winners' Cup could only be achieved by winning a country's major domestic cup, although cup runners-up could represent their country if a team won a domestic double.

United qualified for the 1990-91 European Cup Winners' Cup having beaten Crystal Palace 1-0 in the 1990 FA Cup final replay. Alongside them in the draw were the likes of Red Star Belgrade, who had won the double in Yugoslavia the previous season but were banned from the European Cup by UEFA, and Hadjuk Split, runners-up in the Yugoslav Cup, who were also disqualified from competing in the 1990-91 European Cup as a result of the on-going war in the country. So UEFA invited Bray Wanderers from the Republic of Ireland and Trabzonspur from Turkey to contest a Qualifying Round to make up the 32 team competition. The Turkish side won 3-1 on aggregate over two legs (1-1 away & 2-0 at home).

The competition was packed with quality – Aberdeen, winners under Alex Ferguson in 1982-83, Steaua Bucharest, winners of the European Cup in 1985-86, PSV Eindhoven, European champions in 1987-88, Spanish giants Barcelona who lifted the Cup Winners' Cup in season 1988-89 and who went on to win the first of their 5 European Cups the following season and Italy's Sampdoria who had won the cup the previous season.

United were drawn to play Hungarian cup winners Pesci Munkas in Round 1 and eased through 3-0 on aggregate over two legs. The draw for Round 2 produced a one hour coach journey for United, a 56 mile jaunt down the M56 to face Welsh Cup runners-up Wrexham (winners Hereford could not compete being English). United eased past the Welshmen 3-0 at Old Trafford and 2-0 at The Racecourse Ground.

Round 3 was actually the quarter-final stages of the competition as there were only 32 teams contesting the cup and United drew Coupe de France holders Montpellier. Luckily for United Eric Cantona's one year loan spell from Marseille to Montpellier had been cancelled at the end of the 1989-90 season but the French team still had Colombian Carlos Valderrama in their ranks and would be no pushovers. On 6 March 1991 United drew 1-1 on a frustrating night at Old Trafford and were given little chance of progressing at Stade de la Mosson 13 days later. Yet United defied the odds and left France with a 2-0 win – the turning point was a goal deep into first half added on time, a swerving 30 yard free-kick from Clayton Blackmore that took the French keeper completely by surprise, a late penalty from Steve Bruce settled the tie.

Four teams were left standing: Barcelona, Juventus, Legia Warsaw and United. The semi-final draw was kind to The Reds as United's travelling Red and White Army were drawn to face the Poles. On 10 April 1991 intrepid fans celebrated a 3-1 victory in Warsaw with goals from McClair, Hughes and Bruce. In the other semi-final, Barcelona defeated Juventus 3-1 at Camp Nou. In the home tie United could only manage a 1-1 draw with Lee Sharpe scoring but they had secured their place in the final with a 4-1 aggregate victory and would play Barcelona in the final who lost their second leg 1-0 at Stadio delle Alpi but progressed with a 3-2 win over the two legs.

Tens of thousands of United fans started planning their journey to Feyenoord's home stadium nicknamed "De Kuip" (The Tub). The movie *Planes, Trains and Automobiles* starring John Candy and Steve Martin came to mind as United fans jumped in cars, boarded flights and sailed on ferries to descend on the port city of Rotterdam. This being the height of Madchester the travelling army of Reds wore flares and bucket hats – it was like a footballing Woodstock!

The Catalans were coached by legendary Dutch international Johann Cruyff who had already led the Spanish giants to the 1990-91 La Liga by ten points from Atlético Madrid and would go on to win the next three titles - this was his famous "Dream Team", a side packed with an abundance of talent from captain and playmaker Jose Ramon Alexanko, Holland's Ronald Koeman, Jon Andoni Goikoetxea, widely regarded as the best young player in Europe, and a potent front two of Julio Salinas, who had scored in the 1989 final, and Denmark's Michael Laudrup, a lightning quick and very stylish player with silky skills. Laudrup possessed the same drag back technique followed by a burst of pace that Cruyff himself had made famous some 20 years earlier. However one key player missing was their prolific Bulgarian striker nicknamed "The Gunslinger" Hristo Stoichkov, who was out with a thigh strain. He was the second highest goalscorer in the competition with 8 goals, Juventus's Roberto Baggio had scored 9.

United had finished sixth in the First Division and were hoping to avenge the bitter taste of League Cup final defeat to Sheffield Wednesday just 24 days earlier. United were the team in form in the competition having not lost a game on their way to the final whereas their opponents had lost twice and Brian McClair had scored in every round. When the United team emerged from the tunnel they were wearing a pristine all white kit and the Spanish fans in the stadium must have thought their arch rivals, Real Madrid, had turned up to play them.

United's Starting XI was: Les Sealey, Denis Irwin, Clayton Blackmore, Steve Bruce, Gary Pallister, Bryan Robson (Capt), Mike Phelan, Paul Ince, Lee Sharpe, Brian McClair, Mark Hughes. Subs: Gary Walsh, Mal Donaghy, Neil Webb, Mark Robins, Danny Wallace.

Sealey was only given the all clear to play the day before the game after he suffered concussion in the loss to Sheffield Wednesday but refused to be substituted. Pallister had returned from injury and Alex Ferguson preferred Phelan over Webb to play alongside Robson in midfield. Barcelona were also without their first choice goalkeeper through suspension, Andoni Zubizarreta. His replacement, 23–year old Carles Busquets, was making his first team debut.

The opening 45 minutes was a cagey affair with both sides unwilling to risk a wayward attack which could leave them exposed to a counter but things opened up after half-time with Lee Sharpe making promising runs down the left to stretch the Catalans. In the 67th minute United were awarded a free kick on the left side of the Spanish penalty area, Bryan Robson took it and Steve Bruce rose above a defender and the on–rushing goalkeeper and headed towards goal. Mark Hughes was following in and he tapped the ball over the line and into the empty net – 1–0 to United and as both Bruce and Hughes took the congratulations from their teammates TV replays appeared to show that the ball had just crossed the goal line before Hughes touched it. It was difficult to tell. No doubt VAR would have given the goal to Bruce but the giant scoreboard credited Hughes with the goal. Seven minutes later The Tub almost burst when Hughes added a spectacular second. With Barca pressing for an equaliser United won the ball back and Robson chipped a beautiful pass over the heads of two Barcelona players which Hughes chased after and raced deep into the Spanish half. Goalkeeper Busquets, sensing the danger, ran out of his area and attempted a two footed tackle on the United striker but Sparky saw him coming and body swerved him which took the Welshman wide and over to the right hand side of the box. The Spanish goal was empty but surely the angle was too acute to attempt a shot at goal, nevertheless Sparky fired an arrow like shot with the outside of his right foot which found the back of the net as two defenders arrived a fraction of a second too late to prevent the ball crossing the line.

According to Aristotle, the legendary Greek philosopher, the Pythagoreans used mathematics for solely mystical reasons, devoid of practical application but not even Pythagoras himself could have come up with Hughes's split second calculations to find the finish with that shot! Sparky stood there, imperious, as he held his arms aloft as if to say to the Barcelona fans: "Now do you see what I can do?" Hughes had endured an unsuccessful stint with the Spanish side only a few seasons earlier. Things did not work out for him and in season 1987–88 he was loaned out to Bayern Munich. Thankfully Alex Ferguson persuaded him to return to Old Trafford in May 1988 and this was Sparky's payback and he quite rightly milked every second of it.

Undeterred Barca continued to press and Ronald Koeman made it a nervy ending for United when he beat Sealey with a perfectly flighted free kick from all of 30 yards in the 79th minute. Then in the 84th minute Sparky almost had a hat-trick but he was brought down by Nando who was sent off for a professional foul. It was one of many nasty tackles the Spanish side dished out to Hughes during the game, a sure sign they feared him, but each time Sparky refused to retaliate which incensed his aggressors even more and Nando's tackle was quite rightly dealt with by Bo Karlsson, the Swedish referee. Despite Barca being down to 10 men, United fans had their hearts in their months in the last minutes of the game when the Catalans broke through again and looked certain score but Blackmore cleared Laudrup's shot off the line. United held on and when the referee blew his whistle to end the game, they had won their first European trophy in 23 years and English football's first since the Heysel ban.

Alex Ferguson hugged every one of his players and after the game Sparky said that the first goal was Bruce's as he touched the ball when it had already crossed the line however Bruce was never officially credited with scoring in the final as UEFA awarded the goal to the United striker.

Denis Law, commenting on the game for ITV along with Brian Moore and Jimmy Greaves, was asked by Moore for his thoughts on United's victory. "It is not only a great night for Manchester United. It is also a great night for English football. We have been in the wilderness for the last five years so to come and be allowed back in it and then go on to win it is absolutely magnificent. And, when you look at the game they deserved to win it."

Did You Know That?

Only five clubs have won all three of European football's major trophies, the European Cup/ UEFA Champions League, UEFA Cup/ Europa League and European Cup Winners' Cup and they are Juventus, Ajax Amsterdam, FC Bayern Munich, Chelsea and Manchester United who completed this unique Treble in season 2016–17 when they beat Ajax 2-0 in the Europa League final. The European Cup Winners' Cup is now defunct, SS Lazio were the last ever winners of it in season 1998–99.

GAME NO. 43
UNITED 2-1 TOTTENHAM HOTSPUR
PREMIER LEAGUE
OLD TRAFFORD
16 MAY 1999
ATTENDANCE- 55,189

THE TREBLE PART 1

"It always seems impossible until it is done"
Nelson Mandela

Season 1998-99 is rightly remembered for United's historic treble while the title race that season is largely forgotten but this was a classic as an outstanding Arsenal team went toe-to-toe with United and the race went down to the wire with more twists and turns than an Olympic bobsleigh track.

Before the season Arsenal were bookmakers' favourites to retain their Premier League title. In the summer of 1998, Alex Ferguson added a treble of signings to his squad and brought in Jesper Blomqvist, Jaap Stam and Dwight Yorke and on the opening day of the season United drew 2-2 with Leicester City at Old Trafford (scorers: Teddy Sheringham 79 mins and David Beckham in the 90th minute). It was a particularly satisfying start for Beckham as he the young Londoner had been subject to considerable abuse since receiving a red card against Argentina in the World Cup, his late equaliser would also be the first of many late goals that historic season. Meanwhile Arsenal opened with a 2-1 home win over Nottingham Forest. On the second weekend of the campaign, United drew 0-0 away at West Ham United whilst The Gunners drew 0-0 away at Liverpool. Arsenal then drew their next three games, playing one game more than United before the sides met for the first of four times during the campaign. United had won their two home games during the same period, 4-1 versus Charlton Athletic and 2-0 against Coventry City.

Just as Ferguson had done, Arsenal boss Arsene Wenger had freshened-up his squad by signing the Swedish international midfielder Freddie Ljunberg and Argentina's Nelson Vivas while Ian Wright, who was the club's all-time record goalscorer with 185 goals, joined London rivals West Ham United. The two games against Arsenal could prove to be the difference between the sides yet ahead of this game

United were 8th and Arsenal 10th and it was Arsenal who took the early advantage with a comfortable 3-0 win at Highbury with new recruit Ljunberg among the goalscorers. It looked like the bookies had been right, Arsenal looked to be back to the form of the previous season and were just too powerful for a lacklustre United. After the game Arsene Wenger admitted the victory was crucial saying: "Maybe psychologically we knew we could beat United. If we had lost, we would not have won for five games but a win puts us up towards the top. We found our game in Lens last week (they drew 1-1) and today was our best of the season. The crowd were really behind us and it reminded me of the Everton game last season when we won the title. We have now got our offensive power back and had United under a lot of pressure." A dispirited Ferguson said: "In terms of sheer effort and determination, Arsenal were always better than us. We were second best in every challenge and it was a really disappointing performance. They wanted it more than we did."

Nevertheless after losing at Highbury, United put a 7 game unbeaten run together, winning 5 and drawing 2, the run included a 2-0 victory over bitter rivals Liverpool at Old Trafford with Denis Irwin scoring a penalty and Paul Scholes grabbing the other. Denis Irwin was as reliable from the spot as his fellow Republic of Ireland international Gerry Daly had been during the 1970s, Daly scored 17 penalties for United between 1973-77 while Irwin scored 12 penalties for United during his time at Old Trafford (1990-2002). Wimbledon were then beaten 5-1 at Old Trafford and Everton were swept aside at Goodison Park (4-1). In their following 7 games after beating United, Arsenal lost their next game 1-0 at Sheffield Wednesday, conceding a controversial last minute goal. The Arsenal centre-half Martin Keown was sent off (Arsenal's third red card of the season) before half-time in what was a bruising encounter which will always be remembered for Wednesday's Paolo Di Canio pushing referee Paul Alcock who stumbled backwards and fell to the ground. Arsenal won 4 and drew 2 of the other six including a goalless draw at home to North London rivals Tottenham Hotspur.

On 12 December 1998, a point from a 2-2 draw with Tottenham Hotspur at White Hart Lane was good enough to send United to the top of the Premier League. Aston Villa, the surprise team of the season, were second on 30 points while Arsenal were in sixth place, 5 points adrift of United. Within 24 hours of going top United were displaced by Villa who beat Arsenal 3-2 at Villa Park despite the visitors leading 2-0 at half-time. Two second half goals from Dion Dublin and another from Julian Joachim sent The Villains back to the summit. After they sold Dwight Yorke to United, Villa had spent the £12.6 million fee wisely. John Gregory, the Aston Villa manager, splashed out £5.75 million on a new striker, ex-United player Dion Dublin from Coventry City who had been the Premier League's joint top-scorer with Michael Owen (Liverpool) and Chris Sutton (Blackburn Rovers) in 1997–98 with 18 goals. Gregory then brought in former Arsenal legend Paul Merson, a player who had already won 2 First Division titles, the FA Cup, League Cup and European Cup Winners' Cup with The Gunners. The injection of Dublin and Merson into the Villa attack re-energised the team but their challenge to win their first title since 1980-81 was no match for United and Arsenal and they eventually ended the season sixth. Merson later said that his time with Aston Villa was the best part of his career.

There comes a game in every season when a team which wins the title can look back on and say "that was the defining game of the campaign". It can be a comprehensive home win, a narrow away victory, a derby triumph or beating your closest challengers for the title. On 19 December 1998, United were second in the table when they welcomed Middlesbrough to Old Trafford. The 3-2 loss proved to be United's last defeat of the season which comprised 20 Premier League games (14 wins, 6 draws), 8 FA Cup games (6 wins, 2 draws) and 5 Champions League games (3 wins, 2 draws) – a 33 game unbeaten run at the sharp end of the season. Tottenham Hotspur had ended United's hopes of a Quadruple when they beat them 3-1 at White Hart Lane on 2 December 1998 in Round 5 of the League Cup, Spurs went on to beat Leicester City 1-0 in the final but United would sweep the board and this huge unbeaten run would be the reason.

United had an impeccable January 1999, winning all three games: beating West Ham 4-1 at Old Trafford followed by away victories at Leicester City (6-2) and Charlton Athletic (1-0). In February 1999, United played five Premier League games winning four and drawing once, a 1-1 draw in the return against Arsenal maintained a 5 point gap between the teams in United's favour, United were top, Chelsea second, Arsenal third. The Gunners could point to an under-strength team as they were missing Bergkamp, Petit and Keown and in truth United should have won, Dwight Yorke missed an early penalty before Anelka opened the scoring just after half-time. United were grateful for former Gunner Andy Cole's equaliser on the hour mark.

United played two Premier League games in March 1999 and won both: a 2-1 away win at Newcastle United with Cole scoring twice and a 3-1 home win against Everton. Meanwhile, their London rivals won all 3 of their Premier League outings.

The run-in saw the race tighten when Arsenal beat Blackburn Rovers 1-0 and Wimbledon 5-1 in successive home games. When The Gunners trounced Middlesbrough 6-1 at the Riverside Stadium on 24 April 1999 they overtook United at the top of the table on 69 points to United's 67 but had played two games more. An opportunity to go back to the summit came United's way the next day if they could defeat Leeds United at Elland Road but they failed to capitalise and drew 1-1 (scorer: Cole) but United went back to the top after beating Aston Villa 2-1 at Old Trafford on 1 May, only to be usurped the next day when Arsenal beat Derby County 1-0 at Highbury. The Gunners had three games remaining to United's four and held a slender single point lead at the top.

A key evening came that Wednesday as the title rivals faced huge games against their biggest rivals: United were at Anfield and Arsenal at White Hart Lane – it was an extravaganza for Sky TV who followed both games through every twist and turn. Things seemed to be going well for both teams – United dominated the first hour at Anfield and strolled into a two-goal lead while Arsenal led 2-1 at half-time and were also in complete control but a Jamie Redknapp goal reignited Liverpool and when mild-mannered Denis Irwin was sent-off in the 75th minute despite replays suggesting he accidentally tripped his opponent, the home crowd sensed a comeback. With ten-man United besieged and time running out former United midfielder Paul Ince bundled the ball home in front of the Kop and celebrated in a manner which made a mockery of his former career at Old Trafford and put a huge spanner in the works of United's title charge. On hearing that their rivals had dropped points Arsene Wenger could be seen punching the air after Arsenal's 3-1 win in the North London derby and the away fans celebrated wildly, The Gunners now led the table by 3 points and their goal difference was one better than United's.

Four days later United played their game in hand when they travelled to North Yorkshire to face Middlesbrough – Dwight Yorke scored the only goal of the game meaning United were now on top of the Premier League table by virtue of goals scored (United 78, Arsenal 58) with the teams level on points and goal difference. The fate of Arsenal's season rested on their final two games, if Arsenal could beat

Leeds at Elland Road on 11 May 1999, the pressure would be back on United to beat relegation candidates Blackburn Rovers 24 hours later at Ewood Park. Regardless of the result, Leeds were guaranteed fourth place and qualification for the UEFA Cup in season 1999–2000 so Arsenal were favourites to win the game but the home side had not been reading the script as they defended for their lives before Jimmy Floyd Hasselbaink headed the winner in the 86th minute to earn his team a hard fought 1–0 victory. Now United needed a win and a draw from their remaining 2 games to clinch the title. What a contrast in emotions since the final whistle went in the games the previous midweek!

When asked about his team's chances after the Leeds defeat Arsene Wenger admitted, "Manchester United are favourites now. It is not over, but it will be if they get something from their game against Blackburn on Wednesday night. I am an optimist so we shall wait and see but obviously we are disappointed tonight. It was a huge tactical mistake to concede the goal because even a point would not have been too bad. We still created sufficient chances to win the match, but no-one can say Leeds did not give everything to win and I hope Blackburn and Tottenham now do the same against Manchester United." Wenger's wish almost came true when United could only manage a goalless draw against Blackburn Rovers, managed by former United assistant Brian Kidd. Rovers were relegated at the end of the season just four years after pipping United to the Premier League crown.

And so, with United holding a one point advantage the destiny of the title came down to the last weekend: both teams had won 21 games, United had drawn one more than Arsenal with 13 but crucially The Gunners had lost one game more. Arsenal could still win the title if they beat Aston Villa at Highbury and United failed to beat Tottenham Hotspur at Old Trafford. The fact that Arsenal's North London rivals Spurs were United's opponents led many to believe that this would be a walkover for The Reds with most Spurs fans openly admitting that they'd be delighted to lose if it stopped Arsenal winning the league.

On the final day of the season, 16 May 1999, Ferguson sent his team out at Old Trafford knowing that a win would see him win his fifth Premier League title but more importantly keep his team on track to win the Treble. With the FA Cup final the following Saturday and the Champions League final four days later it would be 11 days in heaven or 11 days in hell for United.

Manchester United: Peter Schmeichel, Gary Neville, Denis Irwin, David May, Ronny Johnsen, David Beckham, Paul Scholes, Roy Keane (Capt), Ryan Giggs, Dwight Yorke, Teddy Sheringham. Substitutes: Raimond van der Gouw, Phil Neville (for Giggs, 80 mins), Nicky Butt (for Scholes, 70 mins), Ole Gunnar Solskjaer, Andy Cole (for Sheringham, 46 mins)

Before the game the Sky cameras interviewed a number of Arsenal fans who openly admitted that they would be, for 90 minutes anyway, Spurs fans that afternoon. Tottenham were managed by former Arsenal boss George Graham who had won two league titles at Highbury as manager. Prior to the game Peter Schmeichel, who was playing his last ever game for United at Old Trafford (his 191st) before his move to Sporting Lisbon, was presented with a commemorative plaque by his manager. When the game kicked off the world held its breath.

Spurs were dealt an early blow when David Ginola, the PFA and FWA Player of the Year, was forced off with an injury. United almost took the lead after four minutes but Ian Walker saved Yorke's shot. Three minutes later a clearance from Walker struck Yorke and the Spurs goalkeeper and all he could do was watch the ball head towards his net. A relieved Walker saw the ball hit the post and rebound to safety. Ryan Giggs then headed straight at Walker and Yorke missed a golden opportunity to score when he was through on goal but blazed his shot wide.

Despite United's early dominance it was evident that Spurs were not going to hand the title to United, even if it meant that a win for them would gift the title to their fiercest rivals, as Steffen Iversen shot over the crossbar from 15 yards out then, in the 24th minute, the visitors took the lead. Les Ferdinand pounced on a long-ball flicked up-field by Iversen and the striker held off the challenge of two defenders and stuck out a boot which sent the ball spinning high into the air and over Schmeichel. United's Danish keeper had been denied his 180th clean sheet for United in his 252nd and last Premier League game as he agonisingly watched the ball trickle over the line and into his net. Some of the Spurs fans did not know whether to cheer at their team taking the lead or think about how delighted the goal would make the Arsenal fans. When news reached North London, the Arsenal fans erupted into cheers of delight as their team were drawing 0-0 with Aston Villa.

United attacked the Spurs defence relentlessly and Walker pulled off a superb double save when he first denied Scholes who fired a thunderbolt of a shot at him which he could only parry away but the ball fell to Yorke whose point blank shot was saved by the Spurs goalkeeper. When Beckham headed over from a Giggs cross it looked like it just wasn't going to be United's day but United never let their heads drop and three minutes before half-time they were level, the ball was passed along the Spurs box and came to Beckham who scored with a vicious curling shot past Walker. Old Trafford erupted with a cacophony of cheering and both games were level at half-time with the game at Highbury goalless.

At half-time Ferguson sent on Andy Cole for Teddy Sheringham, who had been jeered every time he touched the ball by the Spurs fans who had once adored him. Cole's impact was immediate: three minutes later he collected a pass from Gary Neville which he controlled on his right thigh, transferred to his left foot before lobbing it over Walker with his right. It was a sublime finish and sent the United fans into ecstasy – their hopes of winning the title were alive once more. On sixty-six minutes Kanu scored for Arsenal at Highbury and suddenly a Spurs goal would give Arsenal the title. Iversen almost ripped up United's Treble dreams but his shot was saved by Schmeichel. A third goal for United would be enough to see the game out but Yorke had an overhead kick saved and both Butt and Scholes missed when it looked easier to score. Somehow United played out time and got their trophy back and Ferguson matched the number of League titles which Sir Matt Busby won – 5 – in just 12 years as manager. They had just completed the first leg of their 'impossible' treble.

Did You Know That?

Only 10 players have played for Manchester United and Tottenham Hotspur: Jack Hall, Jimmy Brown, Michael Carrick, Dimitar Berbatov, Fraizer Campbell, Teddy Sheringham, Terry Gibson, Alan Brazil, Garth Crooks and Chris McGrath.

GAME NO. 44
LEICESTER CITY 1-3 UNITED
1963 FA CUP FINAL
WEMBLEY STADIUM
5 MAY 1963
ATTENDANCE- 100,000

UNITED MELT THE ICE KINGS

"Leaders aren't born they are made. And they are made just like anything else, through hard work. And that's the price we'll have to pay to achieve that goal, or any goal."

Vince Lombardi

I n season 1961-62 United finished in 15th position in the First Division and, having finished runners-up in 1958-59 and seventh in both 1959-60 and 1960-61, it seemed like Busby's attempt to rebuild after Munich looked doomed with many pundits sceptical whether the manager had the vigour to match the likes of Spurs, Burnley and surprise champions Ipswich managed by Alf Ramsey. The sale of the prolific Dennis Viollet to Stoke City for £25,000 in November 1961, had left the attack struggling for goals – they scored just 54 that season, this after hitting 88 in the previous season. United had already paid £35,000 for Arsenal's David Herd in the summer of '61 but although he had scored 17 in 32 appearances he still needed a quality striker partner and Busby knew just the man!

Busby had already tried to sign fellow Scot Denis Law when he was junior at Second Division Huddersfield Town and as Scotland boss he had given the Aberdonian his international debut aged just 18. Soon Law was off to Manchester City for a season before being lured by Italian Lira to Torino but the Scot didn't enjoy their negative style of football and was soon agitating for a move back to England.

The negotiations to sign Law hogged the back pages of English newspapers throughout the summer of 1962: Busby wanted to sign Law and Law was desperate to sign for United but the Italians used every trick in the book to stop it from happening. In the end it took the perseverance of a go-between to secure the transfer for £115,000 – a British record. Busby believed he'd got a bargain.

Going into the 1962-63 season Busby already had an experienced set of players to call upon including seven Irish internationals:

goalkeeper Harry Gregg, Jimmy Nicholson and Sammy McMillan from Northern Ireland and four Republic of Ireland players, Shay Brennan, Tony Dunne, Johnny Giles and club captain, Noel Cantwell. Busby's squad also included Bill Foulkes, Maurice Setters, Nobby Stiles, Albert Quixall, Bobby Charlton and Law's new strike partner, David Herd. Busby was also keeping a keen eye on the development of the Youth Team players at the club who were being mentored by Busby's right hand man, Jimmy Murphy. Two players from United's Youth Team were already catching Busby's eye, both aged 16, David Sadler and a certain young teenager from Belfast named George Best. However, both would have to wait until the following season to make the breakthrough into the first team.

Denis made his debut on the opening day of the 1962-63 season scoring in a 2-2 draw with West Bromwich Albion at Old Trafford but United had been 2-0 up after just 7 minutes and squandered a point late on. It would be a pattern for the forthcoming season. United lost 9 of the next 13 games including a 5-2 hammering by Burnley at Old Trafford and a 6-2 humiliation at White Hart Lane after which United sat second from bottom of the league and were only above Birmingham City on goal average. From there results seemed to improve, notably a 5-3 win over champions Ipswich at Portman Road and from late October United lost just one game (3-0 at West Brom) and had improved to 13th place by Boxing Day 1962 however they were still just 6 points above the two relegation places.

At this point in the season all football in England stopped because this was the season of football's great freeze. United didn't play a league game again until 23rd February and they hadn't even played their Third Round FA Cup tie – in a normal season they would be at the Fifth Round stage by late February. Fortunately, Matt Busby used the time wisely by adding another key component to his team, paying Glasgow Celtic £56,000 for Pat Crerand on 6 February. Paddy was immediately hurled into a relegation scrap as United lost 6 of their 8 league games between March and April to leave themselves just a point ahead of Birmingham. Solace came in the truncated FA Cup – they beat Huddersfield (5-0), Aston Villa (1-0) and Chelsea (2-1) at home and Coventry City (3-1) away in four cup ties in March to reach the last four, then beat Southampton 1-0 at Villa Park thanks to a typical piece of Denis Law poaching to reach Wembley but it still wasn't clear which division United would be playing their football in the following season.

To work their way through the backlog of fixtures, clubs were now playing 2 or 3 games a week and a run of three defeats out of four in early May saw United lurch towards disaster again, they were now just one point ahead of Manchester City who were second from bottom (Leyton Orient were already relegated) and their next game was the derby at Maine Road.

The Manchester derby of April 1974 is often remembered as one of the most momentous of all-time – Law's backheel and United getting relegated by a former great who had gone to their nearest and dearest, yet what few remember is that Denis had already performed the role of Judas almost exactly 11 years earlier only in reverse. On Wednesday 15th May 1963 United crossed town to play neighbours City and both teams were on the brink. Anything but a home win would almost certainly see City relegated while defeat would push United into the bottom two although The Reds had a game in hand. 52,424 concerned Mancunians were drawn like a magnet to Maine Road to discover the fate of their team and it was the home side who got off to a brilliant start as Alex Harley opened the scoring for City after just 8 minutes. Gaining in confidence the Sky Blues were soon bossing the game but had a goal controversially chalked off before half-time. United tried to come back in the second half but it took an error from a City player for them to find a way back into it. With time running out and City starting to feel the pressure, winger David Wagstaffe attempted a suicidal back pass to keeper Harry Dowd, sharp as ever Denis Law nipped in and went down under a challenge. To this day City fans are convinced that their former player dived but the referee gave the penalty. Albert Quixall scored from the spot, his most important goal for United, and City were all but doomed. United played their game in hand the following Saturday and it looked like a formality as they were facing bottom team Leyton Orient but the O's took a sensational lead in the 9th minute and it took an own goal for United to level and two late goals from Messrs Law and Charlton to secure United's status for the following season. It's tempting to wonder what might have happened to the United Trinity, Matt Busby and the rest of the 1960s team had the result gone the other way…

So it was with some relief that supporters, directors and players got ready for the following weekend's FA Cup final against Leicester City. Busby picked a side containing nine internationals: David Gaskell, Tony Dunne, Noel Cantwell (Capt), Bill Foulkes, Maurice Setters, Pat Crerand, Johnny Giles, Albert Quixall, David Herd, Denis Law, Bobby

Charlton.

Only Gaskell and Setters had not been capped by their country. The Foxes had England's first choice goalkeeper, Gordon Banks, in net and included some quality players including Frank McLintock who would go on to captain Arsenal to the Double in 1970-71. Leicester City were playing in their second FA Cup final in three years having lost the 1961 final 2-0 to double winners Tottenham Hotspur, and the 1949 final 3-1 to Wolverhampton Wanderers. United were seeking their third FA Cup win following triumphs in 1909 and 1948. Leicester were favourites to lift their first FA Cup after drawing 2-2 with United at Old Trafford on 15 April 1963 before beating them 4-3 at Filbert Street the following day with Law netting a hat-trick. The press had dubbed Leicester City "The Ice Kings" during the Big Freeze as their "switch and whirl" system confused defences particularly when McLintock would switch from his right half position with inside right Graham Cross. Between 26 December 1962 and 16 March 1963, The Foxes coped better than any other club with the cold conditions winning all 10 games they played, 7 straight League victories (scored 19 & conceded 1) and wins in Rounds 3, 4 and 5 in the FA Cup (scored 7 & conceded 2), quite a contrast with United who had struggled to adapt to the heavy schedule and heavy pitches.

In the week before the final the clubs faced a coin toss to determine which one would wear their traditional colours, the blue of Leicester City or the red of United. With the final being televised live to an audience of millions in the UK, the blue and red jerseys would look similar on black and white television sets. United won the toss and Leicester City opted for their all white second kit. Both sides had prolific strikers: Ken Keyworth was The Foxes' leading goal scorer in season 1961-62 and 1962-63 (and again in 1963-64) and had scored 23 goals in the League during the season and 5 in the FA Cup as well as bagging a hat-trick in their 4-3 win over United. In Denis Law United had one of the most feared marksmen in Europe. Law ended his first season at Old Trafford as the club's leading goal scorer in the League with 23 goals to his name and he had already scored 5 times in United's journey to the final.

During the 1962-63 season, Busby never had an outright choice as his No.1 goalkeeper. David Gaskell played in United's opening 10 League games before Busby reinstated Harry Gregg for the next 24 games and then handed the green jersey back to Gaskell for the remaining 10 League fixtures. It was a similar story in the FA Cup with the green jersey going to Gregg for Round 3, Round 4, Round 5 and quarter-final ties before Busby replaced the Northern Ireland international with Gaskell for the semi-final and final. Gaskell made a very nervous start to the final and gifted The Foxes' frontmen three golden opportunities to score when he left his net unguarded but Keyworth, Mike Stringfellow and Dave Gibson wasted the chances to put their side in the lead. Crerand and Charlton then took a stranglehold on play and United put their disappointing League form behind them and dominated proceedings. In the 30th minute who else but the mercurial Law fired United into the lead. Banks saved a shot from his England international teammate Charlton, and rolled the ball out to Gibson but Crerand read the situation and latched on to the ball 25 yards out. The Scot found captain Noel Cantwell who then passed to Charlton who fed Law and the Scottish international striker swivelled and turned inside the box to score. Five minutes from half-time Law nearly made it 2-0 but after rounding Banks he was unable to steer the ball into the net as two defenders raced on to the line to keep his shot out.

Just as he had at the start of the first half, Gaskell made a nervy start and dropped the ball at the feet of Cross but the Leicester City player was unable to capitalise but United weathered Leicester's early second half storm and in the 57th minute doubled their lead. Charlton fired a hard shot at Banks who could not hold on to the ball and he spilled it in front of Herd who tapped it into the net. The goal ignited the United fans inside Wembley who burst into singing "When the Reds go marching in." With ten minutes remaining The Foxes were back in the hunt when a shot from McLintock was met with a diving header by Keyworth but any chances of sending the game into extra-time were snuffed out by Herd who scored his second, and United's third, in the 85th minute. United won the game 3-1 and won their third FA Cup, Busby's fifth piece of silverware as United manager (3 League Championships and 2 FA Cups).

United's Irish captain Noel Cantwell was presented with the trophy by Queen Elizabeth II and followed in the footsteps of two former United captains who lifted the FA Cup, Charlie Roberts in 1909, and the first Irishman to hold aloft the FA Cup as a winning captain, Johnny Carey in 1948. United could thank their spearhead of David Herd and Denis Law for the FA Cup victory but many felt another new signing, Pat Crerand, had been the best player on the day. Having survived a relegation dog fight by the skin of their teeth, United could now look forward to the rest of the decade with optimism.

Did You Know That?

Gate receipts for the final amounted to £89,000 which was an all-time British record at the time. Just as it was tradition for the band to play *Abide With Me* it was also FA Cup final tradition to play the National Anthem after the winning captain and his teammates were presented with their winners' medals. However, as the band began to play the National Anthem, with the Queen still inside the stadium, the United players were already back on the pitch and had hoisted Cantwell on to the shoulders of Quixall and Crerand to parade the trophy to the United fans. Some journalists who were close by had to remind the United players of the protocol and in the next day's newspapers, the United players were lambasted for being disrespectful. The following season the Football Association dispensed with the band playing the National Anthem after the FA Cup was presented to the winners. Leicester City reached their fourth and last FA Cup final 6 years later and once again the ribbons of their club colours were left to one side as the cup was held aloft by Tony Book following a 1-0 defeat to Manchester City. The Foxes' manager in the 1969 FA Cup final was Frank O'Farrell, who would later manage Manchester United (1971-72).

GAME NO. 45
UNITED 1-1 NOTTINGHAM FOREST
FIRST DIVISION
OLD TRAFFORD
22 FEBRUARY 1958
ATTENDANCE- 66,124

YOU'LL NEVER WALK ALONE

'United Will Go On' was the optimistic message on the front of the *United Review* for the first game after The Munich Disaster on 19th February 1958 when Assistant Manager Jimmy Murphy's cobbled together team rode a wave of emotion to beat Sheffield Wednesday in the club's postponed Fifth Round FA Cup tie. Matt Busby was still lying in his hospital bed in the Rechts der Isar Hospital in Munich recovering from the horrific injuries he sustained whilst Duncan Edwards was, like his manager, fighting for his life. Murphy, who had been in charge of Wales the night of the Red Star game, had missed the trip but returned to a grave crisis at United – it was a battle to keep the club going amid the grief, high emotion and the attention of the world's press in the days following the disaster.

Murphy had looked to his youth players against Wednesday and they had responded with 21 year-old Shay Brennan scoring twice and 17 year-old Alex Dawson scoring the other. The people of Manchester celebrated as one, red and blue sides of the football divide joined in the euphoria of watching a team rise from the ashes of a slush covered runway less than two weeks earlier. For once United and City fans were united as many of the players who died were local lads and City had also lost a former player in the disaster, goalkeeper Frank Swift who played for the Blues from 1936-39 and was capped 19 times by England (plus 14 Wartime games). Swift had travelled to Yugoslavia as a reporter for *News of the World*.

Two days later, 21 February 1958, Duncan Edwards died in hospital aged just 21 years and 144 days old. The following day a distraught Murphy, having lost yet another one of his boys, had to field a team to play Nottingham Forest. Jimmy was in a daze, he was a distraught man with a broken heart but despite the club being in its darkest hour he had to carry on for his friend, Busby. It was still unclear whether the Boss would pull through. Murphy was unquestionably the greatest ever signing Matt Busby made for Manchester United and it was in these weeks and months following Munich that the fiery Welshman would help revive a club and a city. The Manchester United Jimmy picked that day read: Harry Gregg, Bill Foulkes (Capt), Ian Greaves, Ronald Cope, Stan Crowther, Frederick Goodwin, Colin Webster, Ernie Taylor, Shay Brennan, Alex Dawson, Mark Pearson.

Foulkes, Goodwin, Cope, Dawson, Pearson and Brennan had all played in Murphy's youth teams and that day's opponents Nottingham Forest were just establishing themselves in the top flight having won promotion to the First Division having finished runners-up to Leicester City. Murphy's side was very inexperienced; with Gregg playing in what was only his eighth League game following his transfer from Doncaster Rovers in December 1957, Webster making his seventh League appearance of the season, Goodwin his fifth, Dawson his second whilst Greaves, Cope, Crowther (who made his debut in the Sheffield Wednesday game), Taylor, Pearson and Brennan were all playing their first League game of the season.

The loss of 8 Busby Babes devastated the city of Manchester. What was the most appropriate way to celebrate the lives of 8 young players who just wanted to play football for Manchester United? Many theatres up and down the country were staging versions of Richard Rodgers and Oscar Hammerstein's 1945 musical *Carousel*. A popular song from Carousel was *You'll Never Walk Alone* a song which has since become the anthem of Liverpool Football Club and is despised today by United fans across the globe. Yet in February 1958 the New Mills Operatic Society in Derbyshire were rehearsing to perform Carousel in their local theatre. Jane Hardwick, a United fan and a teenage opera singer with the society, attended the Nottingham Forest game and when she began to sing *You'll Never Walk Alone* in tribute to the lost Busby Babes, her friends joined in and soon a large section of the crowd also joined in the singing. For Jane and her fellow New Mills Operatic Society members they thought that the opening two verses of the song were a fitting tribute to the lost lives of Geoff Bent, Roger Byrne, Eddie Colman, Duncan Edwards, Mark Jones, David Pegg, Tommy Taylor and Liam Whelan.

> *When you walk through a storm*
> *Hold your head up high*
> *And don't be afraid of the dark*
> *At the end of the storm*
> *There's a golden sky*
> *And the sweet silver song of the lark*
> *Walk on, through the wind*
> *Walk on, through the rain*
> *Though your dreams be tossed and blown*
> *Walk on, walk on, with hope in your heart*
> *And you'll never walk alone*
> *You'll never walk alone"*

Murphy had set about steering United through the storm, ensuring his players held their heads up high, ignoring the darkness which clouded Old Trafford, to come out of the darkness and reach a golden sky. The game ended 1-1 with Dawson scoring for United. In the coming weeks Murphy would work a miracle at Old Trafford as he began the process of building a new team for Busby and lift the club like a Phoenix out of the ashes of Munich. United ended the season in 9th place in the League and lost the 1958 FA Cup final 2-0 to Bolton Wanderers and lost 5-2 on aggregate over two legs to AC Milan in the semi-finals of the European Cup. United's top goal scorer in season 1957-58 was Dennis Viollet, who found the back of the net 16 times in the League and 23 times in all competitions despite the fact that he was out of action for two months as he recovered from injuries sustained in the Disaster. On the international scene, Murphy's Wales team qualified for the 1958 World Cup finals where they reached the quarter-finals losing 1-0 to Brazil whose goal was scored by a relatively unknown 17-year old who would go on to become the best player in the world (well until George Best arrived on the football scene), Edson Arantes do Nascimento otherwise known as Pele.

The United fans soon adopted *You'll Never Walk Alone* and would regularly sing it at Old Trafford in the wake of the disaster, their way of remembering the eight players whose lives were so cruelly snatched away from them at such a young age. However, when Gerry & The Pacemakers released the song as a single in November 1963 it gave the band from Liverpool their third consecutive No.1 hit in the UK Music Singles Chart and soon Liverpool fans adopted the song as their anthem.

In 2007 Jane was interviewed by the *Manchester Evening News* about her and her friends singing *You'll Never Walk Alone*, "It has annoyed me so much that people think the song was first sung by the Liverpool fans. The Munich crash was so horrible and everyone was feeling down and despondent and it just seemed an appropriate song to sing. It was an emotional time and I managed to persuade my friends to join in with me. Soon the whole ground was singing it and many people, including me, were in tears. I never dreamed it would become the anthem of our rivals but I wanted to put the record straight about where the song originated from on the terraces."

> *"The greatness of a man is not in how much wealth he acquires,*
> *but in his integrity and his ability*
> *to affect those around him positively."*

Bob Marley

Jimmy Murphy was not born into greatness, his was a journey to greatness and along that path he transformed many young boys from being promising players into great players. He helped Manchester

United to five First Division Championships (1951-52, 1955-56, 1967-57, 1964-65 & 1966-67), two FA Cup wins (1948 & 1963), five FA Charity Shields (1952, 1956, 1957, 1965 shared & 1967 shared), and the European Cup in 1968. As the manager of United's Youth Team his boys won six FA Youth Cups in 1953, 1954, 1955, 1956, 1957 and 1964, the last with two prodigious teenagers under his watchful eye, David Sadler (aged 18) and 17-year old George Best. Murphy's Boys also won the Central League Championship three times in 1946-47, 1955-56 & 1959-60. Sadly, he passed away on 14 November 1989 aged 79. Quite fittingly the club commissioned the "Jimmy Murphy Young Player of the Year Award" in his honour which is presented to the best player in the club's youth system in the previous season. It was first awarded in the summer after Murphy's death, with Lee Martin winning the inaugural award in season 1989-90.

As a coach Jimmy was coveted around the world and despite being linked with taking charge of Arsenal, Juventus and Brazil he never left his boys in Manchester and continued working in the background as the Assistant Manager at Old Trafford until his retirement in 1971. Jimmy still scouted players for managers Tommy Docherty and Ron Atkinson well into the 1980s.

Did You Know That?

Gerry & the Pacemakers were managed by the same two men behind the success of The Beatles, manager Brian Epstein and record producer George Martin, and they almost never released *You'll Never Walk Alone* as their third single. They were supposed to release The Beatles' *Hello Little Girl* but Gerry Marsden, who formed Gerry & the Pacemakers in 1959 along with his brother, Fred, Les Chadwick and Arthur McMahon was a big fan of Carousel and the songs from the musical ever since he first saw it as a young boy. In the second act of Carousel Nettie Fowler, the cousin of the protagonist Julie Jordan, sings the song to comfort and encourage Julie when her husband, Billy Bigelow, the male lead in the show, falls on his knife and dies after a robbery attempt which went wrong. The song is then sung again in the final scene to encourage a graduation class of which Louise (Billy and Julie's daughter) is a member.

GAME NO. 46
CHELSEA 1-1 UNITED AET
UNITED WON 6-5 ON PENALTIES
2008 UEFA CHAMPIONS LEAGUE FINAL
LUZHNIKI STADIUM, MOSCOW
21 MAY 2008
ATTENDANCE- 67,310

BACK IN THE USSR

In 1968 The Beatles released an eponymous double album entitled (also known as "The White Album") and the first song released from the album was *Back in the USSR*. Manchester United conquered Europe in 1968 by winning the European Cup and forty years later Sir Alex Ferguson set his sights on reaching the former USSR to play in the 2008 UEFA Champions League final in Moscow.

Going into the 2007-08 season United were reigning Premier League Champions but Ferguson knew that for his United side, and indeed his own legacy, to be truly regarded in the highest esteem by football critics, the club had to dominate Europe and win European club football's most elite and prestigious trophy, the Champions League. United had not reached a Champions League final since season 1998-99, when they won the trophy in an unforgettable Treble winning season.

After that triumph, many pundits expected the treble team to dominate the Champions League but a disastrous 3-2 quarter-final defeat by Real Madrid at Old Trafford forced Ferguson into a re-think. Madrid dominated the game at Old Trafford exploiting United's traditional 4-4-2 system and Sir Alex recognised that to succeed in Europe over the next decade he would have to change his system. Following defeat to Bayern Munich in 2000-01 they progressed to the semi-final in 2001-02 but an injury to David Beckham against Deportivo La Coruna in the quarter-finals proved disastrous and United tumbled out on away goals to Bayer Leverkusen, Ferguson missing out on a final at Hampden Park in his native Glasgow. The following season they were knocked out by Real Madrid, or more specifically Ronaldo, whose sensational hat-trick at Old Trafford brought the Brazilian a standing ovation then, in 2003-04, they were unfortunate to have a perfectly good Paul Scholes goal disallowed in defeat to Jose Mourinho's Porto and the following year two supine

1-0 defeats to AC Milan in the Last 16 seemed to signal that the club had lost its way at the highest level.

This feeling was reinforced following United's failure to get out of the qualifying group in 2005-06, in which they only managed to score three goals, which suggested an over-reliance on Ruud van Nistlerooy and following his departure in the summer of 2006 United were re-invigorated with Louis Saha at the point of an attack flanked by Wayne Rooney and Cristiano Ronaldo. A 7-1 quarter-final victory over Roma made Europe sit up and take notice but despite Rooney's heroics in the semi-final first leg at Old Trafford against AC Milan, in which he almost single-handedly kept United in the tie, they were blown away in the San Siro, crashing out 3-0 following a masterclass by Dutch midfielder Clarence Seedorf.

Over the summer of 2007 United were busy in the transfer market, out went Kieran Richardson to Sunderland, Giueseppe Rossi to Villareal, Alan Smith to Newcastle United, Gabriel Heinze to Real Madrid while Ole Gunnar Solskjaer retired; in came Owen Hargreaves from Bayern Munich, Anderson from Porto, Nani from Sporting Lisbon and Tomasz Kuszczak from West Bromwich Albion before, on 10 August 2007, United signed a player on loan from Media Sport Investment Limited. Carlos Tevez. Along with his four new recruits, Sir Alex also had the services of Edwin van der Sar, Gary Neville (Capt), Patrice Evra, Wes Brown, Rio Ferdinand, Nemanja Vidic, Paul Scholes, Michael Carrick, Park Ji-sung, Ryan Giggs, Louis Saha and partnering Tevez in a three pronged attack, Wayne Rooney and Cristiano Ronaldo. So United had an elite squad of players, perhaps the best in Europe, but the season that lay ahead would determine just how good they were.

United were drawn in Group F along with Cristiano Ronaldo's former club Sporting Lisbon (Portugal), AS Roma (Italy) and Dynamo Kyiv (Ukraine). On 19 September 2007, the young Portuguese star scored against his boyhood club in the 62nd minute to earn United a 1-0 win. Two weeks later United entertained Roma at Old Trafford on Matchday 2 in a rematch of their quarter-final encounter the previous season when United hammered the Italian side 7-1. United won the game 1-0 with a goal from Wayne Rooney in the 70th minute who had also scored in both legs against the Italians the previous season. Next up was a visit to the capital of the Ukraine where United won 4-2 with goals from Ferdinand (10 mins), Rooney (18 mins) and Ronaldo (41 mins & 68 mins penalty), two weeks later United comfortably won the return 4-0 with goals from Gerard Pique, Tevez, Rooney and Ronaldo. A fortnight later a late Ronaldo free-kick saw United edge out Sporting Lisbon 2-1 at Old Trafford before the final group game, a 1-1 draw in Rome.

The last 16 included some European power houses of clubs such as Barcelona (winners in 2006), Real Madrid (winners in 2002), Porto (winners in 2004 under Jose Mourinho), Inter Milan, Chelsea, Liverpool (winners in 2005), and reigning Champions AC Milan. When the draw was made United got Olympique Lyonnais who won Ligue 1 in France for the sixth consecutive season in 2006-07 and went on to retain their title at the end of the 2007-08 season (they have not been French Champions in any other season since their formation in 1950). On 20 February 2008 a goal from Tevez earned United a 1-1 draw in France's third largest city and two weeks later a goal from Ronaldo in the 41st minute sent United into the quarter-finals. Amazingly, the draw paired United with Roma again. In their last four encounters United had recorded 2 wins, 1 draw and 1 loss against their Italian opponents. The draw for the semi-final stages had also been made simultaneously and the winners of the Anglo-Italian match-up between United and AS Roma would play Schalke 04 or Barcelona in the semi-finals with the winners of Arsenal versus Liverpool facing the winners of Chelsea versus Fenerbahçe. On 1st April 2008, United made fools of their hosts winning their first leg, quarter-final tie 2-0 at Stadio Olimpico in front of more than 60,000 passionate Italian fans — the opener by Ronaldo was spectacular as he rose above the Italian defence before emphatically heading home. When Wayne Rooney added another in the second half the tie was all but over. Eight days later the third member of United's prolific front three, Carlos Tevez, scored the only goal of the second leg to send United into the semi-finals where they would have to overcome the might of Barcelona. Liverpool had beaten Arsenal 5-3 on aggregate and Chelsea squeezed past Fenerbahçe with a slim 3-2 aggregate victory so there was a possibility of an all-English final for the first time in the 52-year history of the competition.

United got off to a sensational start in the Nou Camp when they awarded a penalty after just two minutes when Gabriel Milito was adjudged to have handled the ball. Yet Cristiano Ronaldo, normally so reliable from the spot, fired the penalty wide. Barca responded by forcing van der Sar into a few saves but while the Catalans, who were well off the pace in La Liga, had a lot of possession they produced few chances. When a clearly unfit Lionel Messi was withdrawn early the home side seemed to settle for a 0-0 draw in the hope that the Argentinian's fitness would improve before the second leg. Six days later United welcomed Frank Rijkaard's Barcelona to Old Trafford – it would prove to be a tense evening. When Paul Scholes scored a long range thunderbolt in the 14th minute of play United took the lead but the 75,061 spectators were only too aware that a single goal from the visitors would send the Catalans through. Patrice Evra expertly shackled Messi tracking the little genuis's every twist and turn. With the supply line to Barca's front three cut off United somehow held on. It had been a superb backs-to-the-wall performance and they would now face Chelsea in the Moscow final after the Londoners beat Liverpool 4-3 on aggregate.

Ten days before the 2008 Champions League final United defeated Wigan Athletic 2-0 to win the 2007-08 Premier League, their 10th Premier League crown, and their 17th title in the top flight of English football, which left the club one Championship short of Liverpool's record 18 titles. Chelsea, Premier League Champions in 2004-05 and 2005-06, had dispensed with Jose Mourinho earlier in the season following a poor run of results but under caretaker manager Avram Grant they had rediscovered the form which had made them so formidable under the Portuguese. The 2008 Champions League final was a meeting between English football's two best teams as United won the title by just two points over Chelsea, 87 to 85.

Sir Alex sent out the following side in the red hot heat of an evening in Moscow to play Chelsea: Edwin van der Sar, Wes Brown, Patrice Evra, Nemanja Vidic, Rio Ferdinand (Capt), Owen Hargreaves, Paul Scholes, Michael Carrick, Cristiano Ronaldo, Carlos Tevez, Wayne Rooney. Substitutes: Tomasz Kuszcak, John O'Shea, Mikael Silvestre, Anderson (for Brown 120 +5 mins), Ryan Giggs (for Scholes 87 mins), Nani (for Rooney 101 mins), Darren Fletcher

Chelsea had a galaxy of stars, most of whom had been recruited by Jose Mourinho: Peter Cech, Michel Essien, Ashley Cole, Ricardo Carvalho, John Terry (Capt), Michael Ballack, Claude Makelele, Frank Lampard, Joe Cole, Florent Malouda, Didier Drogba. The Blues' bench comprised Carlo Cudicini, Alex, Juliano Belletti, John Obi Mikel, Andriy Shevchenko, Salomon Kalou and Nicola Anelka.

The supporters of both clubs made the long journey to Moscow for a game that would kick off at 10.45pm local time. The stadium was blessed with English weather for the kick-off as the Luzhniki was deluged with rain. United dominated the first half and deservedly took the lead in the 26th minute – a move down the right found Wes Brown, who had been deputising at full-back for most of the season, his deep cross found Ronaldo who planted a firm header past Petr Cech. It was Ronaldo's 42nd goal of the season and United should have extended their lead soon after but Cech beat away shots from Carrick and Tevez after a flowing move. Then disaster struck as a Michael Essien shot was deflected and fell kindly for Frank Lampard who slipped the ball past van der Sar on the stroke of half-time.

Revitalised, Chelsea suddenly started to enjoy the lion's share of possession and Didier Drogba struck a post before Lampard's chip hit the bar. United were holding on by now and were grateful for the full-time whistle. Extra-time was more frenetic with John Terry clearing a Giggs shot off the line but a key incident right at the end of the additional 30 minute period had a huge impact on deciding the game. A fracas developed by the touchline and during it Carlos Tevez, employing all his Latin cunning, got under the skin of Chelsea striker Didier Drogba who slapped Nemanja Vidic and was instantly dismissed by Slovakian referee Lubos Michel. Minutes later the final whistle went and the game would be decided by penalty kicks.

Both sides scored their first two penalties, Tevez, Ballack, Carrick, Belletti and everyone watching thought United would take a 3-2 advantage when Ronaldo placed the ball on the spot but his tame kick was saved by Cech. Frank Lampard was his usual confidence self from 12 yards out and put Chelsea 3-2, Hargreaves made it 3-3, Cole scored to restore Chelsea's advantage and United's fifth penalty was converted by Nani. The identity of the taker of Chelsea's fifth and decisive penalty was captain John Terry - Avram Grant would not have had Terry listed among his first five penalty takers had Drogba not been dismissed. The United fans had their hearts in their mouths when Terry set the ball down on the penalty spot but as he made contact with the ball his standing foot gave way and his shot hit the post. There was pandemonium in the stadium as United had somehow been given the kiss of life.

The game now entered sudden death and United's fate was now in the hands, or rather the boots, of their back-up penalty kick takers as was Chelsea's. Penalty No.6 for United was converted by Anderson and was followed by a successful spot kick from Kalou. Nest up for United was Giggs, No.7 on the list and the cool Welsh winger slotted the ball home to put United 6–5 up. Anelka was next up for the Blues and the striker was expected to score but the French international hit a poor shot which van der Sar saved to make United Champions of Europe for the third time.

Rio Ferdinand, club captain for the game, and Ryan Giggs, standing in for missing club captain Gary Neville, received the trophy together from UEFA President Michel Platini. Moscow was still Red, Russia was still Red and Alex Ferguson had proved the wisdom in his changing tactics 8 years earlier.

Did You Know That?

United's win in Moscow came 50 years after the fateful Munich Air Disaster. After the game Sir Alex spoke to the media: "I won the Charity Shield that way (on penalties), but that doesn't really count. The European Cup? The FA Cup? The Scottish cups? Never. I've lost three with Aberdeen and three with United, so seventh time lucky — magnificent." Meanwhile a very relieved Cristiano Ronaldo said in his post-match interview: "In my opinion I played well in the game, scored a goal, and then missed the penalty. It would have been the worst day of my life. We deserved to win as we played better in the whole game. It means everything to me, we have won both trophies, it is the best day in my life."

GAME NO. 47
UNITED 1–0 AC MILAN
EUROPEAN CUP, SEMI-FINAL, 2nd LEG
OLD TRAFFORD
15 MAY 1969
ATTENDANCE– 63,103

THE GODFATHER

Mario Puzo's *The Godfather* was published in 1969. It told the tale of the rise of organised crime in the Italian community in New York under the watchful eye of the all-seeing, all-knowing Godfather to whom everyone in the neighbourhood paid their respects. In Matt Busby, Manchester United not only had their very own version of Don Corleone but he was now a knight of the realm following the 1968 European Cup win.

By finally winning the club's Holy Grail the year before, Sir Matt had finally cleared some of the clouds of despond that had engulfed the club in the decade since Munich and the following season's European campaign provided light relief from a domestic campaign that never really got going – United finished 11th that season and were knocked out of the FA Cup at the quarter-final stage by Everton. In truth United looked spent from the amount of physical and emotional energy expended in finally getting to the mountain top in May 1968 and were in dire need of rejuvenation both on and off the pitch.

Still, with a triumvirate of Law, Best and Charlton hopes were high that United could repeat last season's triumph in the 1968–69 European Cup alongside the likes of AC Milan (1963 winners), Ajax Amsterdam, Anderlecht, Fenerbahçe, Glasgow Celtic (1967 winners) Real Madrid (6 times winners including 1966), Red Star Belgrade, Saint Etienne, Benfica (winners in 1961 & 1962) and English champions Manchester City, who Assistant Manager Malcolm Allison claimed would "frighten the cowards of Europe".

The draw pitched United against League of Ireland Champions Waterford, while City had to see off the challenge of Turkish Champions Fenerbahçe. A number of the Eastern Bloc clubs withdrew from the first two rounds when UEFA, by accident or design, paired all of them against one another: Dynamo Kyiv (Soviet Union) v Ruch Chorzow (Poland), Red Star Belgrade (Yugoslavia) v FC Carl Zeiss Jena (East Germany) and PFC Levski Sofia (Bulgaria) v Ferencvaros (Hungary). Only Red Star progressed in the tournament.

United defeated Waterford 10-2 over two legs, winning the away tie 3-1 thanks to a Denis Law hat-trick before a 7-1 hammering of the Republic of Ireland club at Old Trafford with Denis "The Menace" Law netting four times. City had drawn 0-0 with Fenerbahçe at Maine Road in the 1st leg but lost the 2nd leg 2-1 in the Kadikoy district of the Turkish capital and crashed out, much to Malcolm Allison's chagrin. In the draw for the Second Round, United were drawn against the team who had been their first opponents in Europe, Anderlecht, Champions of Belgium. United won the first leg at Old Trafford 3-0 but got the shock of their lives in the return – after Carlo Sartori gave them an early lead the Belgians battled back to win 3-1 and United were holding on at the end as the home team laid siege to their goal.

Round 3 of the competition saw United pitted against Champions of Austria Rapid Wien but before the tie could be played came news that rocked the football world as Sir Matt Busby announced his retirement at the end of the coming season after 24 years. In the following days he named his successor, Wilf McGuinness – this only lent more importance to that season's run in the European Cup.

After beating the Austrians 3-0 in the 1st leg at Old Trafford on 26 February 1969, with two goals from George Best and one from Willie Morgan, United secured a goalless draw in Vienna to reach the last four. The other three teams remaining were AC Milan who beat Glasgow Celtic 1-0 over two legs (they won 1-0 at Celtic Park), Ajax Amsterdam who saw off Benfica in a 3-0 play–off win in Paris after both legs ended 3-1 to the away side and the Champions of Czechoslovakia, Spartak Trnava, who beat AEK Athens from Greece 3-2 on aggregate. The good news was that United were handed an away game for the 1st leg, but the bad news was that AC Milan would be the opposition. On 23 April 1969 United walked out into the San Siro before 80,000 screaming Italians. Their defence held firm until the 33rd minute but then Crerand and Foulkes failed to clear a high ball and it fell for Angelo Sormani who drove it through the legs of Jimmy Rimmer in the United goal. The sound of fireworks rent the air as the Italians pushed for more and were grateful for a huge break when Lodetti sent his header wide of an open goal. Things didn't improve much in the second half and when Swedish striker Kurt Hamrin added a second on 49 minutes many felt the home side were poised to run riot but somehow United managed to keep the score at 2-0 to give themselves a slim chance of progressing at Old Trafford.

Three weeks later 63,103 spectators, nearly all United fans, were drawn like a magnet to Old Trafford hoping to witness one last Busby masterclass of attacking football and no one was more determined to win than Denis Law who had missed the previous year's final and would play a central role in the unfolding drama. Matt Busby picked the following side for the big match: Jimmy Rimmer, Shay Brennan, Francis Burns, Bill Foulkes, Nobby Stiles, Pat Crerand, Willie Morgan, Bobby Charlton (Capt), George Best, Brian Kidd, Denis Law.

United, playing in a change strip of all white, looked to make a fast start but the first half turned into a stalemate with Kidd and Best both going close, then, at the start of the second half, Milan goalkeeper Cudicini went down clutching his head in front of the Stretford End. As the players came across to tend to him toilet rolls rained down into the penalty area and the game was held up for 10 minutes while the player was attended to and the pitch was cleared. Despite United having plenty of possession the Milanese had several chances themselves and always looked dangerous on the counter-attack but just as it looked like the home team would never make the breakthrough, Best jinked his way past two players and played in Charlton who took a touch before beating Cudicini at his near post.

United had hope and now they laid siege to the Stretford End goal; Kidd went close with a header, Crerand shot over then Charlton fired in a wonderful shot that the keeper punched clear. Seconds later came the moment that continues to be debated decades later – Kidd played in Morgan down the right who fired in a cross which was turned towards goal by Law. The ball rolled toward the goal line but did it cross it? Law was convinced but French referee Roger Mâchin thought not. Replays seemed to suggest the Italian defender stopped the ball on the goal line itself but the Scot maintains to this day that he and United were robbed. A goal then and surely United would have won through to the final against Ajax.

Despite numerous corners and near things United never came as close to levelling the aggregate score and the Italians held out and hammered the Dutch 4-1 in Madrid. The following Saturday Sir Matt Busby bid farewell to Old Trafford as manager before the home game against Leicester City which United won 3-2. United wouldn't play another European Cup match at the ground for 24 years.

Did You Know That?

Carlo Sartori was the first non-British player to play for Manchester United. He was born on 10 February 1948, in Caderzone Terme, Italy and made his debut for United on 9th October 1968, a 2-2 draw away to Tottenham Hotspur in (scorers: Paddy Crerand & Denis Law). He played 56 times for United and scored 6 goals and was transferred to the Italian side, Bologna, in January 1973 for £50,000.

GAME NO. 48
NORTHAMPTON TOWN 2-8 UNITED
FA CUP, FIFTH ROUND
THE COUNTY GROUND
7 FEBRUARY 1970
ATTENDANCE- 21,771

BOOZE, BIRDS, FAST CARS... AND GOALS

*"I spent a lot of money on booze, birds and fast cars.
The rest I just squandered."*

George Best

Following the retirement of Sir Matt Busby Manchester United were a club in transition in season 1969-70. They were now being managed by former player Wilf McGuinness and were an ageing side with Paddy Crerand aged 30, Bobby Charlton aged 31, Shay Brennan aged 32 and Bill Foulkes aged 37, all members of the 1968 European Cup winning side. Denis Law, who missed the 1968 triumph over Benfica through injury, was 29 but George Best, who scored in the European Cup final, was still only 23 and still considered to be the best footballer in the world.

McGuinness's side got off to a terrible start that season drawing three and losing three of their opening six league games. On 16 August 1969 Southampton humiliated United at Old Trafford winning 4-1, the visitors' goals were all scored by Ron Davies and after the game, Sir Matt Busby said that Davies "had no peer in Europe" but it was also a game that brought to an end Bill Foulkes incredible United career after a then record 688 first team appearances. Ron Davies had been joint top league goal scorer in 1967-68 along with George Best so he was no mug but he effectively ended Foulkes career in that game. United's league form never threatened the upper reaches of the table and they finished eighth.

The domestic cup competitions were McGuinness's only hopes of proving to the Board of Directors, United fans and his former team-mates, that he was a leader worthy of succeeding Sir Matt. The team had enjoyed a good run in the League Cup but their hopes of winning this competition for the first time were ended by Manchester City; after losing the first leg of their semi-final encounter 2-1 at Maine Road and drawing the home leg 2-2 to go out 4-3 on aggregate.

United's opponents in the opening round of the FA Cup were Ipswich Town, Second Division Champions in 1967–68, and an own goal by Mick O'Neil in the last minute gave United a 1-0 victory at Portman Road. On 24 January 1970 Manchester City arrived at Old Trafford for a Fourth Round game, the fourth derby of the season. This was a period when City dominated derby encounters and were unbeaten in derbies dating back to September 1967. The most recent league encounter on 15 November 1969 saw City romp to a 4-0 win at Maine Road but salt was poured into United wounds when George Best was given a four-week suspension by the Football Association after knocking the ball out of the hands of referee Jack Taylor, during the game. So a Best-less United faced City looking for revenge before a huge crowd of 63,417 at Old Trafford. There wasn't much to chose between the teams league form as eighth placed United were in fact a point and a place ahead of City in the league but the Reds gained some measure of revenge for the League Cup exit with a fine 3-0 victory as Brian Kidd scored twice and Willie Morgan converted a penalty.

The draw for the 5th Round saw United paired away at Northampton Town on 7 February 1970 by which time George had served his suspension and McGuinness put him straight back into the starting XI to face the Fourth Division side. Manchester United: Alex Stepney, Paul Edwards, Tony Dunne, Ian Ure, David Sadler, Paddy Crerand, Willie Morgan, Carlo Sartori, Bobby Charlton (Capt), Brian Kidd, George Best. Substitute: Francis Burns for Charlton.

By 1970 it was clear that George Best was becoming frustrated with football, or more specifically with Manchester United. Having seen mentor Matt Busby retire he believed his replacement Wilf McGuinness was not being supported by Busby and the board. These concerns had come to a head the previous summer when it was rumoured that Wilf had several requests for transfers turned down with the likes of Alan Ball and Mike England linked with a move to United. Best kept a lid on his frustrations for a while but they had boiled over in the derby during that humiliating defeat to City and now George would take his frustrations out on poor old Northampton Town in one of the most mesmerising displays English football has ever seen.

Coming into the game many felt that the Cobblers represented something of a banana skin for McGuinness's side in the kind of muddy conditions and tightly-packed ground that has sown the seeds for many a cup upset and for almost half an hour the home side gave as good as they got before Brian Kidd was released down the right and his cross was misjudged by Kim Book, brother of Manchester City captain Tony, and George nodded in unmarked. Ten minutes later Crerand found Best running in behind the Cobblers defence again to slot home. George completed his hat-trick five minutes after half-time, Kidd's cross was deflected into his path and having hit a defender with his first attempt he made no mistake with his second. Already this was a remarkable comeback having not played since 3rd January but more was to come. A few minutes later Northampton missed the chance to pull one back from the penalty spot and play quickly switched to the other end, Kidd's centre was met with a diving header from Best for his and United's fourth. Kidd made it 5-0 minutes later, turning home a corner before substitute Francis Burns found George with a superb through ball and the Belfast Boy coolly slotted past the hapless Book. Brian Kidd made it seven minutes later, collecting a rebound off the keeper and McNeil pulled one back for the home team before George delivered the coup de grâce – Crerand won the ball back near the penalty area, passed to Best who sold the goalkeeper a dummy and hit the ball into an empty net before kicking the post to remove the mud from his boots. George's double hat-trick equalled the goal scoring record by a United player - Harold Halse had scored six times against Swindon Town on 25 September 1911 in United's 8-4 win at Stamford Bridge in the 1911 FA Charity Shield. The Cobblers added a consolation late on but this had been George's day.

Reflecting on his performance George said, "I don't really class myself as a footballer. I call myself an entertainer. I know a lot of people have paid to see me do something spectacular and that's what I was trying to do on Saturday. It's my job to do something that will send people away feeling that they'd like to see me play again. While I've been suspended I've had letters from cranks saying that the team played better without me. I felt that if we were beaten by Northampton, people would say it was my fault. People think that just because I'm a bit of a showman and lose my temper occasionally I'm not trying but I do as much running as anyone. During the past week I drove myself harder than ever in training and when I went out yesterday I felt really great."

Northampton Town's John "Nobby" Clarke later said of George's performance, "All I kept seeing was George Best's backside disappearing into the distance. He had an amazing game and tore us to ribbons." Ray Fairfax was tasked with marking United's 23-year old former European Player of the Year and said, "Why, oh why, did it have to happen to me? The only time I got close to him was when we went off at half-time and full-time. On top of his baffling skill, Best had all the pent-up energy and frustration of four weeks out of football. And he unloaded the lot on to poor me. What can you do about such a man? We planned for this and that, but in the end it was all so meaningless."

George's outstanding performance earned him an invitation to 10 Downing Street from Prime Minister Harold Wilson, who had regularly written fan letters to him.

Perhaps the last word should go to Northampton keeper Kim Book, "The trouble was that when the scout watched United, George Best was suspended so he didn't mention him. We actually managed to kick Charlton out of the game early on and at half-time I thought we were still in it. But then George put his scoring boots on."

Unfortunately George never got to show off his skills in the biggest game in English football – the FA Cup final. George had still been an apprentice when the club won the cup in 1963 and United were dumped out of that year's competition following defeat to Leeds in the semi-finals but no one will ever forget the day that George scored a double hat-trick in the competition.

Did You Know That?

Denis Law once scored six goals in an FA Cup tie but still ended up on the losing side! The Scot had scored a round half dozen in a cup-tie at Luton in 1961 when he was playing for Manchester City but torrential rain saw the game abandoned after 69 minutes. Typically City lost the replayed game 3-1 and Denis's record was wiped from the books.

GAME NO. 49
UNITED 0-1 MANCHESTER CITY
FIRST DIVISION
OLD TRAFFORD
27 APRIL 1974
ATTENDANCE- 56,996

NOT TOO GOOD TO GO DOWN

After finishing in 18th place in the First Division in season 1972–73, just seven points above Coventry City who were relegated along with bottom placed side West Bromwich Albion, surely things could not get any worse for Manchester United who only five years earlier had been crowned Champions of Europe.

Martin Buchan was the leader of Manchester United but as all great leaders in history learn, they needed an Army behind them. Whilst the United manager, Tommy Docherty, had a Tartan Army behind him in the form of the United fans, Buchan's troops were not capable of putting up a fight. George Best was still at the club but had become unreliable, Sammy McIlroy was only 19-years old and many of the Doc's signings had yet to bed in properly. Buchan was only 24 but already he had captained Aberdeen to a 3-1 Scottish Cup final victory over Glasgow Celtic in 1970 aged just 21, his leadership abilities shone like a beacon.

The 1973-74 season was United's 72nd consecutive season in the Football League and their 29th consecutive season in the top flight. It was Tommy Docherty's first full season in charge of Manchester United after succeeding Frank O'Farrell on 22 December 1972. He already knew that he would start the season a legend down after Bobby Charlton decided to retire at the end of the 1972-73 season and he hamstrung himself even further in the eyes of pundits and supporters by allowing Denis Law to leave the club in a somewhat controversial manner by giving him a free transfer back to Manchester City. The King was the last to know about it, only finding out when he saw the BBC news while he was on holiday in Aberdeen – so two down, one to go…

Docherty only added Martin Buchan's brother George to his squad over the summer but released Wyn Davies to Blackpool, while John Fitzpatrick retired due to injury and Tony Dunne was given a free transfer to Bolton Wanderers. In getting rid of Charlton and Law,

Docherty was looking to stamp his authority on the club but he was also aware that it was a huge gamble with few of his signings so far looking capable of improving the position of the club.

United's opening League game of the 1973-74 season was a 3-0 loss away to Arsenal on 25 August 1973. George Best, who had 'retired' in the summer of 1972, had returned at the start of the 1972-73 season but then went missing again in December 1972 and was transfer-listed for £300,000 but was now back in the fold having come to an agreement with Docherty but was so out of shape that he wouldn't feature for the first two months of the season.

In his place the team still possessed a lot of experience with players such as Alex Stepney, Buchan, Gerry Daly, Jim Holton, Willie Morgan, Lou Macari and ex-Arsenal player George Graham all playing in the loss at Arsenal Stadium. However, despite winning their next two League outings, 1-0 at home to Stoke City and a 2-1 victory over Queens Park Rangers at Old Trafford, United only managed to win three of their first 12 First Division games before securing a home 1-0 victory over Birmingham City with a penalty scored by keeper Alex Stepney, in Best's return that saw 48,937 click through the turnstiles, the second highest gate of the season.

United's troubles lay squarely on the shoulders of the forwards as goalkeeper Stepney was joint top scorer with two penalties, alongside Brian Kidd and Sammy McIlroy, a position the goalkeeper held for ten games. On 29 December 1973, United recorded only their fifth League win of the season after 22 games (Drew 6 & Lost 11) when Macari and McIlroy both scored in a 2-0 home win against Ipswich Town. Three days later George Best played his twelfth game of the season, a 3-0 loss at Loftus Road to Queens Park Rangers on New Year's Day 1974. Little did they know it but the 32,339 fans in attendance had just seen Best's last ever appearance for Manchester United. After making 470 appearances and scoring 179 goals from 1963-74, the third and final member of the famous "United Trinity" had left the building. George was selected for the following game, a Third Round FA Cup tie at Old Trafford against Plymouth Argyle, but manager Docherty sent George away claiming he was drunk. Best and several witnesses refute this but the Irishman never played for United again. The Halcyon Days when Law, Charlton and Best ruled English and European football had come to a dramatic end. In truth the Dynasty had ended some time earlier as the club had never built on the success of 1968 and the top dogs in England were now Leeds, Derby, Arsenal and Liverpool who all won titles in the early 1970s.

Instead, having survived one relegation battle United were battening down the hatches for a second. United didn't win a league game in 1974 until 2nd March (1-0 at Sheffield United) and, following a 1-0 defeat to Spurs at Old Trafford on 23rd March, they were rock bottom with 22 points, 3 adrift of Norwich City and 5 short of safety. Until now Docherty's United hadn't been that different to O'Farrell's. The Doc had put his trust in direct football and defensive solidity and it just hadn't worked so with nine games left of the season The Doc went to see Matt Busby. Sir Matt's solution was typical of the man as he told Docherty "if we're going to go down, let's go down fighting".

For the next game, at Stamford Bridge, United played like a team transformed winning 3-1 to give supporters a glimmer of hope. A 3-3 draw with Burnley, featuring a late equaliser from terrace hero Jim Holton, and a priceless 2-0 win at Carrow Road against fellow strugglers Norwich breathed new life into the club as the club rose to second from bottom now 3 points behind Birmingham and safety. Two wins and a draw followed to leave United a point behind The Blues but defeat at Everton was a huge setback, especially as Birmingham won.

The table going before the Manchester Derby read:

POS	TEAM	P	W	D	L	GF	GA	GD	PTS
18	WEST HAM UNITED	41	11	14	16	53	58	-5	36
19	BIRMINGHAM CITY	41	11	13	17	50	63	-13	35
20	SOUTHAMPTON	41	10	14	17	44	68	-24	34
21	MANCHESTER UNITED	40	10	12	18	38	46	-8	32
22	NORWICH CITY	40	7	15	18	36	57	-21	29

So to take it into the final game of the season United needed a win. Birmingham were playing Norwich, Southampton faced Everton at Goodison and West Ham faced Liverpool at Upton Park. If Birmingham and Southampton won and West Ham drew then United would be down regardless of the result at Old Trafford.

On the final Saturday of the 1973-74 First Division season Docherty placed his trust in 2 Englishmen, 1 Northern Irishman, 1 Republic of Ireland man and 7 fellow Scots to beat City and help save United from being relegated to the Second Division. Manchester

United: Alex Stepney, Alex Forsyth, Stewart Houston, Jim Holton, Martin Buchan (Capt), Brian Greenhoff, Willie Morgan, Lou Macari, Gerry Daly, Sammy McIlroy, Jim McCalliog.

Sensing history in the making, City cheekily made Law their captain on his return to the ground he had graced for a decade. United needed a quick start and forced a few saves from Joe Corrigan but nothing noteworthy. Meanwhile the scores started to come in from Goodison, St. Andrews and Upton Park and there was no good news – Southampton were hammering a mid-table Everton, who were clearly 'on the beach', 3-0. The Hammers were giving as good as they got against a Liverpool team with the FA Cup final very much on their minds, that game would end 2-2 and worst of all Birmingham had turned around a one goal deficit against Norwich and now led 2-1.

It was in this state of resignation that Denis Law delivered his coup de grâce; a City move down the right found Francis Lee who centred towards the Scot. The ball was slightly behind him but Law swivelled and casually back-heeled it goalwards and then watched in horror as it eluded Stepney in the United goal. There were just 8 minutes remaining.

The man nicknamed The King quickly realised what he had done and showed no elation whatsoever in scoring whilst the United fans poured out of the stands and made their way on to the pitch. Law's goal turned out to be his last kick in League Football because when the game re-started three minutes later Phil Henson had come on as a substitute for him. Shortly after the restart United fans invaded the pitch again and with a fire starting in the Stretford End the referee, David Smith, took the decision to abandon the game. The Football League ordered the result to stand with City winning 1-0 and United were relegated but they would have gone down anyway because of the other results. Two days later United lost 1-0 away to Stoke City. It would be their last top flight game for the forseeable future.

Did You Know That?

Manchester United's leading league goal scorer in 1973–74 was Northern Ireland international Sammy McIlroy with 6 goals. McIlroy and United's Scottish international striker, Lou Macari, were the club's top goal scorers in all competitions, with 6 goals each (Macari scored 5 in the League and 1 in the FA Cup).

GAME NO. 50
AJAX AMSTERDAM 0-2 UNITED
2017 UEFA EUROPA LEAGUE FINAL
FRIENDS ARENA, SOLNA, SWEDEN
24 MAY 2017
ATTENDANCE- 46,961

COMPLETING THE SET

Jose Mourinho was appointed the new manager of Manchester United just four days after the dismissal of Louis van Gaal on 23 May 2016 following United's triumph in the FA Cup Final against Crystal Palace. Mourinho had made his reputation with FC Porto guiding them to Champions League success in 2003-04 and first came to English attention when he performed a knee-slide down the Old Trafford touchline following Helder Costinha's 90th minute equaliser that sent his team through. During his first press conference as the new boss of Chelsea that summer he famously said, "Please don't call me arrogant, but I'm European champion and I think I'm a special one." The media quickly dubbed Mourinho "The Special One" and it seemed his showmanship and self-confidence were not misplaced as he won successive league titles with The Blues. Mourinho had since gone on to enjoy success at Internazionale Milan, where he won the Champions League again, and Real Madrid, where he found a way to win La Liga against Pep Guardiola's apparently invincible Barcelona team. Now the two would face off once more as Guardiola was appointed Manchester City boss on 1st February 2016 and would take over that summer.

On 1 July, Zlatan Ibrahimović signed for Manchester United as a free agent on a 1-year contract. Many football pundits questioned Mourinho's decision to acquire a player who was 34 years when he put pen to paper for the Red Devils. When Teddy Sheringham joined Manchester United from Tottenham Hotspur in June 1997 in a £3.5 million deal, many football pundits shook their heads in disbelief that Alex Ferguson had shelled out so much money on a 31-year old striker but as history has proved, they were both inspired decisions. Zlatan was nevertheless labeled a journeyman having played for Malmo (1999-2001, 40 games & 16 goals), Ajax Amsterdam (2001-04, 74 games & 35 goals), Juventus (2004-06, 70 games & 23 goals), Inter Milan (2006-09, 88 games & 57 goals), Barcelona (2009-11, 29 games & 16 goals), AC Milan on loan (2010-11, 29 games & 14 goals),

AC Milan on loan (2011-12, 32 games & 28 goals) and Paris Saint-Germain on loan (2012-16, 122 games & 113 goals) but Jose had worked with Ibrahimović during his tenure in charge of Inter Milan (2008-10) and he knew first hand what the big Swede could bring to the table.

Zlatan made his United debut on 7 August 2016 in the FA Community Shield against surprise winners of the 2015-16 Premier League, Leicester City. Ibrahimović scored the late winner in United's 2-1 win after Jesse Lingard had opened the scoring followed by an equaliser from Jamie Vardy. A week later the Swede made his Premier League debut and scored with a long-range strike in a 3–1 win at Bournemouth on the opening day of the season. On 20 August 2016, he scored both goals, a header in the first half and a penalty in the second, to beat Southampton at Old Trafford on his home debut. Yet United's domestic campaign was underwhelming as they finished sixth in the league 24 points behind runaway winners Chelsea who also knocked United out of the FA Cup. However United did win the League Cup with Ibrahimović playing a starring role in the final, scoring twice including a late winner.

So to qualify for the following season's Champions League, United would have to win the Europa League and the draw for the Group Stages paired them with Dutch Cup winners Feyenoord, Turkish League runners-up Fenerbahçe and Zorya Luhansk who finished fourth in the 2015-16 Ukrainian League. United had faced Fenerbahçe in Europe twice before (1996-97 & 2004-05) and Feyenoord once before (1997-98). United lost their opening game 1-0 in Rotterdam followed by two home victories; 1-0 against Zorya Luhansk and Fenerbahçe 4-1. In Turkey United lost 2-1 with Wayne Rooney netting for the away side which was followed by two wins. On 24 November 2016, United defeated Feyenoord 4-0 at Old Trafford and won the game 2-0 in Odessa thanks to goals from Henrikh Mkhitaryan and Ibrahimović. Fenerbahçe topped the table on 13 points and qualified for the Knockout Phase (Round of 32) along with runners-up United on 12 points.

There was plenty of pedigree left in the competition in the knock-outs which included Ajax, Roma, Athletic Bilbao, AZ Alkmaar, Borussia Monchengladbach, Celta Vigo, Fiorentina, Olympique Lyonnais, RSC Anderlecht, Saint-Etienne, Schalke 04, Shakhtar Donetsk, Sparta Prague, Villareal and Zenit Saint Petersburg. United drew Saint-Etienne in the Round of 32 draw and Ibrahimović scored a hat-trick in United's 3-0 first leg victory at Old Trafford, including a penalty. It was his maiden hat-trick for the club. Six days later United won 1-0 in France thanks to a goal from Mkhitaryan.

In 2017, the Hollywood movie "The Greatest Showman" was released starring Hugh Jackman in the lead role as P. T. Barnum who founded the Barnum & Bailey Circus (1871-2017). It celebrated the visionary Barnum who rose from nothing to create a spectacle that became a worldwide sensation. In Zlatan Ibrahimović, Manchester United possessed football's Greatest Showman, a player who played for six clubs who have won the Champions League, namely Ajax, Juventus, Inter Milan, Barcelona, AC Milan and United, but it is the one trophy that has eluded him in a winners' medal haul which reached No.31 after United's FA Community Shield victory over Leicester. Amazingly he left Inter Milan at the end of the 2008-09 season after helping them win Serie A and the Italian outfit then lifted the Champions League crown in season 2009-10; he left Barcelona at the end of the 2009-10 season after helping them win La Liga and the Spanish club then won the Champions League in season 2010-11.

When the Round of 16 draw was made United avoided the big guns and drew Rostov who finished runners-up to CSKA Moscow in the 2015-16 Russian Premier League. The first leg was played at the Rostov Arena on 9 March 2017. Mkhitaryan scored in the 35th minute to earn United a 1-1 draw. A week later United won the second leg 1-0 with a Mata goal to earn a quarter-final encounter with Anderlecht, the reigning Belgian champions and UEFA Cup winners in 1982-83.

On 13 April 2017 United met Anderlecht at Lotto Park in the first leg of their quarter-final tie. Some 63 years earlier, 12 September 1956, United played the same opponents on the same ground in the club's first ever game in the European Cup. On this occasion United drew the game 1-1 thanks to another goal from their Armenian international Mkhitaryan. In the return at the Theatre of Dreams, United qualified for the semi-finals after a 2-1 victory following extra-time.

The draw for the semi-finals matched Ajax Amsterdam with Olympique Lyonnais and United with La Liga side Celta Vigo. Marcus Rashford scored the only goal of the game in the 1-0 away win at Estadio Municipal de Balaídos. The second leg at Old Trafford ended 1-1 but United were grateful for a last minute Sergio Romero save from former Manchester City striker John Guidetti to send them through. Ajax had squeezed past Lyon 5-4 on aggregate and would play United in the final on 24 May 2017 at Friends Arena, Solna, the home of AIK Fotboll and the Swedish national side.

Mourinho's Manchester United for the final read: Sergio Romero, Antonio Valencia (Capt), Matteo Darmian, Chris Smalling, Daley Blind, Paul Pogba, Juan Mata, Ander Herrera, Henrikh Mkhitaryan, Marouane Fellaini, Marcus Rashford. Substitutes: David De Gea, Timothy Fosu-Mensah, Phil Jones, Michael Carrick, Wayne Rooney (for Mata 90 mins, took over the captaincy), Jesse Lingard (for Mkhitaryan 74 mins), Anthony Martial (for Rashford 84 mins).

It was an emotional night for the United players, backroom staff and supporters following a terrorist attack on the previous Monday during Ariana Grande's performance at the Manchester Arena that claimed the lives of 22 people, many of them children. Eric Bailly was suspended and Zlatan Ibrahimovic, United's leading goal scorer with 28, missed the final after sustaining a serious knee injury in the quarter-final win over Anderlecht. Ajax's team was made up largely of graduates from their famed academy and United were firm favourites.

United fielded three academy graduates themselves with Marcus Rashford in the starting line-up and Jesse Lingard replacing Henrikh Mkhitaryan in the 74th minute but it was another who opened the scoring in Stockholm. Paul Pogba had rejoined United following a £93.2m move from Juventus that summer but he had struggled to make much impact scoring just 8 goals in 50 appearances yet he saved his best performance of the season for the Europa League final – an early shot went inches wide before his flick played in Mata whose cross was just behind Fellaini racing in to the six-yard box. Then Mata found Fellaini who squared the ball to Pogba, the Frenchman's shot took enough of a deflection to beat Onana and put United ahead. Ajax threatened to get level before the break but United's experienced back-line kept the youthful Dutch attackers at bay.

Then, just a minute into the second half, Fellaini forced a corner on the right; from Mata's delivery Smalling nodded goalwards, the ball looped up off Fellaini and Mkhitaryan poked the ball past Onana. In truth United were too strong for their opponents with Fellaini and Pogba towering over their Dutch counterparts in midfield. In the last minute of the game Wayne Rooney came on as a substitute for Antonio Valencia who had started the final as captain but then handed Rooney the captain's armband – it was Rooney's farewell appearance for the club. Rooney lifted the trophy for United and then left the club to re-join his boyhood heroes Everton on 9 July 2017.

At the final whistle Zlatan Ibrahimovic appeared on crutches to join in the celebrations and although he returned briefly the following season he was soon on his way to MLS side LA Galaxy. In his first season at Old Trafford Mourinho had guided the club to a treble of FA Community Shield, League Cup and Europa League while his old rival Pep Guardiola had won nothing as Manchester City boss.

This was United's fifth European trophy and completed the set – the club had now won both versions of the World Club Cup (the official FIFA version and the original Intercontinental Cup), all four European trophies (European Champions Cup, Cup Winners' Cup, UEFA Cup and Super Cup) and all major domestic trophies (League, FA Cup, League Cup and Charity/Community Shield). In the words of the great darts commentator Sid Waddell when describing Eric Bristow, "they had no more worlds to conquer".

Did You Know That?

Zlatan Ibrahimović is the only player to score in the Champions League for 6 different clubs – Ajax, Juventus, Inter Milan, Barcelona, AC Milan and Paris Saint-Germain. Along with Ronaldinho, he is the only footballer to score a goal in Italy's "Derby della Madonnina" (AC Milan v Inter Milan), Spain's "El Classico" (Barcelona v Real Madrid) and France's "Le Classique" (Olympique de Marseilles v Paris Saint-Germain) – he also scored in the Manchester Derby. He is the only footballer to have won 13 League Championships in 4 different Leagues (the Eredivisie with Ajax Amsterdam in 2001-02 & 2003-04, Serie A with Juventus 2004-05 & 2005-06 – both revoked because of the Calciopoli Scandal in Italian football), La Liga with Barcelona in 2009-10 and Ligue 1 with Paris Saint-Germain in 2012-13, 2013-14. He is the only foreign player to have lifted the "Capocannoniere" (top scorer award) with two different clubs, and remarkably for two different teams from the same city, Inter Milan (2008-09 & AC Milan in 2011-12). Zlatan is the only Barcelona player to score in each of his first five La Liga games. He is Sweden's all-time leading goal scorer with 62 goals in his 116 appearances. Ibrahimović is the only Swedish player to score in three consecutive UEFA European Championship tournaments: 2004, 2008 & 2012 a record he could extend as he came out of retirement in March 2021 and made himself available for Sweden at the Euro 2020 championships that will be played in summer 2021.

BIBLIOGRAPHY

Books

Sir Bobby Charlton - My Manchester United Years - The Autobiography; Bobby Charlton with James Lawton – Headline Publishing Group, 2007.

Manchester United: A Complete Record 1878-1992 – Ian Morrison & Alan Shury – The Breedon Books Publishing Company, 1992.

Irish Reds – Iain McCartney – Britespot Publishing Solutions Limited, 2002.

Manchester United Pictorial History & Club Record – Charles Zahra, Joseph Muscat, Iain McCartney and Keith Mellor – Temple Nostalgia, 1986.

The United Alphabet – A Complete Who's Who of Manchester United – Garth Dykes – ACL & Polar Publishing (UK) Limited, 1994.

Harry's Game – The Autobiography by Harry Gregg - Mainstream Publishing, October 2002.

The Official Manchester United Miscellany – John D T White - Carlton Publishing Limited, 2005.

The Official Manchester United Almanac – John D T White - Orion Publishing Limited, 2008.

Irish Devils: The Official Story of Manchester United and the Irish - John D T White - Simon & Schuster Ltd, 2011.

Kicking Through the Troubles: How Manchester United Helped to Heal a Divided Community– John D T White – Empire Publications (UK), 2017.

Websites

https://www.11v11.com/teams/manchester-united/
http://www.mufcinfo.com/
http://englandfootballonline.com/

Made in the USA
Coppell, TX
26 October 2021

64701128R10156